THE DAY OF THE BIG BANG

From a translation of the official Japanese history of the event:

"Then there came a blue-white flash of violent light. Immediately this produced a huge red smoke cloud. At the same time on the ground a yellowish pillar of smoke appeared. It rose gradually until it reached a height of 20,000 meters. Hiroshima city had been changed into an incandescent peak of fire..."

CONTENTS

PREFACE

There is relatively little in this book that is "new" for academic historians, who search in the crannies of the Pacific war archives for little known facts that might change interpretation of the events of those momentous years. I have examined the Japanese official history of the war in reference to the defense measures taken from the winter of 1945 onward in preparation for the landings the Imperial government expected on Honshu and Kyushu islands, but I have not gone into much detail here because the landings did not occur and the movements of Japanese forces are matters of interest primarily to Japanese readers.

What I have tried to do with *Closing the Circle* is show how the Pacific war was changing in the summer of 1945, and how Admiral Halsey carried the war against the enemy. All this was against the backdrop of the other events: the coming of the atomic bomb, the itch of the Russians to get into the war to share in the booty, and the difficult negotiations at Potsdam. Above all, I have tried to put this in perspective with the internal events in Japan as the war worsened for the Japanese people. The sinking of the *Indianapolis* still stands out as a major command error in the Pacific, in the carelessness with which movement of ships was treated as the allies began to believe Japanese seapower was broken. It was certainly nearly destroyed, but a few brave men of the Imperial Navy showed what courage could do, even when resources were exhausted.

Closing the Circle is a synthesis of materials, many of them already published. Whatever value it has is to remind readers of the incredible difficulties in stopping a war short of total disaster for the defeated in the twentieth century. Despite the atomic bomb, despite the Halsey punishment of the Japanese home islands, despite the constant raids of the B-29 force, and the entry of the Soviets into the war, those hard-headed militarists of the Japanese army and navy very nearly prevented the peace faction and the Emperor from ending the struggle. Had they succeeded, the cost to Japan and to the Allies would have been enormous, and the face of the Pacific might have been changed. Had the Russians been given the time to really get moving, they might have been able to force their way into the military government, creating a monstrous situation such as that in Germany, which has dogged the world for almost four decades. In the final analysis, a handful of men, led by the foreign minister, saved the integrity of Japan. As for the Americans, President Truman's wrenching and momentous decision to use the atomic bomb has been attacked in postwar years. Perhaps it is useful to remind readers how it came about and what might have happened had it not.

PROLOGUE

In the spring of 1945, despite the severity of the battle for Okinawa, it was apparent that the Pacific war was drawing to an end. In May the struggle for Europe came to its conclusion with the Soviet capture of Berlin and the death of Adolf Hitler in the bunker of the *Reichkanzlei*. The end of that struggle freed the entire American and British navies and most of the air forces for use in the Pacific. In June the wheels were in motion to bring these forces west, for the coming major assault on Japan.

After months of argument, the Allies had settled on the plan to assault Japan proper, although the navy still hoped against hope to achieve its own objective, a landing in China that would cut Japan off totally from the rest of the world. By June 1945, Japan was nearly cut off as it was. Her empire had been reduced to Formosa, spotty holdings on the China coast, a presence in Indochina, the Netherlands, East Indies, Korea, and Manchuria. But the geography belied the reality; communication between Japan and all these places was more or less cut off, more in the case of Indochina, the Indies, and East China, less in the case of Formosa, Korea, and Manchuria. In that month it became much worse, when the American submarines moved into the Sea of Japan. For the first time, Japan was totally surrounded in the sense that there was no place the enemy could not move.

The true status of the war effort was known to scarcely any person in Japan because of the stratification of Japanese military society. The army might know that the navy was in serious difficulty (it had virtually no seagoing warships left except submarines). But the navy did not reveal to the officials of the army the true and desperate state of its ability to carry on its part of the struggle. The navy stoutly resisted the growing army demand for "unification" of the forces, navy officials knowing they would be totally eclipsed if the truth were out. Except for the submarine force, the navy's real fighting arm was the air force, and this had been largely converted to kamikaze, or suicide, units.

As for the army, although millions of men were in uniform, they were widely scattered. Those units in the south and east had to be written off, even when not under attack: there was no way they could participate in a battle for Japan; the ships to transport them home did not exist, nor did the naval forces to protect them. Troops in the Indies, the bypassed Pacific islands, Formosa, Hainan, Indochina, and China were isolated. Only the great Kwantung Army of Manchuria remained as a major fighting force that could be utilized. But just how greatly utilized was one of the army's secrets. The Kwantung Army had been largely devitalized by the exigencies of the past year. Beginning with the campaign in the Solomons, it had been drawn upon for reinforcements. But by the time of the battle of the Marianas, in June 1944, it had lost many of its best units, sent to shore up the defenses of the inner empire, which began with the Marianas line. Thousands of those troops had never reached a battlefield but had died watery deaths as their transports were sunk by American submarines and bombers. The army concealed this fact from the navy and from the civilian population of Japan. More so than all other elements in Japanese society, the army insisted that the war against the Allies be continued until the bitter end unless the enemy would offer a peace with honor, which meant the preservation of the military clique that ran Japan.

There was a good reason for this army insistence that the "polity" of Japan be retained intact. It was buried beneath the emotional argument that the Imperial system must be preserved, but that was not strictly true. The army's real concern was itself; the professional army officers could not conceive of a Japan in which they were out of power. They could not contemplate a disarmed Japan. What would they do? This feeling was even stronger among the young (thirties and forties) staff officers of the lower senior grades, lieutenant colonels and colonels, than among the generals. After all, the generals had enjoyed their days of glory; the younger men had them yet to enjoy. Rather than surrender and accept disarmament, they would fight to the death, go down fighting and take the nation with them, so that Japan and all things Japanese might end in a holocaust that would leave nothing but a memory for the world. They were quite serious in this attitude, although Westerners found it impossible to come to grips with it. In the bitter days of July and August 1945, this matter became the compelling factor in the life of the Japanese government.

On the Allied side, there was never any question as to how the war must end. Japan must surrender, she must give up the colonies she had begun capturing late in the nineteenth century. She must disarm, and the militarists who had seized and held power since the 1920s must be wiped out. The military system must be destroyed in such a fashion that it could never rise again. (The ultimate success of this venture is indicated in the 1980s; an America whose attitudes had changed now wanted a revitalized Japanese military, while the Japanese were most reluctant to return to military ways.)

The attitude of the Japanese military and that of the Allied leaders worked hand in glove to make the ending of the war a monumentally difficult task.

My previous books about the Pacific War have scarcely mentioned political affairs. In that sense the books represented the realities of the time; in 1941 and 1942, American forces in the Pacific were beleagured, and the major concern was to carry the fight to the enemy. The army as exemplified by General Douglas MacArthur, and the navy as exemplified by Admiral Chester W.

Nimitz, each wanted to run the show, but the Joint Chiefs of Staff made the decisions. Only after the battle for the Marianas in the central Pacific did a major political decision about the war have to be made. President Franklin D. Roosevelt made it: the major emphasis in the Pacific war would move next to the Philippines, to redeem MacArthur's promise (and America's) to return and thus show the world that Japan would soon be conquered.

The battles for Saipan, Tinian, and Guam had represented the edge of change. On these islands, for the first time army infantry tactics could be more or less properly utilized. With the invasion of the large island of Leyte, there was no question but that the Pacific war had become more an army war. Okinawa was another example; Iwo Jima and Peleliu were in that sense anachronisms. When it came to the next major politico-military decision—who would command the invasion of Japan—the army had the upper hand and General MacArthur received the command. By the summer of 1945, the political decisions were as important as the military ones, and much more farreaching in their consequences. Thus, *Closing the Circle* is not a completely military history in the sense that my previous books were. What was happening at Potsdam and in Tokyo and Moscow and Washington was as important as what was happening in the U.S. Third Fleet and in the U.S. Pacific Air Forces.

I expect to be faulted by academic historians for not going to the sources in the political matters, but the fact is that a number of authors have quite competently brought forth the necessary materials. I have gone to the sources in the conduct of the American forces assaulting Japan in June, July, and August 1945 —particularly the navy, which in the last days was given the responsibility for occupying Japan, a plan rescinded a few days before the time came for politico-military reasons. Admiral William F. Halsey had no conception of the atomic bomb that spring when he set out to try to destroy Japan's capacity to carry on the war. Up until that last day, when American fliers were killed completely unnecessarily after the surrender was agreed upon, he did not falter in that resolve. Nor did the Japanese military machine.

Since the war, the historical section of the Japanese Self-Defense Agency has published some 100 volumes of historical material on aspects of the Great East Asia War, going back to the beginnings. Two volumes of this enormous study are devoted to the preparations of Japan for the last great battle. When the Americans finally landed in the Japanese home islands and began moving about, assessing what they saw, they started to learn just how committed the military was to a defense that would have involved the entire civilian population. Suicide craft of all sorts had been assembled for the desperate struggle. Food and ammunition dumps had been moved around the country. Military plans for almost all sorts of defense were committed to paper. It was apparent that there had been no bluffing in the Japanese military position. If the civilian politicians, and particularly Foreign Minister Shigenori Togo, had not been successful in finessing the surrender plan through the total resistance of the military, the results would have been a bloodbath in Japan that would have made the dreadful losses in the Nazi-Soviet war seem pale, at least to Western eyes.

That is the burden of this book, to indicate what happened, how it happened, and what might have happened.

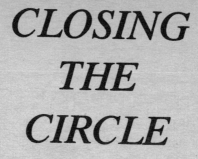

CLOSING THE CIRCLE

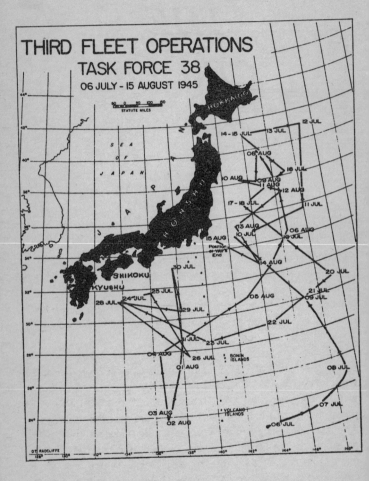

THIRD FLEET OPERATIONS
TASK FORCE 38
06 JULY - 15 AUGUST 1945

STATUTE MILES

HOKKAIDO

HONSHU

SEA OF JAPAN

SHIKOKU

KYUSHU

BONIN ISLANDS

VOLCANO ISLANDS

12 JUL
14 - 15 JUL   13 JUL
06 AUG
16 JUL
10 AUG   09 AUG
11 AUG   12 AUG
17 - 18 JUL   11 JUL
13 AUG   06 AUG
10 JUL   19 JUL
15 AUG
Position
of War's
End   14 AUG
30 JUL   20 JUL
28 JUL   21 JUL
28 JUL   24 JUL   05 AUG   09 JUL
29 JUL   22 JUL
31 JUL   25 JUL
04 AUG   26 JUL
01 AUG   08 JUL
03 AUG   07 JUL
02 AUG   06 JUL

DT RADCLIFFE

1

RE-ENTER HALSEY

The battle for Okinawa had been raging for fifty-six days, and for the first time in the Pacific war, the U.S. navy was suffering high casualties with no way of striking back to avoid them. The problem was the kamikaze forces operating from Formosa and Honshu and Kyushu islands—young Japanese men dedicated to the idea that by sacrificing their lives in a flying bomb they could change the course of the war that was going so desperately against them.

For the past six weeks, Admiral William H. Halsey had been laying plans for a whole new series of naval operations in the far western Pacific. At the highest levels the future conduct of the war against Japan was being hammered out, but before that last phase, the Joint Chiefs of Staff planned several other operations. And yet even the planning was extremely tentative, until April. At that point Admiral Ernest J. King appointed Halsey commander of the Mid-Pacific Striking Force, which was to be composed of all surface units in the Hawaiian islands and on the West Coast. Halsey's responsibility, which seems absurd in light of history, was to repel an expected Japanese carrier strike against San Francisco at the time of the United Nations organizational meeting there. When King described the problem to

Halsey, that admiral began to laugh, although it was not generally good form to laugh in the face of the commander-in-chief. But even King's stony face broke into a smile for, as the top naval officers knew very well, the striking power of the Japanese aircraft carriers had been almost completely destroyed by Halsey at the Battle of Leyte Gulf. But the politicians worried, and when they did, the navy had to respond, so Halsey put his staff to work planning for an eventuality that he knew could never arise.

In this matter King was dealing directly with Halsey instead of through Admiral Chester Nimitz, commander of the Pacific Fleet, because Nimitz had moved his advance headquarters to Guam to be closer to the scene of naval action, and closer to General MacArthur, who had assumed the leadership role for the Allies in recent months despite an active campaign by the navy to retain command of Pacific operations.

Part of the reason for the shift away from the navy leadership that had taken the Americans as far as Iwo Jima was a bitter quarrel between Lieutenant General Holland M. Smith of the Marine Corps and Major General Ralph Smith of the United States Army. After "Howling Mad" Smith relieved General Ralph Smith during the battle for Saipan, the highest officers of the army asserted that they would not again serve under marine command. That was an emotional issue, but a very real one; it was buttressed by the change in the war with the invasion of the Philippines, the largest land mass the Americans had assaulted in the drive across the Pacific. The navy and its shock troops of the United States Marines were admirably suited for assaults on islands and island groups where the fighting must move fast and furiously. But the army with its more ponderous methods was equally admirably suited for operations across wide swathes of terrain, where tens of thousands, not hundreds, of troops were to be employed and where the logistics would stagger a marine officer. So in that spring of 1945 the Joint Chiefs of Staff had determined that when the next assaults came, they would be under army direction. One plan called for assault on the China coast. Another plan indicated an assault on Formosa.

In one sense Admiral William F. Halsey was the ideal figure to undertake the planning. Whatever came from his efforts, all would know that Halsey was choosing the path that he believed led most directly to Tokyo. He had never been one to take the least line of resistance. He was the first carrier admiral in America to follow the doctrine of risk. While his contemporaries (Annapolis, class of 1904) were avoiding battle in the Pacific lest they lose their carriers, Halsey went out looking for the Japanese and trouble. In the earliest days he did not find it, held back by his timid superiors, but beginning in February 1942, he did go into trouble, first in a daring raid on the Marshall Islands. There he violated the accepted (American) rule of carrier warfare: instead of holding his carrier back from the front line and sending the planes out at maximum distance, he brought the *Enterprise* right into Japanese waters, struck hard, and then pulled out to strike again. "Haul Ass with Halsey" was the phrase created by the bluejackets that day to describe their commander. "The admiral will get us in and the captain will get us out" was another saying aboard the carrier.

From the days at the U.S. Naval Academy, Halsey had been one of the popular ones in the navy. His broad grin and irrepressible style appealed to everyone, it seemed. To be sure, he was in the bottom third of the class scholastically, but what he seemed to lack in intellectual fervor he made up in pure guts. "He looks like a figurehead of Neptune," his classmates said even then.

Early in Halsey's career he had been exposed to the Japanese and their way of thinking. He had been a very junior ensign aboard the battleship *Kansas* when she joined "The Great White Fleet" of American capital ships that sailed around the world in 1906 to impress all nations—and particularly the Japanese—with America's growing naval might. It was a show, no more, no less. Halsey's memorable part in it came in Tokyo Bay when Japanese Admiral Heihachiro Togo gave a party for the officers of the American fleet aboard his flagship the battleship *Mikasa.* After the formalities and the dignified dinner and toasts, the junior

Japanese officers gave Admiral Charles S. Sperry a special
accolade—one they reserved for their most cherished leaders.
They seized him and tossed him three times in a blanket,
shouting *"Banzai"* (May you live 10,000 years) as they did so.
Admiral Sperry emerged a bit shaken from the apparent indignity,
but bearing up. His senior American officers were annoyed and
they were prepared to take a hasty departure. It was Ensign
Halsey who saw the looks on Japanese faces, and acted to prevent
an insult to Admiral Togo. He seized the blanket, shouted,
"Come on, boys," and grabbed Admiral Togo. In a moment the
other young officers were with him, and Admiral Togo got his
ceremonial tossing in the blanket and three hurrahs. Thus was
protocol preserved by the quick thinking of a junior officer.

Admiral Halsey's career antedated the naval air force. He
served in destroyers before and during World War I. He had a
hitch in naval intelligence and one as naval attaché in Berlin. In
1930, at the exalted prewar rank of captain of the navy, Halsey
decided to take pilot training. He failed the eye examination
and could not take the course. But in 1934 Admiral King, then
chief of the Bureau of Aeronautics, offered Halsey command of
the carrier *Saratoga* if he would take the naval observer's course.
In those days carriers were regarded as secondary units of the fleet,
extremely vulnerable to attack, and the men who commanded
them followed fleet tactics. It was not expected that they
would think as airmen; it was not understood that aviators
would have any different view of war tactics from any other
naval officer. Since carriers had come along after World War I,
to secure commanders for the vessels meant the navy had to
do a bit of shuffling.

The officers senior enough to command a major warship were
also too old to be pilots. Halsey, for example, was fifty-one years
old when he decided to take "observer's training." The course
only required that he familiarize himself with navy flying; he
was to sit in the rear seat while a pilot flew him around, practicing
loops and turns, military tactics, and deadstick landings. That
way, after studying engines, radio, aerial navigation, gunnery,

bombing and torpedoes, an observer was supposed to be able to at least keep up with the talk of the aviators. But Halsey was not interested in form without content. He insisted that his designation be changed from "student observer" to "student pilot," and since he was in the program and the physical examination no longer controlled his activity, it was, through a bit of a shenanigan winked at by authority. He knew very well that he could never pass the pilot's test, but he argued forcefully that he could not understand the problems of a pilot unless he was one. So off he went, into the wild blue yonder.

His instructor was Lieutenant Bromfield B. Nichol, whose major comment on his protegé's aerial progress was "The worse the weather, the better he flew." Perhaps it only seemed better by comparison. He took the maximum twelve hours of dual instruction, then soloed in a navy seaplane, somehow managed to get it off the water, into the air, and around the required course, and back down onto the top of the water again. He was the last of his class to make it, and they lined up at the ramp of Squadron One and gave a collective sigh of relief as Captain William Halsey brought his plane safely up. They pulled him out and tossed him into "the drink," just as they had all been tossed before, and when he emerged, dripping wet, he was a full-fledged naval aviator.

"What do you think the old fool is doing now?" his wife asked their daughter one day. "He's learning to fly!" And she muttered something about old men and monkey glands.

Halsey persisted through the next part of the aviation program, although it was not necessary for him to do so to keep those gold wings. He learned to fly land planes, of the sort that would be used on carriers. He ground-looped one, which taught him a little bit about humility. He got lost on a cross-country flight. Flying service planes after the trainers, he turned one over on its back, refused medical attention, and went aloft again immediately to prove he could do it. He learned to fly torpedo bombers, carrying torpedoes. He flew fighters and learned aerobatics. One day he won the training squadron emblem for stupidity: the Flying Jackass, a large aluminum likeness of a donkey, awarded to anyone who broke a safety regulation. He wore it for two weeks until another student pilot won it away from him. But he insisted on keeping that particular badge. When he took command of the *Saratoga,* he said, he would hang it on the bulkhead of his cabin. Any time he got ready to raise hell with some pilot for an infraction of rules, he was going to look at that Flying Jackass and think twice.

Such tales began the legend of Bill Halsey, the only really flying commander of a carrier, and the true aviators got to love him. When he took over his carrier, he continued to add bits to the legend. From the *Saratoga* he went to the *Enterprise,* one of the new carriers of the fleet, as commander of Carrier Division Two and he was promoted to admiral. One day a young officer made an error that delayed the launch of planes. Admiral King was present at the time, and King was a noted disciplinarian (who put an end to the advancement of one naval captain because he ran a cruiser aground in a fog trying to get King back to Washington to make an appointment).

"Who was responsible for the delay?" King demanded by signal, and on the bridge of the *Enterprise* souls quaked as the message was taken to Admiral Halsey's bridge.

"COMCARDIV Two," was the reply.

There was no further word from the flagship. But on board the *Enterprise* the story went from keel to masthead. Admiral Halsey was the sort of officer who protected his men, it said.

He was always an officer to bend the regulations (or even fracture them) to bring humanity to steel decks. After Pearl Harbor, when navy flying had become a deadly business, Halsey decided that on his ship there would be no nonsense, as about "prohibition." Back in 1914 Navy Secretary Josephus Daniels had prohibited alcoholic beverages aboard ships. His action was the result of a long struggle between America's Calvinists and the rest of the country. The nation adopted Prohibition entirely after World War I and struggled under the ridiculous system that made criminals of half the population until the 1930s.

Afterward Prohibitionists continued to fight the navy battle and won it on the basis that an officer might make an error of judgment under the influence of alcohol. (Had that been true then Britain could never have developed the Royal Navy into the world's greatest fleet of the 1930s or the Russians have challenged the Americans for suzerainty of the seas in the 1980s.) But politicians' decisions, as Halsey knew very well, did not have to be based on fact or reason. The prohibition rule was still in effect (as it is today) and the rule was broken as often as the men in charge would let it be. Halsey in 1942 had the title of Commander, Aircraft Battle Force, and in that guise he ordered up one hundred gallons of bourbon whiskey. It was for the flight surgeons to issue to the pilots, he said. There was some complaint in high quarters, but a fighting admiral was not to be gainsaid in 1942, when there were so few of them, and Halsey had his way. The practice became standard throughout the carrier fleet (and in the air force).

After Pearl Harbor, when Admiral Nimitz took over command of the Pacific Fleet, he quickly realized that the one carrier admiral he could trust with any mission was Bill Halsey. It was Halsey who was chosen for the difficult and dangerous task of transporting Lieutenant Colonel James Doolittle and his squadron of army B-25 medium bombers to attack Japan for American morale purposes. Halsey jumped at the chance: his country's enemies were his personal enemies. That extremely personal view of the war dominated all Halsey's actions from the day of Pearl Harbor's attack onward. He was undoubtedly the most aggressive commander in the navy. When Halsey learned that three of Doolittle's fliers had been executed by the Japanese in violation of all the laws of war, he took the matter extremely personally. As biographer J. Bryan III noted in *Admiral Halsey's Story*, the book he wrote with the admiral, "All he could choke out was, 'We'll make the bastards pay! We'll make 'em pay.' "

Halsey's singleminded devotion to the war made him sick—actually—and on May 28, 1942, he was shipped off to the hospital suffering from a nervous disease. He was hospitalized until the fall of 1942, then immediately he was thrust into new responsibility as commander of the failing American effort in the South Pacific. In August the marines had invaded Guadalcanal Island in the Solomon Islands to prevent Japanese buildup of an airfield there that could dominate the sea lanes between the U.S. and Australia, thus cutting off General Douglas MacArthur from supplies. When the invasion was staged everyone concerned knew it was a risky business: General MacArthur said it was a disaster, and Admiral Robert Ghormley, dispatched as Nimitz' commander for the South Pacific, agreed with him completely. In the next two months, the Americans suffered one defeat after another at sea (the Japanese tactical superiority was alarming), and something had to be done. So King and Nimitz called on Halsey. He appeared at Nouméa, the headquarters of the South Pacific command, figuratively breathing fire and brimstone. Signs sprouted around the command bearing a new slogan: "Kill Japs, Kill Japs, Kill More Japs." In a month Halsey turned the situation around, *before* he began to get the material supplies and new ships he needed to win that campaign.

Halsey soon became the darling of the newspaper correspondents. The reason was simple enough: he was always good copy, he never hid behind official pronouncements (as Nimitz and Spruance were wont to do), and he seemed to say anything that came into his head. One day late in 1942 he announced (by way of answering a demand for predictions) that the Americans would be in Tokyo at the end of 1943. Back home in America, the civilian leaders broke out in sweats; Halsey, they said, was endangering the war effort with his rash statements. But the fact was that Halsey was fighting the war in the South Pacific, and that is where the morale booster was needed. What angered the civilians at home gave new strength to the men who were doing the fighting, and Halsey never backed down and never complained about what was said. He was particularly worried at that time about a rumor spreading through the fleet of Japanese "invincibility." Anyone who studied the naval actions of Guadalcanal could have come to that conclusion after the first month or so. The Japanese had superior torpedoes, superior fighting planes (the Zero), and were superior at night fighting because they had trained for it when the Americans had not. But on the ground, the marines showed that they were superior to the Japanese in the jungle. In the air the marines and navy pilots and a handful of army air corps pilots showed that they could learn, and after a time they secured new aircraft that made the odds closer to even.

By January 1943, the problem was still serious, however. Halsey gave an unflinching interview in New Zealand, predicting a Japanese general retreat. It came at a time when Admiral Yamamoto had just decided to make of New Georgia the base that was supposed to go into Guadalcanal. The Japanese had been defeated in their attempt to recapture Guadalcanal, but they did not at that time regard the defeat as any more than a fluke. The Allied area's morale needed shoring up, and Admiral Halsey did it.

Because of all this, Halsey became known as "Bull" Halsey. It was a name tagged on him by a newspaper correspondent, and it stuck. To some it meant the powerful bull of the bull ring, who put down his enemies with ease. To others it meant the "Bull in the China Shop," who went about breaking the crockery. Halsey always said he did not mind being accused of breaking the crockery—as long as it was Japanese.

So Halsey fought his personal war against the Japanese. He won it in the South Pacific, and was then given command of the carrier fleet on an alternative basis with Admiral Raymond Spruance. When Spruance had the fleet it was called the Fifth Fleet. Nimitz took care to be sure that Spruance had the fleet when his various island invasions were under way, because he knew that the conservative Spruance would not exceed his instructions and try to win the war overnight. He was never quite sure about Halsey. The difficulty came to a head during the Battle of Leyte Gulf when Halsey, entrusted to defend the invasion of Leyte, chose to do so by chasing after the Japanese force of carriers and battleships under Admiral Ozawa. The force had been sent northward to draw Halsey off, but it was none the less dangerous for that. Two other Japanese striking forces were engaged by Halsey's planes and by the ships of Admiral Thomas C. Kinkaid, the commander of the new Seventh Fleet (MacArthur's navy). Kinkaid was surprised and shocked, and furious with Halsey for moving off in pursuit of one force and not sticking around to cover the eastern flank of Leyte Island. The Japanese sneaked through San Bernardino strait, north of Leyte, and came down like wolves with their battleships and cruisers on the escort carrier force that was guarding that flank. There was an enormous outcry by the strategists against Halsey, but the fact was that he did destroy the Ozawa force, the Americans won the battle, the U.S. loss was one small carrier and several destroyers and escorts. The trouble was that by this time the American strength was so great that no one seemed to think ships should be put at risk any more. Halsey could not have disagreed more. In the battle for the Philippines, Halsey had virtually wiped out the Japanese navy, and had so smashed the Japanese air potential on Formosa that it was never restored; the end of the war found that island's airfields in shambles created by Halsey's carrier planes.

In the spring of 1945, interviewed in Washington, Admiral Halsey struck a new chord with a statement that he would like to ride Emperor Hirohito's white horse. For years, on ceremonial occasions, the Emperor had been shown in military uniform riding a snow-white horse, and it had become a symbol of Japanese militarism and power. Halsey's statement caused a ripple of enthusiasm in America, and people and groups began sending him saddles, bridles, spurs, and other equipment; all designed for his ride on the white horse, preferably through the Imperial Palace. The whole story was blown up by the press, it reached Japan and infuriated the propagandists there. Halsey had always been able to "get the Japanese goat" and this time, by committing lèse majesté against the Emperor, he made personal enemies of all the militarists in the island kingdom, and that meant many, many thousands of officers.

So in this spring of 1945, Admiral Halsey's war against the Japanese was a very personal matter, and in a way it symbolized even more than the calm arrogance of General MacArthur the American spirit about the war.

In April, having shored up the defenses of San Francisco against ghosts, Admiral Halsey and his staff occupied themselves with plans for four different operations in the Pacific.

One, Admiral Spruance had suggested that the amphibious force make a landing on the China coast about 100 miles south of Shanghai. Halsey snorted at this concept as a waste of time, but orders were orders. The plan was drawn.

Two, Admiral Nimitz liked the idea of landing on the Shantung peninsula, 350 miles north of Shanghai, and then looking over to Japan. Halsey felt that this too was a waste of time, but again, he planned.

Three, establishment of a line of communications with Russia across the North Pacific, through the Sea of Japan. This was a book plan, necessary just in case the Russians began to move. No one liked that plan, but it was a contingency that must be taken into account.

Four, an attack on the Sea of Japan and Kyushu. This was right down Halsey's alley; strike the enemy at his heart and do not fool around with the preliminaries. This plan brought forth the best efforts of the Halsey staff.

But in the interim, the Joint Chiefs of Staff had been improving all these plans and those submitted by General MacArthur's staff, and out of the effort came a joint operation: Halsey would have his Kyushu landing; one force would land there and a second on Honshu in the Tokyo area. The navy planning became meaningless.

At the end of April, Admiral Halsey went up to Guam to see Admiral Nimitz who was beset with the difficulties of trying to keep from being swallowed alive by General MacArthur. At about that time Admiral Spruance indicated his growing restlessness with the Okinawa campaign, now that it had settled down to a slugging match on the land and the Fifth Fleet was largely confined to defensive operations against the kamikaze planes. For any offensive purposes, the Japanese fleet had ceased to exist as a fighting unit. A handful of ships floated, many of them maimed and in harbor, and the Japanese submarine service was still strong, but there was nothing else.

Nimitz wanted Spruance back at headquarters to begin planning for the Pacific Fleet role in the invasion of Japan that had to be contemplated for the autumn. Also, Halsey and not Spruance was the ideal commander for what Admirals Nimitz and King wanted the fleet to do next: conduct a series of strikes at the Japanese on their very doorstep. Halsey could be expected to go in close, exceed his instructions if anything, while Spruance would have played the exercise by the book and been worried all along about enemy attack.

Nimitz then told Halsey that he was to take over the fleet again the next month. Halsey, as always, was delighted with the prospect of action. He was not quite so pleased with the information that his flagship would be the battleship *Missouri* because he was used to sailing in the *New Jersey*, but the latter was being overhauled and there was no recourse. It meant training a new captain and his officers in the admiral's ways, but Halsey had done that before, too.

From Guam, Halsey made a brief trip to Okinawa to confer with Admiral Spruance on his flagship offshore and discuss the change of command. There was nothing complicated about it but nothing easy, either. The Japanese had persisted in their kamikaze attacks on the naval force and Halsey could be expected to have to do the same, Spruance indicated. Since it was not time for the change of command, Halsey only grunted, and listened to the various reports of the difficulties the picket destroyers and the carriers were having with the suicide planes. Then he went back to Pearl Harbor to tidy up the plans he had made for Nimitz and prepare for sea once again. He was there on May 7 when the Germans signed the unconditional surrender agreement and the war in Europe came to an end.

The reports from Okinawa were delivered to Halsey these days, and read avidly by his staff. Generally speaking, it was a pretty dull war by Halsey's standards. On April 27, Admiral J. J. Clark's Task Group 58.1 was ordered to the new base at Ulithi for a ten-day period of overhaul and resupply. Admiral Marc Mitscher was not too concerned about detaching five carriers just then; the task group had been at sea continuously for more than forty days, but that was not a record by any means—Rear Admiral Frederick Sherman's Task Group 58.3 went eighty-seven days without hitting port. With the new methods of resupply by support ships and plane delivery by jeep carriers, the amount of time a carrier could spend at sea in 1945 depended on morale and the luck of not being hit by a suicide plane. Only one of Clark's ships, the *Wasp*, had been hit by a kamikaze, and while the damage had been extensive, by wartime standards that was a long time before, back in March, and the damage had been repaired. What was really essential was an occasional "blow" from the war, and they had a series of rousing parties on the island of Mogmog, including one "wall-banger" on the night that the German surrender in Europe was announced.

On May 9, as Admiral Halsey was pulling his staff together to take over at Okinawa, Clark's task group left Ulithi for the three-day voyage to Okinawa. It was back to the old grind, sending combat air patrol up at dawn, and then responding to various ships as they came under air attack from the Japanese suicide units. As Clark's group reappeared on the scene Admiral Radford's task group left for Ulithi. There was a weary feeling in the fleet that this hammering could go on forever unless the brass at the top did something to stop the Japanese suicide flights. One captain who was also a Biblical student summed it up with a quotation: Hebrews 13, Verse 8 and in reply to a question from Jocko Clark, Admiral Nimitz announced, "We are a high-speed stationary target for the Japanese air force."

That about summed up the carrier men's reaction to the role in which they were used. They argued that the job of defending the landing force and its supply ships could as easily have been done by the army air force, thus freeing the carriers to do something the army planes could not do, range the seas around the Japanese bases and stop the flow of planes at the source. But with Spruance in charge, all concerned had to expect a narrow interpretation of orders. His orders had been to launch and protect the invasion of Okinawa, and that is precisely what the carrier task force was doing, at considerable cost. During the first two weeks of May, the Japanese launched their fifth and sixth *kikusui* attacks—organized units of suicide planes coming in from several directions. The result, even as the final victory on the land at Okinawa was in sight, was to give Admiral Nimitz at Guam great concern. In the fifth attack he lost two destroyers, two landing ships, and 370 officers and men. In the sixth attack on May 11, more than 150 Japanese planes came in. The destroyer *Evans* was hit by eight different suicide planes. The destroyer *Hugh W. Hadley* was attacked simultaneously by ten kamikazes, and four of them were effective. It was sad enough to contemplate the damage and the losses in men at Okinawa, but what would it be like on the beaches of Japan if the enemy continued to behave in this fashion—and there was no reason to believe the Japanese approach was about to change.

Admiral Nimitz' intelligence indicated quite the opposite, and it was correct intelligence the Japanese were preparing. In the last few months before Okinawa, the Japanese had begun to concentrate on the defense of their home islands—*hondo*, Japan proper—as they called them. All else, including Okinawa, might be lost. But the Japanese people found it incomprehensible that they could be defeated on the shores of Japan itself. In April, the Imperial General Headquarters had taken note of the succession of defeats. No matter how valiantly the commanders and their men had fought, at Leyte, at Iwo Jima, and most recently at Okinawa, the American juggernaut moved on. It was apparent in April that it was only a matter of time before a landing was attempted on the shores of Kyushu and Honshu islands. Kyushu's special defense began then, even as the kamikaze corps used that island's airfields as the major takeoff area (along with Formosa) for the attacks on the American ships off Okinawa. As Admiral Halsey laid plans for future operations against Japan that spring, so the Japanese planned to halt the Americans on the beaches of the Japanese islands. On April 5, General Kuniaki Koiso resigned as premier of the Japanese government. He had been the successor chosen when General Tojo resigned after the fall of Saipan, the first important point breached within the Japanese home empire. Koiso was followed by Baron Kantaro Suzuki, an eighty-year-old statesman who, like Admiral Yamamoto almost alone among the Japanese officials of World War II, had experience that went back to the Russo-Japanese war. Koiso could remember—as Japanese history teachers had conveniently forgotten—that at the end Japan had been very close to bankrupt and bereft of the materials to continue the war against Russia. In the spring of 1945 the situation was far worse, and yet the old baron was forced to promise the army generals that he would "prosecute the war to a victorious finish." He knew such a course was impossible, but the general staff showed no sensible recognition even as the Okinawa defenses crumbled, so the premier's public utterances all indicated that Japan was not far from forcing the Americans to an "honorable peace" although the truth was precisely the opposite. And so, as Halsey prepared to surge into Japanese waters and carry on his personal campaign of attrition against the enemy, the Japanese were digging entrenchments along the cliffs above the beaches of Kyushu and Honshu islands and filling the harbors and estuaries with small plywood motorboats equipped with explosive charges. The suicide corps had begun to become a way of life in the Japanese military.

On May 18, Admiral Halsey climbed the companionway up to the deck of the *Missouri* and was piped aboard. A few hours later the flagship sailed for Okinawa. The changes were already coming fast in that command in anticipation of Halsey's arrival. Admiral Richmond Kelly Turner, the primary amphibious commander in the U.S. Navy, had been relieved the day before by his deputy, Admiral Harry W. Hill. The prime objective of putting the troops ashore at Okinawa and making sure they could stay had been achieved, and Turner's abilities were needed back at Nimitz' headquarters to plan for the invasion of Japan.

As Halsey steamed toward Okinawa he was making his plans. He could see no sense in the static defense that Admiral Spruance had been offering. He intended to go out and "get 'em" where it would hurt, in the Japanese homeland.

At Okinawa the kamikaze threat was greatly diminished during the last half of the month of May. One reason was the generally poor flying weather throughout the western Pacific. The spring rains came on May 16 and began dumping inches of water onto the ground, and the cloud cover made it difficult for the suicide planes to find a target. Since they carried only enough fuel for a one-way trip, many were lost in the sea before they reached the island. But the attempts to fight back did not diminish. The seventh attack of the *kikusui*, the "floating chrysanthemums," was under way, although its effects were largely diminished by the weather. The Americans made the mistake of believing the lesser activity indicated a weakening of the Japanese. This was true only in the sense that the plans were made to defend the homeland, and all available resources were husbanded for that purpose except those already committed to the Okinawa battle. The kamikazes kept flying, and although many were lost without an attack, enough damage was done in the last ten days of May to give Admiral Nimitz more cause for concern.

On May 26, Admiral Halsey arrived at Hagushi on the west coast of Okinawa, and the *Missouri* anchored offshore. That day, on the other side of the island, the Japanese attacks from the air continued. The eighth organized kamikaze assault was in progress.

On the same day, Admiral Halsey conferred with Admiral Spruance to complete his understanding of what had been done, and later he went ashore to meet Lieutenant General Simon Bolivar Buckner, commander of the Tenth Army, which was charged with the capture of the island. From Buckner and his generals, Halsey learned that no one with whom he would be dealing had a vested interest in continuation of the "static defense," as he called it. Halsey decided he would blanket the enemy airfields and destroy every single plane that could be found before it took off on a mission against the fleet. He made arrangements with the army to install new radar at various points on Okinawa and on other islands of the group, to replace the picket destroyers which had been taking such a beating. On May 27 just after midnight, as the Japanese suicide pilots prepared for the next day's strikes back on Formosa and Kyushu, Admiral Halsey took command of the American naval forces. The fleet that had been called Fifth Fleet once again became Third Fleet. Halsey promised a different kind of war against the Japanese.

HIT THE ENEMY: GET THOSE PLANES!

Halsey arrived at the anchorage off Okinawa with one half-resolved idea, and before that first day was out, the resolution was complete. In his usual cautious fashion, Admiral Spruance had allowed the enemy to take the initiative; the rain of hell on the ships, and particularly the picket destroyers, was the result. The way to stop it, Halsey said, was to take the carriers to Formosa and to the Japanese shores themselves, and strike hard to knock out the enemy air forces. He intended to blanket the enemy airfields and burn every plane his pilots could find.

One of Halsey's first requests went to Admiral Nimitz: could he assign Marine Air Group 14 to Okinawa, thus relieving the task force of the protective duty until army planes could be brought in? Nimitz was quick to agree; he did not like the exposed position of those destroyers that was bringing so much grief and so many casualties.

As soon as Admiral Radford's group returned from replenishment at Ulithi on May 28, the *Missouri* joined up and took position at the center of the task group. Admiral Sherman's ships were sent off to Leyte then, for a rest, and the second big change in command was made: Vice Admiral Mitscher was relieved of control of the carriers and began the long trip back to Washington to take over the direction of the navy's air forces. Vice Admiral J. S. McCain, who had held that job, replaced him. McCain and Halsey were old friends, and they had served together at Guadalcanal, where McCain had been for a short time after Halsey's arrival as commander of land-based air forces. McCain's recall to Washington had been partly because of suspicions by Admiral King that McCain might be responsible for some of the many mistakes made by the air forces in the early days of the campaign, but in the desk job McCain had performed so superbly that he was given the chance to go back to sea—something that did not happen to officers who lost the trust of Admiral King.

For two days the task force lingered around Okinawa, in protection of the landing force while awaiting the coming of the marines. Then, on June 1 the task force headed for enemy waters. Halsey was not going to fool around; he intended to strike the Japanese at their heart. At 6:00 on the morning of June 2, while Admiral Clark's task group remained off Okinawa, Halsey sent Admiral Radford's planes against the airfields of Kyushu.

The task force just then was about 350 miles off southern Japan, and the instructions to the pilots were to move in, strike hard, and move out. The fighters were armed with machine guns, rockets, and bombs.

Aboard the light carrier *Independence* that morning the pilots got their briefing and were in the air at 6:04. Their target was to be the airfields at Miyazaki, Iwakawa, and Miyakonojo. A dozen Grumman fighters were assigned the task, joined by eight fighters from the fleet carrier *Yorktown*. Other planes from the *Yorktown* struck Kanoya and East Kanoya airfields, and those from the remaining carriers in the force hit still more of the dozens of Japanese airfields on Kyushu island.

The carrier force was operating from a point northeast of Okinawa in the open sea, but since these were very much enemy waters there was a certain amount of nervousness, particularly on the part of the ship captains in the destroyer screen. Just at takeoff that morning, the *Remey* reported a sound contact ahead of the task force, and the carriers made an emergency turn to avoid what seemed to be a submarine. The *Remey* went out to investigate, but an hour later reported that there was no submarine; all was secure.

In the afternoon as the pilots returned to their carriers and reported on the activity, Halsey was pleased. *Yorktown*'s planes had burned five single-engine and one twin-engine plane on the ground, had destroyed other installations, and claimed to have damaged eighteen other planes, all on the ground. They also claimed one locomotive, victim of a strafing attack that must have been a surprise to the Japanese engineer as he sped along native ground. For although the B-29s had been coming over Japanese territory for months, attack by carrier planes on the homeland was something new.

It had not occurred for more than three years, since this same commander, Admiral Halsey, had taken Lieutenant Colonel Jimmy Doolittle of the army air forces within striking distance of Japan and Doolittle and his pilots had flown off a squadron of B-25 medium bombers to hit the Japanese islands. The Doolittle raid's damage to Japanese industry was slight, but the emotional impact on Japan had been enormous; the Japanese government had made much of the "fluke" (which it was), and had promised the people of Japan that there would be no more such incidents.

With the coming of the B-29s the promise had lost its force, but still the sight of F6F fighters zooming across the Japanese sky and strafing trains was a shocker in Japan.

Halsey's returning pilots reported no air opposition although the antiaircraft was strong and accurate. For example, one *Yorktown* pilot, Ensign Roy C. Koeller, had to ditch his plane in the sea after it was hit by antiaircraft fire over the target. Koeller put the plane down in rough sea, as far from Kyushu as he could get. The plane sank swiftly, and his rubber boat was lost. He then tried to save himself by using his parachute pack as a life raft, but the parachute soon became waterlogged and sank. One of his fellow pilots, circling to direct rescue, saw Koeller's plight and dropped an empty 58-gallon wingtank close by. Koeller managed to swim out to the tank and clung to it desperately for an hour, when a Dumbo amphibian from the carrier found him, landed, took him aboard, and brought him back to the *Yorktown.*

For Halsey, the results of the June 2 action were satisfying—as a beginning. He ordered flight operations off Kyushu to continue the next day. The destroyer captains, not very comfortable in Japanese waters, would just have to be nervous and on the alert. They were. That night, *Remey* encountered a floating mine and destroyed it. This minelaying in open water was a new desperate Japanese technique, but a very sensible one under the circumstances. No Japanese shipping now dared operate in the waters between Japan and Okinawa, and so it might be expected that any ship sunk by mines would be American or British, since the British Pacific Fleet had sent a carrier task force to operate with the Americans. At this point, the British force was heading for Sydney and a "blow" after having spent more than a month in action at Okinawa and having contributed heavily to the defenses of the landing force, at considerable expense in men and planes and heavy damage to several ships.

Before 6:00 the next morning, Halsey's planes were flying again, against the same targets, the southern Kyushu airfields. Halsey figured the Japanese might expect an attack elsewhere and thus would have replaced the destroyed and damaged planes, preparing for another suicide air armada against Okinawa. This second day, as the launching began, the task force radar picked up bogeys a hundred miles away, heading north, which meant away from the task force. But that was not very meaningful because the bogeys might turn, so *Yorktown's* combat air patrol tried to intercept the enemy planes, but failed. Probably it was a flight bound from Formosa to Honshu.

On this second day of the strike, the Americans met a little air opposition (*Yorktown's* pilots shot down two Japanese fighters) and other carriers reported the same.

More important, the pilots returned to their ships to report that the pickings were very poor on the ground. Instead of re-spotting aircraft on the fields after the first raids, the Japanese had gone to greater lengths to conceal them. They had con-structed a complex system of underground revetments, and their camouflage techniques were greatly improved. *Yorktown* pilots, for example, reported only damaging two twin-engine planes and two single-engine planes on the ground, and these might have been left over from the first day's raids.

The weather was changing rapidly, and for the worse. On June 2, the weathermen reported a frontal zone between the carriers and Kyushu, and the pilots confirmed it. At 28 degrees North latitude, a broad front of cloud and fog extended from several thousand feet down to the water, just north of Amami Gunto, one of the most northerly of the Ryukyu islands. They flew over the front—it did not bother them too much—but they reported an altostratus cloud overcast above Kyushu and the towering cumulus clouds of thunderstorms in broken patches.

On June 3, the front began to move south so that by 0700, just as the last planes were launching, the wind began to shift and came around to northeast and east, and increased to ten knots. At noon the task force began to move through rain, and at times it became so heavy that it impaired air operations. On the flight to Kyushu on this second day the pilots reported foul weather, but when they reached Japan it cleared and they had good visibility over the targets.

So the storm front did not seriously bother the American flight operations on the second day. But during the night of June 3 the weather worsened, and in the morning when opera-tions began, a typhoon was reported in the general area.

Several reports about the weather had been sent out by various units of the fleet, from Pearl Harbor and from the

Philippines, but they were conflicting. The different reports covered an area of 34,000 square miles. Admiral Halsey's actions in relation to the storm were limited because to the north and west he would be moving into enemy waters, and already the discovery of mines had indicated the sort of dangers he would face there. Better than any other man in the Pacific, Admiral Halsey understood the dangers of fierce Pacific tropical storms. He had been caught in a typhoon on December 17, 1944, when the Third Fleet was fuelling between strikes. At that time, the fleet was about 500 miles east of Luzon island. After checking with his aerographer, Admiral Halsey decided to move 200 miles to the northwest. The aerographer told him that the storm was then just about over Luzon and that it would soon strike an incoming cold front and turn northeast. But instead, the typhoon—for that is what it was—had changed course. Fleet communications were so unwieldy, involving decoding and complicated message priority ratings (weather messages were not very high on the list then), that Halsey did not have access to a dispatch that said the storm center was not 500 miles to the east but 200 miles southeast.

Faced with changing reports, Halsey changed his orders, and finally the fleet was running southwest to try to avoid the storm.

The course change, as it happened, took the fleet into the eye of the storm, and the ships took a tremendous beating that day. Some of the waves were seventy feet high, up above the topmasts of the small ships. The fury of the typhoon was not the only problem. Over the years of the war, many improvements in ships and techniques of warfare had brought changes to the older vessels, and the changes had altered the metricentric balance, or the center of gravity of the ships. They were, in other words, top-heavy. In the course of the storm three of the topheavy destroyers, loaded with radar and other devices, turned over on their sides, and the water poured down the funnels and sank them as a child sinks his toy boats in the bathtub. They were the destroyers *Spence, Hull,* and *Monaghan.* Besides these tragic sinkings, the cruiser *Miami* was badly hurt, and so were the carriers *Monterey*, *Cowpens*, and *San Jacinto*. The escort carriers *Cape Esperance* and *Altmaha* were also badly damaged and the destroyers *Aylwin*, *Dewey*, and *Hickok* looked as though they had been in battle. Altogether twenty-nine other ships than those sunk were damaged by the storm, 150 planes were lost, and nearly 800 men were killed. Admiral Nimitz called it the greatest loss they had taken in the Pacific since the desperate days of Guadalcanal.

Halsey was responsible for the disaster; that was the way command went in the navy, and he never tried to avoid responsibility. But as for the cause—he attributed the decisions that carried the fleet into the storm to bad information management by the fleet at Pearl Harbor. There was enough truth in what he said so that he avoided a court-martial although his enemies cried out for his head.

After it was all over, Halsey recommended a number of changes in the weather reporting system. He wanted weather reconnaissance planes to fly constantly in the battle zone, to track typhoons and report on their movements. This was not done. He wanted weather messages given the highest priority. Again this was not done. And so, while Admiral Halsey tried to figure out the course of the June typhoon, the old system was still in effect and his weathermen did not have the benefit of the latest information as they made their decisions: the messages were bottled up in the radio room of the flagship.

At noon on June 3, a Seventh Fleet weather plane operating out of the Philippines reported on the move of the typhoon to weather central station at Leyte, but the information was delayed twenty-four hours before it reached Admiral Halsey. No further information of visual sighting was received by Halsey until the USS *Ancon*, moving south from Okinawa, made a radar fix on the storm center late on the evening of June 4. By that time, Halsey was already in the wrong place and the Third Fleet was in trouble.

The planes returning from the fighter sweep on June 3 had some difficulty with weather. On June 4 the task groups were scheduled to refuel and then to resume the attacks on the Japanese homeland. At 9:30 on the morning of June 4 Halsey ordered the fuelling stopped and told Admiral Clark to head southwest. By afternoon the weather seemed better and the refuelling was begun again. But the storm continued to build up as the ships headed into it instead of away. Halsey suggested late that night that they take a course of 150 degrees or further south and west, but Admiral McCain said he could not see any particular gain to be achieved by it, and a few hours later he suggested that the best course would lie eastward.

Halsey consulted his weatherman, who replied that to go east would only keep them running before the storm, and he suggested that they head almost due north. So Halsey issued that order, and the Task Force headed northwest at sixteen knots. Soon, ship captains began to report that they were heading into the teeth of the storm, and Admiral McCain ordered a change in course to due north. But at 3:00 in the morning, Rear Admiral Beary, commander of the logistics group, reported that his escort carriers were taking water on the flight decks and that he was heading back to the northwest again. At 4:00 in the morning, Admiral Clark announced that the storm center was on his radar and that it was forty miles away and almost due north. Twenty minutes later Admiral Clark suggested that he could get out of the storm by heading southeast. Admiral McCain said he saw no such indications, but let Clark go if he wished. What Clark wished was just that, but the weather grew heavier every few minutes. At 6:30 that morning of June 5 the bow of the old cruiser *Pittsburgh* was wrenched off by a wave. They had come into the storm center. Admiral Clark ordered the task group to stop engines and lie to, and half an hour later he reported the heavy weather to the task force commander. By 7:30 they were able to make a little headway and began moving south at about five knots. The seas began to fall a little as the barometer rose. The weather continued to improve, and by 8:00 that night they were out of the storm and heading toward a fleet rendezvous at twenty knots.

Once again the fleet suffered more damage from the storm than it had from the Japanese in recent surface actions. The escort carriers *Salamaua* and *Windham Bay* were badly hurt. The *Salamaua*'s entire flight deck was destroyed, the catapult supports were ruptured. The *Windham Bay*'s flight deck was rolled up like a pancake for the first twenty feet and it then collapsed on the forecastle. The big carriers *Hornet* and *Bennington* each lost the forward twenty-five feet of their flight decks and could not use their catapults. The cruisers *Pittsburgh* and *Duluth* were both damaged, as was the destroyer *Moore,* the *Blue,* and the destroyer escort *Conklin.* Damage in this case meant the sort that would have to be dealt with by a shipyard. Twenty-five other ships were damaged, but not so seriously. Still, once again there would have to be a court of inquiry, and some of Halsey's junior admirals, particularly the outspoken and irrepressible Jocko Clark, were extremely critical of Halsey's management of the fleet during the storm. Vice Admiral John Hoover ran the court of inquiry and he wanted Halsey and McCain court-martialed, but Admirals King and Nimitz, whose ambitions had all been fulfilled, took a different view. Nimitz recognized that Halsey had complained about the failure of fleet headquarters to provide adequate storm information after the last typhoon. This time, steps were taken to correct the errors.

THE WATERS
OF JAPAN

Had either of Halsey's typhoons occurred during the first two years of the war, the blows they dealt the American fleet would have been extremely serious. But in the summer of 1945 the U.S. had so much capacity to produce and repair ships that even the serious damage was not a major problem in terms of pressing the war. On June 7, Admiral Halsey reported to Nimitz that he was ready to carry out the fleet's assigned task of striking the enemy at home to support the Okinawa operations, rather than sit back at Okinawa and take punishment.

Already, however, Halsey had learned something new about the effective operation of carriers in a war that had changed remarkably in the past year. As he put it, "The glorious days of the carrier spearheading the Pacific offensive ended when the spear entered the heart of the Empire."

As had become apparent in the first two days' raids, Japanese strategy had undergone a complete change. The Japanese were not coming forth to fight; air opposition had been negligible, although Halsey knew that the Japanese aircraft factories were still turning out planes by the thousands. The answer was inescapable: the Japanese were holding their strength and waiting for the invasion forces. By holding back they not only conserved resources, they also concealed from the Americans any accurate estimates of the Japanese strength and will to fight.

Halsey warned that it was no longer a matter of sending out the planes to hit whatever they found, but that careful planning was necessary to find targets that were worth the enormous effort of a carrier strike. The same would be true, Halsey predicted, of submarine targets.

Already Halsey had observed that the Japanese air force was avoiding combat to conserve resources. He saw that the vast armada that would move against Japan would need constant air cover by all available resources, to mitigate against a kamikaze attack that would make Okinawa look easy. The escort carriers would no longer be enough, but the fast carrier force would have to do the job for many weeks. So the roles of the pilots would be changing, and the important matter would be to have enough fighters, fighter bombers, and night fighters to protect the fleet and the landing forces. The torpedo bombers and dive bombers would take a back seat. In future, Halsey said, the carriers would want about 80 percent fighters and 20 percent bombers.

As Halsey approached Japan on June 8 he began planning for operations around the islands. The first strike, sent out that day, was a regular carrier strike, concentrating on fighters. From 250 miles off Kyushu, the planes were launched—200 fighters and fighter bombers from the carriers of Task Force 38. The planes came from *Ticonderoga, Bennington, Hornet, Shangri-la,* and *Yorktown.* The *Yorktown* supplied the photographic planes, and they encountered the only opposition of the day. Over Shibushu, they ran into five Zeros in the air, and shot down two of them and damaged another. Then the fighters and fighter bombers came in over the airfields and strafed and bombed without any opposition in the air, although the antiaircraft fire was severe. Three American planes were damaged and forced to ditch, but not a single pilot or crew member was lost; all were rescued by the Dumbos.

Indeed, "operational casualties" rather than casualties of enemy action were causing most of the plane and personnel losses. For example, two of the pilots of the carrier *Independence* were lost on June 3 as the weather worsened in the flight area, not to enemy action, but to weather and possibly because of a midair collision of pilots not familiar with flying in bad weather. The two went into a cloud along with their flight about sixty miles east of Okinawa, and they did not come out.

It was, indeed, becoming a different sort of war.

On June 9 Halsey decided to try bombardment of the Japanese islands, to see what sort of targets and result might be obtained. He assigned the big cruisers *Guam* and *Alaska* to the mission. They were to hit Okino Daito Shima, a small target, just to see what could be done and to train the men of the ship for more difficult action later. The next day, several battleships carried out a bombardment mission against Minami Daito Shima. The targets were not very important in the big picture, but the training was. The bombardments were accompanied by air missions, and the pilots were equipped with variable-timed bombs, some of them going off on impact and some delayed. Some planes used napalm to see what effect it would have against various sorts of targets. All this was in training for the assult on Japan proper. What Halsey was trying to do, particularly, was to find effective means of knocking out the Japanese antiaircraft installations.

On June 10 the carriers struck the islands again, but late in the afternoon it was announced that the ships were heading for Leyte for two weeks of repair and upkeep. Leyte was hardly "Pearl" or "Dago" but it was land, and the enlisted men and junior officers would be able to get a drink. The navy's celebrated prohibition of alcoholic beverages aboard ship was honored at the lower levels, and by breach at the higher. Aboard the carriers the flight surgeons always had control of a certain amount of "medicinal" liquor, but the use of it was a painful process and could be grounds for court-martial, so the ships were generally dry and any surcease was more than welcome.

As Halsey and his men retired to the Philippines for a rest, Japan was moving rapidly to gird the national loins for the greatest struggle of the war.

In a series of military conferences the Imperial General Staff decided to augment the military forces of Kyushu even more. Actually the buildup had begun in earnest a year earlier, with the American invasion of Saipan. The Satsuma Peninsula was seen by the staff as the most probable invasion point for the Americans even then and three major army units had been deployed there under command of the Fortieth Army. One unit was the 14th Division, reinforced, and another was the 8th Independent Mixed Brigade. In all, 900,000 men were committed to the area, with all the equipment and planes and guns this indicated. When the American fighters had come zooming across the Japanese air fields and had spotted only a few planes on the runways and scattered about the fields, they were the victims of Japanese camouflage, for the planes were there; they were simply in hiding.

But it was certainly true, in Kyushu and the rest of Japan, that the war effort had become most difficult. The growing number and effectiveness of B-29 bomber raids was telling on the Japanese economy. Already in June 1945, the military men were complaining because the transportation facilities had been destroyed, and they said that their efforts were half paralyzed. The population had begun to suffer seriously from the fire bombing and the effects of fires and high explosives on the industrial areas. The civilians were beginning to feel real distress in terms of hunger and clothing and, as the paper and wooden houses burned, from shortage of housing.

The course of the war in Okinawa had brought about a renewal of the defense efforts in the south in May 1945, and

Halsey's raids on Kyushu at the beginning of June brought an even greater effort. The Japanese were certain that invasion would come that fall, probably in November.

When Halsey's ships arrived in San Pedro Bay, the fleet was still not out of action. The minesweepers were out to clear the area of mines before the task force returned to the East China Sea. The area concerned was cleared by the third week of June. Also, as Halsey's men rested for the coming fight, the Okinawa campaign came to an end. The Japanese commander, Lieutenant General Mitsuru Ushijima, dispatched his last message to Imperial General Headquarters on June 21. The battle was over, he told Tokyo, and it had been lost. They would not hear from him again. The Japanese force was reduced to two small units in caves, after Ushijima committed suicide the next day. Organized resistance on Okinawa was finished.

That announcement had an electrifying effect on the Japanese air forces in Kyushu and on Formosa. No longer was there any excuse to continue to send forays over Okinawa. With the departure of the carriers and the battleships for Halsey's new plan to hit Japan at home, there was no further reason for the sacrifice. The Japanese air forces had hoped for a long time that they could knock out enough of the American carriers to force the U.S. navy to slow down its approach to Japan. But the battle was obviously a losing one. Fleet Air Wing One's flying boats and land-based aircraft continued to hit Japanese shipping in the Yellow Sea and the Sea of Japan as Admiral Halsey's carriers were repaired and refurbished, so there was no end to naval air activity, and of course the B-29 raids continued. So did the American submarine forays into the Japanese home waters and along the coast of China, to prevent Japan from receiving the supplies of oil and ores that she needed so desperately to continue the struggle. As spring moved into summer, the Japanese position continued to deteriorate. The Japanese casualty rates, of civilians as well as military, were rising, and millions were homeless. In May alone, air raids had hit 370,000 buildings and made 1,300,000 people homeless. The raids caused the factory workers to stay home from their jobs, and aircraft production by the end of the spring had fallen from a high in 1944 of 2,500 planes a month to 1,600 a month in June. But 1,600 planes a month was still a lot of aircraft, particularly when added to the stockpiles the Japanese army had been holding onto so tightly during all those months when the navy's air forces were being decimated in the battle of the outer empire.

As Halsey rested, his enemies in Tokyo assessed their problem. The worst of it, Imperial General Headquarters discovered, was a war-weariness on the part of the general public that must somehow be overcome if the military men were to continue the fight. Some of the most ardent among the generals truly believed against all logic that a victory was possible. But most held onto a far more slender hope: that by causing enough casualties and enough trouble for the Americans, they could secure a negotiated peace that would leave them whatever remained of the empire. It was not much: Korea, Manchuria, and Formosa. Okinawa, for years considered to be a part of the homeland, was now gone, and China would have to be given up, but these other territories had been Japanese for a long time.

As for Manchuria, the Japanese had built up almost all the heavy industry, and at a conference table could argue that point.

One of the most serious problems in Japan in the spring of 1945 was troop discipline. As the trains and roads were destroyed and the shortages grew, the troops tended to forage and abuse the civilian population to get what they needed. This activity, in turn, caused so much difficulty that War Minister Korechika Anami cautioned the army again and again that it must behave if it wished the support of the people when the final decisive battle came on the beaches of Japan.

The Japanese navy now existed almost entirely on paper. To be sure, a number of ships remained afloat, but virtually none of the capital ships were in condition for combat. Combined fleet headquaters, for years a seagoing command, was now ashore at a land installation near Tokyo, and the army was insisting on the unification of the services. For all practical purposes this meant the naval air force would begin operating under army command and the remaining naval troops would become soldiers. In fact this was not accomplished, but it was not particularly important, because there simply was not enough left of the navy to make that much difference.

A survey of the civilian economy in the spring of 1945 showed that there was no way the Japanese government could successfully raise the number of men in uniform. Before the war the civilian economy had commanded the service of five million men in business. The number in June 1945 was down to two million. Of the whole work force, 79 percent of the workers were engaged in war work or in agriculture, and they certainly could not be drafted. Of the remaining 21 percent, most of the "civilian industries" that survived pertained directly to the military effort. Japan had, in effect, been turned into a military machine in these past five years.

The war had brought dreadful casualties to the Japanese officer corps. The number of officers who were graduates of the military academy—the professionals, in other words—was down to 12 percent of the total.

And as for supply for the major effort that must be made to defend the homeland, where would it come from? Imperial General Headquarters had to swallow some very unpleasant figures. The military supply of fuel was almost exhausted. There was virtually no aviation gasoline left in the islands; after September there would be nothing but alcohol. The supply of gasoline for trucks was already gone and they were running—if at all—on alcohol.

The food prospects were equally serious: The American submarines and the bombers made it impossible to import foreign rice. Rice could still be brought across from Korea and the whole South Korean rice crop was requisitioned this year, but for years Japan had been importing rice from Indochina and

Thailand, and this had become impossible. Those rice ships were almost invariably sent to the bottom by the Americans.

All spring long, as the Americans concerned themselves with Okinawa, the Japanese reorganized their defense. In May, nineteen new divisions were activated, eight of them to be of a new sort, a kind of flying division able to operate over great distances, and provided with extra firepower.

The air arm, newly consolidated, proposed to fit out 500 squadrons of fighting planes. About half of these were to be ordinary squadrons, dealing with reconnaissance, transport, coastal search, fighters for protection and interdiction of enemy planes, and bombers. But the other half would be suicide squadrons; in June 2,000 suicide planes were ready for action, and 187 daylight attack units and 43 night attack units were being organized.

Steel was short (production was down to one quarter of that of 1944) so the concentration of weaponry had to be changed. Instead of field guns, the infantry units would have many more mortars, which were cheap to produce. New units were organized even before weapons were available, but southern Kyushu, where Halsey had been operating, was regarded as the focal point of danger, and so all available weapons were shifted there. Halsey's attacks of early June only emphasized the importance the Japanese were placing on the Kyushu position. All the contingency plans were in effect by then: the 12th Area Army was responsible for the defense of the Tokyo region, but another army, the Tokyo Defense Army, was established to secure the area around the Imperial Palace. A provisional Imperial Palace was set up in the suburbs of the city of Nagano and an Imperial General Headquarters was established in caves in the town of Matsushiro in Nagano prefecture.

By June the Imperial General Staff put out a new estimate of the war situation. With the end of operations on Okinawa, the next step (here the navy agreed wholeheartedly) would be landings on the China coast and then on islands near the Japanese homeland—sometime in midsummer. November was still the month when an American attempt to land on Japan proper was to be expected. Probably, said the experts, landing would first be made on Kyushu, but the final battle would be fought on the Tokyo plain.

There were some in Japan this summer who remembered with great regret the Imperial General Staff's refusal to consider Admiral Yamamoto's proposal that the army attack the Russians in 1942. The Russian experts on the staff warned that while Russia could not be expected to help the Americans, still the Russians would seize any opportunity to take Manchuria; when the Americans landed in Japan, this move could be expected. So Japan must expect Soviet intervention at the time when it would be most disagreeable. Partly to shore up the home defenses, and partly to preserve the forces involved, three armies were moved from Manchuria down to Japan. Manchuria, with all its industry, simply had to be written off, and it was.

In the Japanese fashion, a good deal of bombast was written into the appraisals and orders—"doom the American forces," "fight on to glorious victory"—but for anyone prepared to skirt these patriotic phrases, the actual assessment of conditions was accurate enough. All efforts possible would be made to destroy the American capability to invade Japan, but the massive effort was reserved for that moment when the U.S. forces began the amphibious assault. This was to be the *ketsu go* (decisive operation). Because the navy, even in these desperate hours, still had more planes and more skilled pilots than the army, the major effort in the air would be navy. It would field more than 5,000 planes to the army's 3,300. At least half of all planes would be suicide bombers, and judging from the effectiveness of the *kikusui* squadrons at Okinawa (of which the Japanese were perfectly aware) with the shorter distances and increased will to destroy, the effectiveness of the suicide weapons would be great. Back at Guam and in Washington the American planners had no doubt of that; in the middle of the Okinawa campaign Admiral Nimitz succeeded in persuading Admiral King to establish a special planning office in Boston whose task was to devise an effective defense against the suicide plane. Up to this time, no defense had been perfected, nor would one be; the fact remained that a determined man, piloting a simple plane and committed to giving his life to destroy a ship, had an excellent chance of success. In its way the Japanese effort was a vindication of the samurai theory that the will could overcome superior force.

To augment the attacks from the air, the navy devoted its remaining resources to creation of its own suicide forces. At Otsujima, the navy organized its most experienced young officers of midget submarines into a *kaiten* unit. For a year the navy had been experimenting with the launching of these small submarine bombs from mother submarines. The results had not been encouraging, but the effort persisted. On June 4, as the typhoon struck Admiral Halsey's fleet, the *I-36* left Otsujima with a load of *kaiten*. The submarine command had previously sent out twenty-three sets of *kaiten* in big submarines, and had compiled records that showed that thirty ships, including several aircraft carriers and battleships, had been sunk by the midget submarines. It was wishful thinking, but it buoyed Japanese navy morale.

The *I-36* headed east of Saipan to cover the U.S. shipping route that ran from Pearl Harbor to the Marianas. For two weeks the submarine patrolled, spending much of its time down deep to avoid American destroyers and destroyer escorts. Also as was the case with most of the other *kaiten*, these midgets were far from perfect. One day, Captain Sugamasa of the *I-36* ordered a *kaiten* drill. Each suicide pilot rushed to his machine, three pairs on each side of the submarine—and not one of the *kaiten* was found to be operational. Only three of them could be repaired immediately.

On June 17, as the men of the Third U.S. Fleet were beginning their shore leave in the Philippines, the *I-36* made a *kaiten* attack on a pair of transports. But the submarine could not get close enough to the targets to launch. On June 23 the captain spotted an American tanker and launched two *kaiten* against it. One failed to operate, and then a second failed. Captain Sugamasa launched a torpedo attack and claimed at least one hit, but the tanker neither burned nor sank; it speeded up and moved away. On June 28, Sugamasa made another attack on a transport, but was surprised by an American destroyer just after he launched his first *kaiten*. The submarine went down and was subjected to a hail of depth charges. She was damaged but managed to escape, waterlogged and slow. She survived nearly a hundred depth charges. Sugamasa managed to surface and launch another *kaiten*. But once launched, both suicide weapons failed. Two more lives were lost to no avail. On June 29, the *I-36* was back in Japanese waters, only to have a tremendous shock. Before the boat could get back to her submarine base in the Bungo strait, between Kyushu and Shikoku islands, she was attacked by an American submarine which fired four torpedoes. It was as if a Japanese submarine had entered San Francisco Bay.

On the day that *I-36* ceased operations, Admiral Halsey learned that the bodies of General Ushijima and his chief of staff Lieutenant General Isamu Cho had been found on Okinawa. The body count of Japanese came to 107,000 men, and 11,000 prisoners of war. Another 25,000 men were apparently killed and sealed in caves. The Japanese had lost 7,800 planes in the concentrated attacks on the island and its environs, or ten times as many as the Americans, but the American casualties in the taking of Okinawa had been heavy enough: about 75,000 officers and men.

On the last day of June 1945, Admiral Halsey was ready to get back into action, and the Third Fleet's ships had been repaired from the damage caused by the natural kamikaze—divine wind—of the typhoon. Halsey had what he called "comprehensive plans for the destruction of the remainder of the Japanese navy." He was living up to a promise he had made back in the early days of the battle of Guadalcanal, when he told reporters he proposed to ride into Tokyo one day on a white horse of the sort Emperor Hirohito rode. Halsey was ready, all right, with blood in his eye.

DESTINATION: TOKYO

With thirteen carriers and eight battleships, and all the cruisers, destroyers, escorts, and support ships of a major modern fleet, Admiral Halsey set forth from the Philippines on July 1, bound for the heart of Japan.

For weeks, while the ships were repaired, Halsey and his staff had made careful plans for this operation. No one knew what the Japanese reaction to an air strike by carrier on the Tokyo region might be. It just could turn out that the enemy would react violently and put up all the force at his disposal, and that could be extremely hazardous for the operation.

To insure the highest margin of protection, Halsey had used every means at his disposal to see precisely what he was getting into. B-29 Superfortresses had made a series of reconnaissance flights over northern Honshu and Hokkaido to locate airfields and other installations. Four-engined Liberator bombers (B-24) had covered the Tokyo area, photographing every part of it, and on their return photo experts had examined the results with minute care. At sea, several American submarines were sent into Japanese coastal waters to check for mine fields. Halsey intended to move his battleships and cruisers close in to shore to bombard Japanese military and defense production installations, and he wanted to make sure the water would be safe for them.

As the fleet headed toward Japan, all these preparations continued, and the men of the planes and the ships conducted training operations: largely gunnery practice and air defense against what might be a rain of kamikaze attackers against the fleet. As the ships moved toward the enemy homeland the smaller ones were refuelled from the larger, a technique perfected in the third year of the war. The carrier *Yorktown*, for example, refuelled fourteen destroyers and escorts before July 8, and then refuelled herself when the task force met its logistic contingent on that day at a rendezvous. This technique made it possible for the Third Fleet to range over an enormous area of sea.

On July 8, the carriers and battleships and cruisers took on fuel from the tankers, and food and ammunition from other supply ships. Replacement planes were supplied by the escort carriers in the task force. It all went so smoothly it looked easy, a far cry from those desperate days in 1941 and 1942 when Admirals Fletcher and Brown had missed chances to strike the enemy because of fuel problems and their inability to fuel properly at sea.

On July 9 the tension in the fleet increased as the ships moved up to the point east of Honshu island where they would launch planes early the next day for the Tokyo strike. As the ships moved onto station, they were not observed by the Japanese. The Japanese picket boats did not operate so far out these days, the submarine force was reduced to a handful of operational I-boats, and under orders from the Imperial General Staff nearly all aircraft were grounded because of the fuel shortage. But there was another reason: stealthy approach of the Americans; they came up through a front of bad weather and only emerged into the clear at 2:00 on the morning of July 10. Two Japanese flying boats were out at dawn patrolling the coastal waters, but they were easily handled by the combat air patrols, and both were shot down in short order. Apparently the patrol planes had not seen the fleet, for no reports reached Tokyo.

The carrier pilots and crewmen were up by 3:00 that morning, and shortly before 4:00 the carriers began to launch. The targets on this sweep were to be airfields for the most part. The *Yorktown*, for example, was assigned to strike twelve different airfields.

The pilots took off in clear skies, and as the sun came up the day brightened. The planes droned on inward, over the Japanese shoreline, and still no Zeros or other fighters rose to meet them. As they headed inland, there was very little antiaircraft fire. Only as the bombers and fighters approached the airfield targets did the antiaircraft guns around the fields come to life, and then the fire was surprisingly light. But the pickings were also very light this day. There was no doubt about the completeness of the Japanese surprise. Many planes were found on enemy fields, more were seen in revetments, widely dispersed. Most of these planes seemed to have been degassed, since when the fighters strafed them they showed damage but did not flame.

The pilots were carrying fused bombs and general purpose bombs, and it was difficult to tell what damage was caused to the planes in their enclosures. The most successful strikes were made by planes with machine guns and rockets. The trouble with the fuse was that it required a fall of about 5,000 feet to arm the bomb, and the pilots generally could not find the concealed planes at that altitude. The pilots also discovered that the Japanese had begun moving their planes far away from the airfields themselves in order to protect the planes better. So the fliers came back to report that what was needed were low-level attacks with forward-firing weapons.

Still, Halsey had reason to be pleased at the end of the day. A conservative estimate, which he insisted on these days, indicated that about 100 planes had actually been destroyed and perhaps another 225 damaged. But installations were hit hard, hangars were burned, and shops were knocked out. Based on his experiences in the past, it was surprising to Admiral Halsey that the Japanese did not come up to fight, but on consideration he realized that they were saving everything for that "decisive battle" which had been so long in the offing.

For more than a year the Japanese had clung to that tiny hope. They had tried to create the decisive battle during the Saipan invasion, and the result had been Admiral Mitscher's "Marianas Turkey Shoot," which would have been more successful had Mitscher not been restrained from pursuit of the Japanese carriers by Admiral Spruance. The "decisive battle" had again been planned for the time of the American invasion of Leyte, and Halsey had destroyed nearly all the remaining carrier force in his run up north during that battle. So now, indeed, here in the Japanese homeland the decision was nearly at hand.

About a dozen planes were lost in this strike, mostly from antiaircraft fire. At the time no one could tell precisely how many pilots were lost, because of the operations of Dumbo rescue aircraft within the fleet and of submarines on lifeguard duty. But the loss of only a dozen planes in a major strike by thirteen carriers would have been unbelievable even a year earlier.

Until July 1 the Japanese had also clung to the belief that the Americans would first assault the China coast, and that was another reason the attack of July 10 on the Tokyo area came as a complete surprise to Imperial General Headquarters.

On July 11, the American ships retired to a previously planned fuelling rendezvous, and Admiral Halsey considered his planning. The strikes against the airfields even around Tokyo had not been productive enough to continue as long as better targets were available. On the thirteenth he would hit northern Honshu and Hokkaido, areas that had previously been almost immune to air attacks, since the B-29s were concentrating on the southern industrial area.

On July 12, the fuelling continued. Just two hours after midnight the destroyer *Melvin* reported a torpedo wake 200 yards off her beam, and a few minutes later the destroyer *Norman Scott* reported a torpedo wake, too. These may have been *kaiten* launched from the submarine *I-53*. She was out at that time, one of the two or three submarines then operational in the entire Japanese navy. In any event the torpedoes missed and no damage was done, although *I-53* claimed a destroyer.

On July 13, when the first strike was supposed to hit northern Honshu, the weather closed in and the carriers could not operate. After all, the ceiling was only 900 feet and visibility was less than two miles. It was not long before the ceiling was zero and visibility was a quarter of a mile. This situation continued until after sunset, so the carriers waited. The weather seemed to be growing worse by the hour, and Halsey was not immune to concern about weather after two typhoons, so he gave the order to retire eastward and return to the operating area later. On the morning of July 14, the wind dropped and the sky cleared, and operations began before dawn. The strike area this day was northeastern Honshu.

Everyone concerned was nervous about operating so close to the Japanese homeland. The basic concerns were over submarines and mines, and although the submarines did not make much of an appearance, the mines certainly did. The Japanese had released hundreds if not thousands of floating mines to keep the enemy ships away from the islands. Every day the destroyers and escorts exploded half a dozen mines with gunfire. And there were some scares caused by the big round glass fishing floats the Japanese had used for years.

Once again, the pilots of the carrier planes discovered that in this Japanese homeland there was no opposition at all. It must have been hard for the Japanese fighter pilots to restrain themselves and obey the orders that insisted they must stay on the ground and watch as their enemies moved unopposed through Japanese air. But Imperial Headquarters demanded absolute compliance: no planes were to be wasted, no fuel and ammunition expended until the ultimate battle.

The American planes did their job well. They were assigned to destruction of aircraft on fields in the industrial areas around

Muroran, Hakodate, and Otaru. The Japanese planes, they found, were again very few, but there was a good deal of coastal shipping on the seas and in the ports, and the pilots destroyed a number of small vessels. The *Yorktown's* pilots claimed to have destroyed fourteen locomotives and damaged two. They also claimed six direct bomb hits on the Wanishi Ironworks at Muroran. They lost one pilot that day, a favorite in Air Group 88, and member of a navy family that had suffered heavily during the war through the deaths of several of the five brothers: on this day Lieutenant Commander Richard Crommelin's Hellcat collided with another fighter in a cloud, and Crommelin, the commander of Fighting 88, went spinning into the sea. The other pilot's plane was only slightly damaged, and he continued on the attack mission.

The pilots of the *Independence* and several other carriers struck targets in southern Hokkaido. One pilot reported that he forced a small steamer to beach. Other pilots reported attacks on destroyer escorts, patrol craft, and one 5,000-ton freighter.

Altogether that day Task Force 38 flew off 871 attack planes, plus the usual antisubmarine and combat air patrol; that accounted for another 300 flights. They dropped 330 tons of bombs and fired 1,800 rockets at Japanese targets. The task force claimed to have sunk twenty-four ships and fifty-one small craft. The most serious damage (although they did not then know it) was the destruction of seven ferries that carried goods and people from northern Honshu to Hokkaido island. The attack of July 14 knocked out the ferry service and brought havoc to Hokkaido. Nearly all the damage done this day was to civilian industry and shipping. One destroyer escort was sunk at Fukushima; and three picket boats in the Tsugaru strait, one patrol craft at Kamaishi and one destroyer escort north of Hachinohe were damaged, along with two others near Hakodate and one near Erimo Saki. But there were no battleships, cruisers, or carriers to be found that day.

They found only one two-engined Betty bomber in the air and another on the ground. Halsey now knew that the Japanese were playing a waiting game.

On July 15 the action took about the same form. The carrier planes had to concentrate on shipping and industry because there were no visible air installations worth striking. The anti-aircraft opposition was heavier than it had been earlier. Three of the pilots off the *Yorktown* were shot down. Pilots from some of the carriers had difficulty finding adequate targets. The *Independence* sent off nine torpedo planes loaded with bombs to go after shipping. They sank one destroyer escort southeast of Hakodate, and then when the other planes could not find shipping, they attacked bridges and viaducts west of Hakodate. At the end of the day, the Aomori-Hakodate ferry system was a shambles. The Japanese brought huge supplies of coal down from Hokkaido for the industrial plants of Honshu island, and it travelled between the island by ferry and a system of colliers. The carrier planes in two days put all of the twelve ferries out of action and sank or seriously damaged a third of the ships that carried the coal. After this raid, the coal supplies of Japanese industry were reduced so severely that steel production and aircraft production dropped another third.

Simultaneously, the American battleship fleet was brought into action against the Japanese homeland. Rear Admiral John F. Shafroth led the first naval gunfire in the home islands of Japan with a strike on the Kamaishi ironworks of the Japan Iron Company, one of the Empire's largest steel producers. Admiral Shafroth had a difficult problem: the Kamaishi works was located in a narrow valley of the Otatari River, with steep hills on both sides of the stream. Shafroth would have liked to have come in as close as possible, but the Japanese mining of the coastal waters kept him outside the 100-fathom curve, where destroyers and escorts had been able to protect the ships from floating mines launched out from shore. Inside that curve they could expect to find anchored-mine fields, and since Halsey did not have the minesweepers to clear the area, Shafroth had to improvise. He did so, taking three battleships, two heavy cruisers, and nine destroyers in to shell the Kamaishi steel plant for two hours in broad daylight.

The American bombardment force stood sixteen miles off the coast and passed back and forth across the harbor front. There was no opposition of any kind; it was as if they were shooting at targets on Kahoolawe island in Hawaii. The accuracy of the bombardment was remarkable, but this was possible because of expert aerial mapping and target spotting after scores of aircraft from the B-29 command and the fighters and bombers of the carriers had flown across the region taking aerial photos. Most of the shelling fell within the target area, but as always, there was damage to civilian installations as well. One unforeseen result was a firestorm in the town, created by concussion and the spreading of cooking fires through the paperwalled houses of the Japanese.

Every unit employed in this Halsey strike against Japan was amazed by the lack of opposition. Rear Admiral J. Cary Jones was sent out with four cruisers and six destroyers to find shipping along the coast and destroy it. Halsey figured that possibly the Japanese were holing up by day and moving at night. But on July 15 Admiral Jones reported that he had swept the east coast of Honshu island—without finding a single target. So antishipping strikes were not productive. But Shafroth's success in damaging the Kamaishi works was confirmed by aerial photographs, and Halsey decided more of this activity was in order.

On July 15, Admiral Oscar C. Badger employed three battleships, including the Halsey flagship *Missouri,* two cruisers and eight destroyers against the Nihon Steel Company plant and the Wanishi Ironworks at Muroran on Hokkaido for an hour. Badger had a harder job than Shafroth because the weather closed in on his activity until the ceiling was down to a thousand feet by the time he finished. The clouds obscured the visibility, but at one point, when shells were falling at the Nihon Steel Plant, an enormous cloud of smoke arose, as some buildings exploded. And when the action was over, four of the eight smokestacks at the Wanishi Ironworks had fallen.

The failure of the Japanese to defend themselves in these attacks changed Admiral Halsey's mind. His staff held that the

Japanese were keeping back their planes and pilots in reserve for the great battle. Halsey snorted and said the Japanese were almost licked. He thought they could not last through the fall—and militarily speaking, Halsey was probably right, except for one factor. It might be called national pride, or honor, or the spirit of *bushido*, but whatever it was called, this strong national spirit existed and was being exploited to the fullest by the military. One reason it was so easy for the military to control the civilian population was the militarist government that had taken power in the late 1930s. But an underlying reason might even have been stronger: the Japanese were a homogenous people, for hundreds of years back from the same basic racial stock. So far removed from beginnings were they that they were contemptuous of the Koreans, although the lineage of the Japanese royal house stemmed from Korea. As postwar evaluation proved, Japan might be impoverished and her resources destroyed, but her people were prepared to die rather than surrender, and that was a fact not appreciated by Halsey. After the strike at Muroran, Halsey felt certain that the war had nearly come to an end.

For Halsey's own peace of mind, it was just as well that he did not have access to the discussions of the Imperial General Staff or the plans of the generals, as they worked to prepare "the proper mental attitude" of the people for the "decisive campaign in Japan proper."

In Tokyo, the generals were planning for every eventuality. The intelligence bureau of the army began making peace overtures to Mao Tse-tung in the far reaches of Yenan. The plan called for an accommodation with the Chinese Communists that would prevent the Soviet Union from entering the war and would thoroughly confuse the Allied position in China. Meanwhile, almost a year before the end of the war, Japanese army officials were negotiating with Chinese officials in Honan province for a separate peace with Chiang Kai-shek's China. (These rumors, by the way, were known in Chungking to the foreign population but were stoutly denied by the Nationalist government.)

But in the midsummer of 1945, the negotiations had come to nothing. The army high command pinned its hopes for the preservation of the army and the Japanese system as it existed on a stout resistance against the American invasion, so stout that it would have political repercussions in the U.S., and Washington would force an end of the war on conditions that would cause Japan little more pain than she had already suffered.

The reason the planes were being preserved in their revetments and hidden sheds was to save them for an immense attack, suicide and otherwise, on the American transport ships as they attempted to unload troops on the Japanese islands in the fall.

If the American landings could not be stopped at the water's edge, then the whole army system would be changed and a volunteer army, consisting of military officers and men, the political forces, and the people at large, would continue resistance inland. The program for each district was laid out. The military hoped by such effort to cause the Americans to abandon the attack even after they had reached the shores of Japan.

The military reasoning that this was possible went thus: Japan's big problem was shipping. She had lost the island campaigns because the Americans had gained control of the sea and air above the sea. But the Americans did not know the true strength of the air forces of Japan or about the new airfields that had been built. The main strength of the Japanese army remained virtually intact, and over the last few months millions of troops had been moved back to Japan proper from points afield. At that time the Japanese army consisted of 169 divisions of infantry, four divisions of tanks, and fifteen air divisions. Altogether there were more than five million men under arms, and most of these were in the homeland. American landing operations would require an enormous number of ships, and the U.S. supply lines would be long and tenuous. So the generals could see how their limited resources could still stop the enemy, and they kept talking of "the certain way to victory." But in spite of their high hopes, they became elusive when asked to show precisely how the Americans were to be defeated; they

spoke then of the establishment of a "metaphysical spirit."
"What should be remembered above all in carrying out the general
decisive battle," said Lieutenant General Yoshijiro Umezu, "is
adherence to a vigorous spirit of attack."

As if to outline and emphasize this position, on July 13 the
Imperial General Headquarters laid out the war plan for the combined forces. It was expected that the attack would come in the
west. The navy air force was to take primary responsibility for destruction of the American fleet; then, when the transports came into the beach, the attack was to be made on them and they were to
be driven off. At all costs, imperial soil was to be defended. If that
meant "ramming" or suicide attacks, then that was what it had to
be, and in effect suicide became a national military policy.

The plans announced on July 13 had a certain ethereal
quality about them. They were high on rhetoric and very low
on practicality; each step was planned out with the implication
that it must bring certain victory. First, the carriers and the
battleships would all be sunk off the coast. Then, an observer
might ask, why go further? But once the Americans launched
their seaborne invasion, attention was to be diverted to the
transports and they were to be sunk and everyone annihilated.
Then, the observer might ask again, why go further? But after
the transports had landed the troops, then every obstacle was to
be placed in their way and the civilians would be called to assist
in annihilating them. So it went, with plans for movement of
the Emperor and of the government out of Tokyo—all in the
name of annihilation of the enemy. The war plans showed how
far removed from reality the General Staff had allowed itself to
become. But that must not be construed as reflecting disorgani-
zation, for quite the opposite was true. All spring long the
military leaders had been making even more demands on the
economy and on the civilian population. Civilians were to be
taught to throw grenades and use mortars and to give their lives
in suicide attacks if need be.

So, as Admiral Halsey sat back in his cabin and planned to
strike the enemy where it would hurt most, calm in his assessment

that he had come very near the end of this war, the Japanese faced desperation and death with an almost equal calmness. The most levelheaded of them saw that there was no hope of defeating the Americans, but even they conceded to the warmakers that it might be possible to influence the terms of peace by a convincing display of national determination to die rather than submit. As every Japanese knew, the American war policy called for "unconditional surrender," and to the Japanese, schooled to fear the American barbarians, this policy conjured a vision of mass murder, the deposition of the Emperor and destruction of the imperial system, and an existence marked by slavery to the foreigners. It was not hard for the military men to convince the public that the rape of their daughters and wives was to be expected, and that life under American rule would be not worth living. So, since honorable death was so highly regarded in the society, the military men had fertile ground for their determined effort to resist to the last. Back in Guam Admiral Nimitz was contemplating this possibility with more than his usual gravity. In Washington Admiral King was talking about casualties that would go into the hundreds of thousands, perhaps a million or more, to subdue the Japanese enemy.

On July 16, Halsey's Third Fleet was out of action, fuelling. That day the fast carrier task force of the British Royal Navy's Pacific Fleet showed up again for duty. The task force, termed by the Americans Task Force 37, consisted of a battleship, *King George V*, four fleet carriers, six light cruisers, and eighteen destroyers. The commander of the fleet was Vice Admiral Sir Bernard Rawlings, and the leader of the carrier force was Vice Admiral Sir Philip Vian. The British and American admirals then made plans for more air attacks against the Tokyo area. Halsey was particularly interested in knocking out the slender remains of the Japanese fleet. For example, the battleship *Nagato* was still afloat, under repair at Yokosuka naval base in Tokyo Bay. Halsey wanted that ship, the last symbol of Japanese supremacy as the largest battleship in the world.

Had Halsey on July 16 been apprised of the plans of the remnants of the Japanese submarine force, he would not have been quite so confident of the coming end of operations. It was true that the Japanese were having difficulty in completing submarines. But they had all the latest technology, a gift from their German friends before the surrender of the Third Reich. They had the latest in schnorkels, and in the spring the boats *I-401, I-13,* and *I-14* were given schnorkels and antimagnetic devices to ward off mines. These three submarines were joined by *I-400.* The four were the largest submarines in the world, and they were developed as underwater aircraft carriers. Each carried a number of low-winged monoplane bombers fitted with floats, called *seiran.* Captain T. Ariizumi, the commander of Submarine Division One, proposed a startling plan to cripple or at least delay American operations against Japan. He wanted to bomb the Panama Canal, rendering it nonoperational, and he suggested that such a move would delay the arrival of the American Atlantic Fleet in Pacific waters for at least three months. The Japanese knew that they had to expect all the naval resources of the U.S. and Britain to be turned against Japan now that Germany had surrendered. Captain Ariizumi had full-sized models of the Panama Canal locks built at the Maizuru navy yard. They were towed to Nanao Bay where the submarine crews and pilots were training. An operational plan was authorized and a July date was established. The submarines would head eastward toward the Hawaiian islands, and then turn south and follow a line along 9 degrees north latitude, the position of the Panama Canal. Ten aircraft would be launched on X day, each carrying a 1,700-pound bomb or a "long-lance" torpedo. Japanese intelligence assured Captain Ariizumi that there was nothing much to fear from the coastal defenses. Years earlier the Americans had maintained a stout defense of the Caribbean and Panamanian waters, but following the defeat of Germany this had been relaxed sharply.

As Captain Ariizumi planned and prepared, his operation came under close scrutiny at Imperial General Headquarters. No one doubted that it would strike a heavy blow at the United States, and the advocates of the plan said it would be the most effective blow possible under the circumstances, delivered with a minimal cost. But Panama was a long way away and Japan was having serious difficulty with the forces already in the Pacific theater. It seemed more important to the advocates of area warfare that a target be struck closer at hand. They suggested Ulithi, the forward American naval base. Captain Ariizumi's supporters argued that Ulithi was bound to be defended in force, while Panama was not. But the argument fell on deaf ears. The men who could seriously contemplate a war with civilians fighting tanks, flamethrowers, and napalm on the beaches of Japan could not be deterred by that sort of logic. The Panama plan was scrapped and the Ulithi orders were given.

Ariizumi then made his plans to strike Ulithi, and in July he set out for Truk. The once-powerful Japanese naval base was still in Japanese hands, but only because Admirals Nimitz and King had decided, after the fall of the Marianas, that Truk was no longer important and need not be defended. The Combined Fleet had long since deserted the island and nothing existed there except a few operational patrol boats, an occasional visiting submarine, and a harbor full of wrecks. The naval garrison at Truk was reduced to living off the land, and gunners and armorers now spoke about their taro patches and their coconuts and not about the weapons of war.

Captain Ariizumi set out personally in *I-13* to command the operation. *I-14* accompanied the flagship. *I-400* and *I-401* were to go to Ponape and await orders. From Truk, Captain Ariizumi would issue new directions for the final assault on Ulithi.

Thus, as Admiral Halsey searched about for targets for his aircraft and ships, had he but known there were vital ones to be found at the submarine bases. The broad American dragnet did manage to catch some "fish." On the morning of July 16, a search plane from the escort carrier *Anzio* spotted a Japanese submarine on the surface. The *Anzio* and its planes belonged to one of the relatively new (to the Pacific) hunter-killer teams of escort carrier plus destroyer escorts. The bomber attacked the submarine, which was *I-13*, and left it trailing oil. However, the I-boat managed to dive and get away. The oil trail, however, was followed by the plane and the course and speed were given to the escorts *Lawrence C. Taylor* and *Robert F. Keller*. Soon they arrived on the general scene and were directed to the trail. Following the directions from still another plane that had taken over the watchman's duties, the two destroyer escorts attacked. At 11:40 that morning the *Lawrence C. Taylor* launched an attack with another relatively new weapon, the hedgehog. This was a rocket-fired device that threw several depth charges into the water in a broad pattern that interlocked in area and depth. The *Taylor* launched several groups of charges and explosions were heard, including the heavy explosion made by a charge when it blew up against something solid. After a time, the destroyer escorts found debris floating on the surface and identified the submarine as *I-13*. So the Ulithi bombardment mission was leaderless. The *I-14* managed without difficulty to reach Truk, and there unloaded the aircraft it had brought across the sea, and waited. But no word came, and so *I-14* remained at Truk, waiting. At about the time Captain Ariizumi was fighting his last battle, *I-400* and *I-401* set out for a long journey to the Carolines to take station off Ponape and wait for word. They too stayed, waiting.

Admiral Halsey would not have been pleased either to learn of the augmentation, just then in the middle of July 1945, of the Japanese submarine arm by half a dozen German U-boats, which were renamed *I-501, I-502, I-503, I-504, I-505,* and *I-506*. Japanese crews were flown to Singapore, Kobe, Jakarta, and Surabaya, where the submarines had put in, and began taking over from the German crews.

On July 16, as Admiral Halsey prepared to take the fleet into another major attack against Tokyo, the Japanese were also reorganizing their suicide air squadrons at Kanoya naval air base in Kyushu. The problem was planes. The American attacks on metal industries and the aircraft plants had cut production without a doubt, not eliminated it, but cut it so that certain priorities had to be observed. The Jinrai Butai, or kamikaze unit, had reorganized into four squadrons at Konoya and they wanted Zero fighters, which were still extremely effective weapons in the Pacific war. But they would get no Zeros for suicide use. Instead they would get new Nakajima bombers and Ginga bombers, to escort the Ohka, or flying bombs. A new Model 22 Ohka was a combined jet rocket plane with a speed of 300 knots and a range of 120 miles, which meant that the parent bomber could release the "flying bomb" outside the actual combat area. Obviously this would give the crew of the parent bomber a much better change of survival, and the pilot of the Ohka a much better chance of finding, tracking, and striking his target. On the testing fields in July were two other models of flying bomb, which were designed as jet aircraft that would not depend on a mother plane to launch them. They would take off from an airfield and carry out their mission as had the propeller-driven craft of the early days of the war. But the mission, of course, was still to be suicidal.

On the night of July 16 the carrier task force moved southwest to get into position for dawn strikes on the Tokyo area.

BATTLESHIP SHOCK

On July 16, as Admiral Halsey and the British admirals conferred and their fleets prepared for action, at Alamogordo, New Mexico, some 500 scientists, technicians, and government officials prepared to test a new sort of explosive device, an atomic bomb. Work on the weapon had begun in December 1941, just the day before the Japanese attack on Pearl Harbor, when President Roosevelt authorized funds for a project that many of his military men believed to be the height of folly. Three and a half years later the scientists believed they had managed to control atomic forces of plutonium to the extent that they could trigger a bomb that would explode far enough below a bomber that the crew would not be endangered. But that was about all the scientists could predict about the weapon. It would be enormously destructive in its blast power and its radiation results. They did not know what might happen. They were ready for a final test of the atomic bomb, which was placed on a tall steel scaffolding in the middle of the desert. Admiral Halsey knew nothing about this development, nor did his British counterparts. News of the atomic project had been carefully protected from any but the participants and the highest levels of the military in the U.S. Admiral King knew about the project as a member of the Joint Chiefs of Staff, but Admiral Nimitz knew nothing, nor did

General Douglas MacArthur. They did not need to know until this point.

Nor did the military figures in the Pacific know of the efforts being made in Europe to bring an end to the Pacific war. Several months earlier, after the fall of Iwo Jima, the Emperor had realized that the war could not but end in disaster for Japan. The collapse of the Japanese defenses in Okinawa had been the finishing touch, and he had asked the government to begin feeling out the Russians. On June 22 the Emperor spoke and two days later one of his closest confidants met with Jacob Malik, the Soviet ambassador to Tokyo. But the Russians were more interested in getting into the war in its final phases than in pulling the Japanese chestnuts out of the fire. There was Manchuria with its enormously valuable industrial plant—which would in some bit replace that destroyed by the Japanese allies, the Nazis. So the approach to Malik came to nothing. But in Switzerland, Lieutenant General Seigo Okamoto, the Japanese attaché at Bern and assistant to the chief of Japanese military intelligence, was dealing with a Swedish banker, Per Jacobsson, who in turn was in touch with Allen Dulles, the European chief of the American Office of Strategic Services, and they were all dickering over terms for a peace between Japan and the United States. In Europe, peace was definitely in the air.

With the successful explosion of the atomic bomb at Alamogordo that day, word of the new weapon began to proliferate. Among others present were newspaper reporters, and although they were all sworn to secrecy, everyone knew it could not be long before the rumors began to flow. It did not make much difference now, because the wheels were already in motion to deliver that atomic bomb—its counterpart or counterparts—to the enemy from a base in the Marianas by means of one of the B-29 Superfortress bombers that made the almost daily runs across Japan. Within hours after the successful explosion at Alamogordo, a fifteen-foot long crate was loaded aboard the cruiser *Indianapolis* and she sailed out of San Francisco Bay, bound for Tinian island in the Marianas. A proper story about the mighty flash in the desert had been given the press—explosion of an ammunition dump, it said—and the captain of the *Indianapolis* did not know what he was carrying, but all these little bits of information would soon begin to add up. Time was of the essence —no lawyer ever knew it better than President Truman. He was discussing the bomb and the difference it would make in the war plans with his Joint Chiefs of Staff, but he did not know what difference it would make once it was used, so the plans went on.

On that night of July 16, also, an ordinary Japanese submarine set forth from Kure on an ordinary—or what had now become an ordinary—sort of mission. It was the *I-58*, commanded by Commander Moshitsura Hashimoto, and she was going out on a mission of destruction, carrying a contingent of six *kaiten* submarine suicide weapons.

Early on the morning of July 17 the carriers of the American and British task forces were in position and they launched planes. But after two strikes had gotten away the word began to come back: as the pilots neared the Japanese coast they found a heavy layer of cloud between them and the Tokyo plain. It rose to 13,000 feet, which made it too much of a problem to cross, so the strikes of that day were suspended and the carriers waited for better weather. Those first two waves of planes got through, but what damage they did was not readily assessable.

The most effective Allied work that day was done by the battleships. Rear Admiral Badger was ordered to bombard the factories of Hitachi Industries in the Mito area of Honshu, about eighty miles northeast of Tokyo.

Admiral Badger was in charge, although Admiral Halsey was riding along as a passenger in the *Missouri*. The flagship for this mission was the *Iowa*, and the other ships were the *Alabama*, *North Carolina*, *Wisconsin*, *Atlanta*, *Dayton*, and a number of destroyers, as well as the *Missouri*. The ships set out toward the coast at 4:45 that afternoon. The sky was overcast, as it had been all day, and the ceiling was 2,000 feet, with a ten-knot wind. The barometer began to drop and so did the thermometer, and Badger soon knew he was in for a storm.

At 8:00 that night the admiral called for General Quarters and the ships came to attention. An hour later they were adopting their bombardment formation and approaching the shore at eighteen knots. They began firing from a distance of seventeen miles through the heavy overcast, directed entirely by radar. The first target was the Hitachi refinery. The second target was the Hitachi Engineering Works plant at Densen, and the third was the Hitachi Engineering Works Taga plant. The fourth target was the Hitachi arms factory. By midnight the bombardment had ended and the ships were retiring. At 2:00 in the morning the flagship lost radar contact with Honshu island.

There was no way Admiral Badger could assess the damage caused by his ships' guns that night in that storm. Two days later the area was hit again by B-29s and so the damage was not ever really assessable except in broad terms. After the B-29 raid the production of the Hitachi plants was almost wiped out and the electricity, rail, and water connections were destroyed. Later, Japanese civilians testified that the ship bombardment had caused by far the most damage.

On July 18 the weather began to clear, and Admiral Halsey sent his planes in after the ships at Yokosuka navy base—their primary target was the battleship *Nagato*. The planes of the *Yorktown* and several other carriers went after the *Nagato*. But Admiral Halsey could not concentrate all his effort on a battleship; other aircraft went for the airfields in the Tokyo area. They hit the *Nagato*, but when the air strike was over she was still afloat. They hit the airfields, and claimed forty-three enemy planes with damage to seventy-seven, a number of small ships, and several locomotives. No air opposition developed but the antiaircraft fire was the strongest the pilots had yet experienced; the Americans and British together lost fourteen planes and eighteen fliers that day. It was certainly obvious that the Japanese had not lost the will to fight but were lying quietly, conserving their resources no matter how maddening the attacks might be. The pilots were particularly unhappy (*Yorktown's* bombers had been assigned the *Nagato*) to see that they had not done the job, but Admiral Halsey had not really expected so much, or he would have sent the planes in with torpedoes. Considering the antiaircraft defenses around Yokosuka naval base, such an attack would have been enormously expensive in lives and planes, for it could only be launched at low level in confined space. The excuse for it might have been that the *Nagato* was preparing to go out and fight again, but everyone knew that was not true; she was too badly damaged by previous attack for that.

The Yokosuka attack had one result that the Americans did not suspect at the moment. Lieutenant Shingo Takahashi was just preparing to take *I-352* out to do battle on a *kaiten* raid. One of the bombs from the *Yorktown* planes struck her squarely and sank her. Fortunately most of the crew was ashore and not a man was lost, but the submarine was a total loss. Not so the *I-58*. On making a deep dive at the entrance to the Bungo Channel, Captain Hashimoto discovered that the periscopes on the *kaiten* were all defective, and he turned about and returned to Kure naval base. By the afternoon of July 18 they had been replaced and the submarine went to sea, zigzagging through the channel in the night.

So powerful were the American forces at sea and in the air that many could be assigned specialized jobs these days. Admiral Oldendorf was made commander of a new striking force with headquarters at Buckner Bay, Okinawa, and given seven battleships and many cruisers and destroyers to wipe out enemy shipping in the East China Sea and the Yellow Sea. The B-29 unit, the 20th Air Force, was divided into units with special missions. One of these was the 315th Wing, which was given the special task of destroying Japan's oil installations. In preparation for the coming decisive battle of Japan, the Americans were attempting to immobilize Japan's defenses by destroying her capacity to resupply with oil from the East Indies and her storage capacities at home. The 315th Wing's raid of July 16 on the Maruzen refinery showed what the potential for destruction still was: Colonel Boyd Hubbard, Jr., led a raid of fifty-eight B-29s which bombed the refinery and claimed to have destroyed 95 percent of the plant. The 313th Wing was devoted almost entirely to laying mines, largely in Shimonoseki Strait, between Honshu and Kyushu. (It is quite probable that many of those mines that bothered Halsey's ships so much in operations off Kyushu were laid by the American B-29s.) The 509th Group came to Tinian as a mystery organization whose task no one quite knew, except for its commander Colonel Paul Tibbets and General Curtis LeMay, the commander of the air force. On July 18 Colonel Tibbets was planning a series of raids for his pilots. They would be odd missions; each would involve only a single plane, which would bomb from an extremely high altitude.

On July 17 the Potsdam Conference of Allied leaders had begun informally with a luncheon given by President Harry Truman for Soviet premier Josef Stalin. The luncheon was marked by sparring and diplomatic folderol. The major issue of the moment was the status of Japan, and Truman knew that Stalin was stalling on Japanese attempts to open negotiation for surrender, while Stalin knew that the Americans were very close to developing an atomic bomb, although he did not know it had been exploded successfully. The Japanese representative in Moscow, Ambassador Naotaki Sato, was cooling his heels and waiting for some word on new overtures he was trying to make to the Russians. He was well enough informed to warn Tokyo that the Russians were really more interested in getting into the war and invading Manchuria than in stopping the fighting. In Tokyo the government made it quite clear that it was not interested in surrendering unless the conditions were generous.

"Not only our High Command," said a message from the foreign office to Sato, "but also our Government firmly believes even now our war potential is still sufficient to deal the enemy a severe blow. . . . If only the United States would recognize Japan's honor and existence we would terminate the war. . . . But if the enemy insists on unconditional surrender to the very end, then our country and His Majesty would unanimously resolve to fight a war of resistance to the bitter end. . . ."

On July 18, President Truman and Prime Minister Churchill conferred and agreed not to tell Stalin anything about the atomic bomb at the moment. Truman called on Stalin and they talked about Japan but resolved nothing, since Stalin did not want the war to end until he had a chance to get into Manchuria and seize the industrial plants there for shipment back to the western U.S.S.R. The big problem in the minds of the American negotiators was to establish the actual (as opposed to propaganda) conditions the Japanese must face, and it all came down to the sort of life Japan could expect. The Americans at least were agreed among themselves that the Japanese should be treated humanely. The big sticking point was what was to be done with the Emperor, since many American experts believed that the imperial system had brought about the emergence of the Japanese militaristic policies that led to war.

On the night of July 18 Rear Admiral Cary Jones's cruisers made a sweep around Cape Nojima on the peninsula southeast of Tokyo, looking for naval targets or even cargo ships. They found nothing.

Admiral Halsey was disgusted with these results, and a bit concerned about the large number of mines his ships were encountering in this area. Several of the destroyers and escorts spent many hours blowing up mines found floating in the path of the task force. On July 19 he moved offshore to fuel, and fuelling of the whole fleet was carried out without incident between that date and July 22. The massive replenishment was the greatest such operation in history. The task force took on 6,300 tons of ammunition, 380,000 barrels of fuel oil, 550,000 gallons of aviation gas, 1,600 tons of stores, and 99 new aircraft replacing those lost or damaged. Halsey was then ready to turn his attention to Kyushu and the Inland Sea area, where he hoped to find more targets.

6

THE ULTIMATUM

On July 19, 1945, as Admiral Halsey's fleet refuelled and the Japanese contemplated the enormous destruction that was being wreaked across their land daily, the Americans, Russians, and British sparred at Potsdam. No one really trusted anyone else. The Americans thought the Japanese ought to be told something soon, and the Russians must be told something about the conduct of the Pacific war. The British believed the information given the Russians should be done by a joint U.S.-British spokesman team. The Americans suspected this was a ploy by the British to secure a voice in the direction of military operations against Japan. In the end the British told the Russians what they wanted to tell them, and the Americans told the Russians what they thought they should hear.

Meanwhile, on Tinian island, the B-29s of the 509th Group were gearing up for their special missions. Admiral Halsey knew nothing about this, of course, nor did very many other people. On the night of July 18 Colonel Tibbets had the word from General Leslie Groves that the atomic bomb explosion had come off according to schedule. There had been some doubt: no one knew quite what might have happened when the power of the plutonium atom was suddenly released in a shock wave. It had all come out all right, Groves said, and nothing had occurred that would interfere with the forth-coming mission.

There was, however, difficulty in the Marianas. General Curtis LeMay, the commander of the B-29 force, was not happy that a unit completely untried in combat should be brought in to perform on a special mission while his "boys" were left out of it. He and Colonel Tibbets quarreled, and high authority had to intervene to prevent LeMay from breaking up the 509th Group and assigning the secret project to someone under his own control.

In Guam and Manila the radio messages piled up as Admiral Nimitz and General MacArthur tried to settle the basic differ-ences between their two services about who should command in the forthcoming operations against Japan. MacArthur insisted that he must be the supreme commander. But not on the sea, said Nimitz. And on July 19 that is where matters stood, and no amount of jockeying or conferring made any changes in the vital position. It seemed apparent that before the landings, President Truman would have to make one of those high-level political decisions, such as that made by President Roosevelt when he gave MacArthur supreme command of the Philippines invasion and diverted the thrust of the war from the navy's Central Pacific drive, headed toward China.

At Kanoya on Kyushu island, the pilots of the reorganized kamikaze program sat and waited. A large open field ran along the stream that was located south of the pilots' quarters. The pilots spent a good deal of time wandering through the bamboo groves on the stream, and enjoyed the sight of the white roses that bloomed wild along the banks. They felt much at one with nature and very poetic for the most part. They lived in a world of their own, a semihypnotic world, and looked from their base to the outside. They were forbidden to leave the base, but the stream was not officially "off limits." One day in mid-July a pilot strolling along the stream stopped to watch the wheat harvest in the field across from the bamboo grove. He saw that the work was being done entirely by women and small children—there was not a full-grown man in sight. Overcome with compassion, he went back to his billet and asked Commander Tadashi Nakajima for permission to work in the fields. It was given, the pilot spread the word, and soon some thirty suicide pilots were working alongside the women and children in a patriotic fervor to bring in the harvest; it was somehow satisfying and symbolic to those who were preparing to die that they give that effort to the survival of others.

The suicide pilots were making occasional flights to Okinawa, and on July 19 several planes took off from Kanoya. The escort pilots returned to announce that two kamikazes had crashed into a destroyer, causing serious damage. The American reports did not show any such action.

On the morning of July 20, ten B-29s from the 509th Group took off to fly their first missions against Japan. Each flew separately, and one pilot, Captain Claude Eatherly, decided he would drop a 10,000-pound high-explosive bomb on the Emperor's palace. Had Eatherly been successful in his mission he might have resolved the problem facing the Potsdam conferees: what was to be done with the Emperor of Japan? But the weather closed in, the B-29 jettisoned its bomb, and no one in the plane knew where it fell. Most certainly it did not fall on the Imperial Palace. The troubles of the Potsdam conference continued. Captain Eatherly's deliberate violation of his orders and the constraints on bombing of the Palace had come to nothing.

On July 20, a discouraged Ambassador Sato sent a message home to Japan from Moscow, stating that there was no way, in his opinion (for which he apologized profusely), of preventing the total defeat of Japan. The best that could be done was to secure a peace quickly with the allies, hopefully before the Soviet Union could enter the war and complicate matters.

This was the day of the fifth official session of the Allied conference at Potsdam. Nothing was said to Stalin about the atomic bomb, but President Truman had the word that day that the bomb makers were preparing the first bomb for Japan and it would be ready for delivery in about two weeks.

Late that day, on receipt of Ambassador Sato's unhappy message, Foreign Minister Shigenori Togo replied that Japan could not accept unconditional surrender under any conditions. This was a sticker. The Soviets had announced to Sato that they could not act as intermediaries unless they knew the conditions the Japanese would accept for surrender. The statement, of course, was a Soviet ploy, but it served its purpose. Now Togo told Ambassador Sato that he might as well give up. Prince Konoye, a senior statesman and intimate of the Emperor, would have to come to Moscow and transmit to the leaders of the U.S.S.R. the Japanese feelings.

The fact was that in Tokyo, the Imperial General Staff was still holding out for concrete and continued resistance to the Allied advance. The Supreme War Council, which included the cabinet and was theoretically responsible only to the Emperor, was so badly divided that every meeting ended in a squabble and nothing could be done to present a firm policy.

On July 21 there was no political change in the climate. Admiral Halsey's Third Fleet was still taking on stores. Admiral McCain, commander of the carrier task force, used this period to reassess the methods of the pilots; the damage done in the past few strikes had not been satisfactory. It was apparent that the Japanese tactics of dispersal and lying "doggo" were more effective than anyone had thought they would be.

From the dreadful experience at Okinawa, the carrier force had learned the importance of a more powerful combat air patrol. McCain could expect the Japanese to swarm about his carriers like bees when the amphibious landings in Japan were beginning, so he reexamined the defenses. Over each task group of three to five carriers and supporting ships, twenty fighters were be to placed at various altitudes up to 30,000 feet. Out at the perimeter, over each radar picket ship, McCain would put eight fighters at 10,000 to 15,000 feet and four more at 30,000 feet to prevent high-altitude surprise attack.

Okinawa, by McCain's standards, had led the carrier commanders into some "loose thinking." In a sense it was not the
fault of any task group commander but that of Admiral Spruance,
who had insisted that that carriers be employed in the immediate vicinity of the Okinawa landing force. This restriction had
created defensive thinking on the part of the carrier commanders. It did not take many incidents like those of March 18
and 19 to make a carrier commander edgy about kamikaze
attacks. On that day the Americans had been operating off
Kyushu to minimize the Japanese attack expected against the
Okinawa invasion force. The *Enterprise* had been hit by a
bomb that did not explode but did some damage. A kamikaze
scooted across the deck of the *Intrepid* at so low an altitude
that several men were killed and injured, and then crashed into
the sea. The *Yorktown* was bombed and thirty men were killed
or injured. The *Wasp* suffered nearly 400 casualties in a bombing attack, and the *Franklin* was hurt so badly that Admiral
Davison, the commander of the task group, told the captain he
ought to abandon the ship. She had a thousand casualties.
She was virtually abandoned, but Captain L. H. Gehres and a
skeleton crew managed to save the ship. After that experience, it
was not very surprising that the carrier captains were nervous
and thought "defensively" when they knew they were not
going to be able to operate offensively.

So Okinawa had put some negative notions in the heads of
the carrier commanders, and Admiral McCain, fresh from his
Washington post, was quick to see what was wrong.

He reminded all concerned that any task force in enemy
waters was an offensive force, and this talk about "offensive"
operations and "defensive" operations had no place in carrier
doctrine. Every plane launched was on an offensive mission,
and this meant there was no different psychology whether the
assignment of the pilot was to attack enemy targets at a distance—the usual role of a carrier pilot under Halsey at least—to
ambush kamikaze or bombing planes as they took off or were
discovered in the middle of the mission, or to shoot down enemy

planes that were trying to attack the task force. This last was the "defensive" role so many carriers had assumed in recent months.

The carrier, said McCain, was a base of operations, the only one in the world that was projected into the front lines. If a carrier is put out of action that means a hundred planes operating twice a day are out of action, and that must be multiplied by the number of days the carrier is out of action to understand the true import. So protection of the task force, passed off by too many pilots as a necessary evil, should instead be regarded as an insurance policy on the carriers.

Admiral McCain, like Admiral Halsey, was extremely critical of the Spruance policy regarding the use of carriers and air forces. Once again, in the criticisms of these two air admirals there was emphasis on Spruance's great weakness, his failure to realize the potential of air power in this naval war. The McCain criticism was not personal, nor was it made to carp at actions of the past. The Americans were facing the most important military operations of the war in a few months. Operation Olympic, the invasion of the Japanese homeland, would make D-Day at Normandy seem like a picnic. The Germans had maintained only a part of their force in France, but most of the five-million-man Japanese army was in the homeland by the summer of 1945, and simply waiting for invasion. There was no way that surprise could be brought about, no way that the Americans could hope to avoid casualties on landing.

All this might have been very different had the commanders of the Okinawa operation struck early and hard against the Japanese at home during March and April. The moment Okinawa was invaded, said McCain, all available air forces—the carries, the escort carriers, the marines, the army air forces—should have been thrown against Japanese airfields and aircraft factories with the overriding purpose of destroying the Japanese air effort. It could have been done in less than a month and perhaps in two weeks. That it could be done was shown absolutely to McCain by what the Halsey force had done since it went on the offensive. Had it been done, the casualties to ships and personnel at Okinawa could have been cut to a minimum.

McCain was sure that the Japanese were planning an all-out attack on transports and carriers when the time came. His evidence was the number of planes burned in the last three days of operations against the Honshu airfields. He was expecting more trouble when Olympic was staged.

McCain was concerned about interference from Admiral Nimitz with the operations of the task force. As he sat in his cabin during these days of replenishment, he mulled over the problem. It was of a piece with the criticism that Halsey had received for going after Admiral Ozawa and the Japanese carriers at Leyte. Indeed, the success of the suicide attacks that had begun that very day of Leyte operations could largely be attributed to offensive failure by the fleet. During the Philippines campaign, MacArthur had established an artificial boundary line between his forces and those of Nimitz, and Halsey was forbidden to strike dangerous enemy air concentrations because they were in MacArthur's territory. Someone back at Cincpac had insisted that Halsey's Third Fleet concentrate on shipping and that had allowed the Japanese to make best use of their slender air resources in the Philippines to create the kamikaze threat.

With only one major exception (*Borie*) when the fleet operated as Third Fleet under Halsey, no ships of Task Force 38 were hit in an entire year. The reason for this was the method of attack that Halsey favored. The secret, if one could call it that, was first to send in low-altitude photo planes to photograph all air installations in the operating area. When the strikes were launched, they were timed so that blanket attacks were carried out against these fields, keeping the Japanese on the ground during the American strikes.

Also, the carrier force maintained a watch system with combat air patrol planes fifty and sixty miles out from the force, which gave time for the carriers to launch extra fighters if any Japanese attack came along.

Another effective measure was rigid control of returning strikes. In some previous operations the Japanese had followed American planes back to their carriers, but under the Task Force 38 system the returning strikes came up under the eyes of the "Tomcats" of the combat air patrol, who observed every plane coming in. A Japanese plane would be shot down miles from the carrier. And experience had taught the combat intelligence officers that every Japanese snooper must be sought out and destroyed. For years the Japanese snoopers had come around the task forces, and no one had paid much attention as long as they stayed out of bombing range. That was a serious error. Task Force 38 had proved it.

From this point on, said McCain, he could not overemphasize the importance of aerial photography as their primary weapon to discover the Japanese air forces and destroy them. No pilot could be expected to manage his aircraft and carry out the sort of visual search that would be necessary to spot Japanese planes concealed on the ground. But photo intepretation men, in the relative leisure of the intelligence cabin, could examine films with the utmost care. That was how they were going to find their enemies in the coming months.

Just then, one of those enemies, almost disregarded now, was moving along the American shipping route between Okinawa and Guam. She was the submarine *I-58*, loaded with her half dozen human torpedoes and a complement of the long-lance torpedoes as well. The sea was calm and the moonlight nights were bright, perfect for attack. But the American enemy stubbornly failed to appear. There would be one more good night, July 22, the night of the full moon. After that the moon would wane, and hunting would be harder. Captain Hashimoto spent part of the night of July 21 praying in the tiny ship's shrine. His prayer was for a major target.

While Captain Hashimoto prayed and Admiral McCain considered the changes that should be made in carrier policy, in Potsdam the political figures were worrying over decisions that would affect them all. Admiral Leahy, who had been the official naval aide and advisor to President Roosevelt and now served President Truman in the same capacity, had always opposed the atomic bomb. He believed Japan could be forced to surrender by continuation of the devastating aerial attacks on her, plus the submarine war. He had not changed his opinion in all the months of preparation of the A-bomb. At Potsdam, General H. H. Arnold, chief of the army air forces, agreed with Leahy, but General George C. Marshall, head of the army, said that an invasion was absolutely necessary.

All this discussion on July 22 revolved around the enormously important decision that President Truman was going to have to make, now that the scientists at Los Alamos had reported the atomic bomb was completed and had been tested successfully, and that one had been shipped aboard the *Indianapolis* to the delivery point of the Marianas. At noon President Truman consulted Prime Minister Churchill about the matter, and Churchill pointed out that the casualties they might expect from an invasion would be enormous. Of course Truman must authorize the dropping of the bomb. Then all the nightmare about the invasion would vanish, and in its place could be seen a vision of the end of the war with one or two violent shocks to Japan. There need be no protracted slaughter. And further, the Russians—who had not been around when the allies needed them to start a new front against Japan, even though in the last six months Germany's ability to fight had been minimal—those Russians need no longer be wooed or consulted. They could be kept out of the war.

Truman was not so sure of that. The whole idea of the atomic bomb was so new to him that he was still thinking along the old lines, and the old lines called for Russian participation in the invasion of Japan, to keep the American casualties down.

On the night of July 22, Admiral Halsey was ready to move again. The fleet was fuelled and the ships' bellies were full of ammunition and supplies. He sent out two destroyer forces to Nojima Zaki, near Tokyo, to let the Japanese know they were coming. One force came in close and bombarded shore installations. The other found a convoy of four Japanese ships sneaking along the coastline, and sank two of them and damaged the others. This sort of bombardment and patrol became from that point on a nightly occurrence, weather permitting. And in July weather was the biggest problem the fleet faced, for the typhoon season was at its height. The bombardment of Omura that night by Destroyer Squadron 57 was a real shock to the Japanese along the coast. So was the shipping strike of Squadron 61.

On July 23 the weather was still fine on the Okinawa-Saipan lane, but there were still no American ships in sight. Disgustedly, Captain Hashimoto turned *I-58* toward the Guam-Leyte route, where he hoped to find targets. *I-53* under Lieutenant Commander Saichi Oba was operating in this area, but, Hashimoto hoped, closer to Leyte. In fact, Oba was much closer to Leyte, about 250 miles east of Cape Engano. That night of July 23, Lieutenant Commander Oba began tracking an American convoy escorted by a destroyer escort, the *Underhill*, and a patrol craft, *PC-804*.

On the morning of July 24, Admiral Halsey moved the Third Fleet to the south of Honshu, from which his planes could strike targets on Honshu and Kyushu and Shikoku islands. The planes concentrated on the Inland Sea area, and most of them were looking for what remained of the Japanese navy. Thus, the Kure naval base was a major target. The *Yorktown*, for example, sent off 120 missions and the other carriers did about the same. At the end of the day, they reported damage to twenty-two warships, including a battleship, several cruisers, and two destroyers. They also sank more than fifty merchant ships and, in sweeps across the airfields in the area, destroyed seventy-four planes and damaged another 135. For a change there was some air opposition over Kyushu, mostly army fighter planes. Most of these were shot down, but not without losing some men of the U.S. force. The *Yorktown* lost three planes, two of them in the Bungo-Suido area where the fighters were encountered. The third pilot was involved in a midair collision with a plane from the carrier *Shangri-la*, and spun into the water from 14,000 feet.

That night, Halsey sent out night fighters and ships to conduct a sweep of the Kii Suido area. They also struck the Kushimoto seaplane base and Shimonoseki field. The strikes were only marginally successful, largely because the weather had turned foul again.

On that day the Allied leaders at Potsdam were still skirmishing; the Russians were demanding influence over Turkey and the former Italian bases in the Mediterranean. President Truman stood firm against these claims, secure in the knowledge of his new superweapon. The Russians had massed troops along the Manchurian border, and this prevented the Japanese from moving even more of their forces down to the home islands, a matter that gave General Marshall much satisfaction. He was torn: like President Truman he rather wished the Russians would not come into the war, but as matters stood, with the contemplation of the enormous casualties that must be expected in the Olympic Operation against the Japanese homeland, he had to be glad for any help. To Truman's objections, Marshall cogently pointed out that even if the Russians did not come into the war there was really nothing to stop them from moving into Manchuria and taking anything they wanted. It was apparent at Potsdam that Stalin intended to strip the Manchurian industrial establishment for the Soviet homeland.

There was one strong difference of opinion between the Americans and the British on military policy. Because of prestige, the British wanted a much larger role in the Pacific war than they were playing with the utilization of the British Pacific Fleet in Halsey's operations. But the American Joint Chiefs of Staff stoutly resisted any change in authority. They did not tell the British that they still had not solved their own problems: that General MacArthur and Admiral Nimitz were still jockeying for control of the Pacific war. The Americans were willing to give the British control of military operations in Southeast Asia, where the British were in control anyhow and where they had the preponderance of troops. But as for the fight against Japan, the answer was no. And after considerable discussion that is how it was agreed. The landings against Kyushu would come first, then the landings on Honshu, and the Americans would be in control. The British would provide long-range bombers, the naval task force in the Pacific would be built up, and a ground force of some sort would be added to the American might. The Russians would be encouraged to come into the war. The French were eager to have a finger in the pie, but the Americans made it clear that this was not much wanted in view of the French behavior in Europe, where General DeGaulle had created enormous confusion by insisting that the control of the French forces be under his command, and then refusing to accept orders from General Eisenhower. There would be none of that. The French offer was accepted in principle, but the French were told that they would have to serve under the Americans or the British, and that in any case their troops could not be used until the spring of 1946. The same sort of offer was made by the Dutch who wanted to liberate their own Dutch East Indies, and the same sort of reply was given.

The Russians announced this day that they were ready to enter the war against Japan and that Soviet troops would begin to move in the last half of August. General Alexei Antonov, the chief of staff of the Red army, said that the Soviet forces would withdraw their troops as soon as Japan was defeated. They wanted assurances that the Japanese would be prevented from moving troops from China or the home island to fight in Manchuria. Admiral King, General Marshall, and General Arnold told the Russians that this was definitely being prevented and King went into some detail about Halsey's operations at the moment and the work of the American submarines.

The submarines were moving ever more forcefully into Japanese waters. In late May, Admiral Charles Lockwood, the commander of submarines for the Pacific Fleet, had sent in the first boats to the Sea of Japan. Borrowing a tactic from the Germans, the Americans used a "wolfpack." Nine submarines, called "Hydeman's Hellcats," sailed from Guam on May 27. Their commander, E. T. Hydeman, was ordered to do the utmost damage and then come home and report. Lockwood watched this operation with renewed interest because it was something special.

Such was the confidence of the Americans in these last days of the war that when the *Tinosa*, one of the submarines, picked up ten men from a B-29 which had ditched south of Kyushu and the survivors learned that they were being taken on a mission into the Sea of Japan, they asked to be put back into their rubber rafts to wait for another submarine to come along and get them home quicker. The submarines of the Pacific fleet, operating as "lifeguards," had given the airmen almost complete confidence in survival.

In fact, it was not hard to do what the airmen wanted, and the submarine *Scabbardfish*, which was on patrol nearby, was called up and the aircrew was transferred to this submarine that was about to head home.

The wolfpack then headed into Tsushima strait, and between June 9 and 20 sank twenty-seven ships and a Japanese submarine, the *I-122*. They lost one boat, the *Bonefish*.

Since June the undersea war had seen the Americans penetrating further and further into Japanese waters. The *Tirante* had gone into Nagasaki harbor to attack one ship. The *Barb* sailed up and down the coast of Hokkaido and as far as the Sakhalin islands. By mid-July, the Joint Chiefs could assure the Russians that U.S. submarines were finding it hard to get targets, so completely had Japanese shipping been knocked out. No, the Russians need have no fear that the Japanese would be moving any troops by sea from China into Manchuria. As for the communication between Japan and the Korean peninsula of the Asian continent, it had been cut off to all but the smallest junks and sampans. There need be no fear there either, especially since the Japanese were building up power in Japan to counter the American invasion expected in the fall. "As a result of increased naval action and mining by super-bombers, there is little likelihood of any Japanese troops movements between Japan and Manchuria," General Marshall told the Soviet officers. As for China, there was evidence that the Japanese had been withdrawing from the countryside, leaving garrisons at Hong Kong, Shanghai, and Hankow. The Chinese communist guerillas could be expected to stop any use of the rail lines that led up to Manchuria. The Japanese were as badly off in terms of shipping along the China coast as they were in the main islands of Japan.

The Americans and Soviet military leaders then planned out the course of military operations for the summer and autumn. The Americans would move into the Kurile Islands to open a line of communications to Siberia, so that American supplies could be shipped to Siberia. It was inherent in the discussion that the Americans would provide much of the supply for the Soviet armies. It could not be otherwise; the Soviet economy had not yet begun to recover from the war against the Germans.

This July 24 was also the day that President Truman and the Chiefs of Staff had the word from General Groves in Washington: the two atomic bombs that could be prepared immediately would be ready on Tinian island on August 1 and August 6 respectively. A third would be ready on August 24, and others would be ready in larger numbers beginning in September. The targets would be Hiroshima, Kokura, Niigata, and Nagasaki, not necessarily in that order. Kyoto had been on the list, but because of objection by Secretary of War Stimson, it had been dropped since it was Japan's old capital and a major cultural shrine. Back in Washington Groves' staff was busily preparing to deliver a whole series of atomic bombs! That attitude, of course, was normal because no one knew what the atomic bomb would actually do or what reaction the Japanese would have to it. It was certainly known to be immensely powerful, but such matters as radiation effect were virtually unknown. The full horror was not even suspected.

Armed with all this information, President Truman was prepared on July 24 to declare the terms of Japanese surrender.

The declaration of terms of surrender was to be agreed to by the Americans, British, and Chinese governments. The Soviets were not asked to participate because they were not at war with the Japanese government (although Stalin later indicated that if he had been asked the Soviets would have declared war, perhaps earlier than they did).

The terms were cold and harsh.

The authority and influence of the military in Japan was to be wiped out and eliminated for all time. Allied forces would occupy "key Japanese points." Obviously that meant Japan, Korea, and Formosa, and such other islands as they chose. Japan would be stripped down to the homeland—*hondo:* the four islands of Honshu, Kyushu, Shikoku, Hokkaido, and the small islands immediately surrounding. That meant Korea, Manchuria, Formosa, Hainan, the Ryukyus, Sakhalin, would all be sacrificed, as would be the Marianas and the rest of the Japanese mandate in the Pacific.

That was the hard part. To soften it was the assurance, demanded by the Americans and British, that Japan would not be "enslaved." The soldiers would be allowed to return home after their disarmament "with the opportunity to lead peaceful and productive lives." War criminals would be prosecuted, but freedom of speech, religion, and thought would be established.

Japan would be forbidden to rearm, but she could reestablish industries to sustain her economy. (This responded to a Japanese fear that if defeated, Japan would be stripped of her industrial potential, forbidden to engage in such industries as steel, and turned, thus, into a captive market for the industrial nations of the world.)

The occupation would not last forever, but only until the objective of establishing a peacefully inclined and responsible government was attained. Inherent in this of course was the intention of the Allies to wipe out all vestiges of militarism, including the officer class and especially the revived samurai tradition.

The alternative to such surrender, President Truman could say with assurance by the last week in July, would be "prompt and utter destruction." But what did that mean? The American propagandists had been promising the Japanese military "utter destruction" for many months and the word "prompt" did not seem to change much. President Truman would have liked nothing better than to be able to telegraph his punch, to tell the Japanese of the existence of an atomic bomb—a number of atomic bombs—in American hands. The Japanese were well aware of the potential destructive power of the atom, and at Tokyo University and other scientific centers, some research on atomic weapons had been undertaken during the war. But it had not come to much, largely because of Japan's limited resources. Still, if the Imperial General Staff were to consult the leading physicists of the country when told about an atomic bomb, the physicists would have told them that it certainly was possible, and if given a few details they might have confirmed the existence of such a bomb in American hands.

But the trouble was that based on recent events in Europe, the slender ties between the Western Allies and the Soviet Union were strained already. President Truman did not want to pass on information about the atomic bomb to the Russians, because he did not trust them. General Marshall in particular was uneasy about Soviet intentions, and the discussions at Potsdam about the Soviet demands for influence over all the countries on their perimeter brought an increase in American suspicions. The problem then was that without a demonstration the Japanese would not believe the Americans had an atomic bomb, unless the Americans told them generally how it was made. But to tell the Japanese was impossible without telling the Russians, and the Americans felt that to give the Russians any hints in this regard was too dangerous to contemplate. (They did not know that British and American traitors had already revealed some of the secrets and that Soviet espionage agents had a good idea of the stage of progress of the American bomb.)

That July 24, after the formal session of the Potsdam conference had ended, Truman walked over to Stalin, and remarked casually that the Americans had developed a new weapon of unusual destructive force. Stalin did not seem much interested (which might have been a tipoff to a more imaginative person), but Truman believed that Stalin had not understood the importance of what was said. Events indicate the contrary, and Herbert Feis in his *Japan Subdued* suggested that to have told the Russians all might have been a wiser course. Perhaps, but the Allies' growing distrust of one another was a matter that not one of the Allied leaders managed to understand fully in those difficult days. Quite probably the course of the Soviet Union, with the combined distrust by the Communist Party of all others and by Russians of all outsiders, would hardly have been changed. The Soviets have never accepted allies, in the sense that America and Britain were allies, but have held that their own security demanded domination of all around them, and perhaps, if possible, all the world. An examination of history shows it is not an unusual view.

Early on that morning of July 24, Lieutenant Commander R. M. Newcomb, the captain of the *Underhill*, had the word from radar plot on the destroyer escort that there was a "bogey" out ten miles from the convoy. That meant a plane. The aircraft circled around out there and did not seem inclined to attack. It might even be a PBY on some strange mission. Captain Newcomb did not pay too much attention. The convoy kept moving along toward Okinawa. Nothing more was observed, and in half an hour or so the aircraft went away.

At 2:00 in the afternoon all was quiet, but just under an hour later one of the patrol craft sighted a floating mine. These were becoming more common as the B-29s dropped mines off Kyushu. Many of them drifted south and east and became dangers for the American ships in the vicinity. The *Underhill* came up and tried to sink the mine with gunfire but did not succeed. She was still trying when a sound contact was made, and Captain Newcomb sent *PC-804* out to check. The patrol craft confirmed the contact, and the destroyer escort then came up to launch a depth charge attack on what Newcomb thought was a human torpedo.

The depth charge attack brought up debris and oil, and Lieutenant Commander Newcomb was sure he had sunk the human torpedo. But as he was looking about, his radar and sonar men reported another contact, and he went off after it. Almost at that moment, the crew of *PC-804* reported sighting a periscope and then a submarine just under the water (where *I-53* would be, to launch *kaiten*). Lieutenant Commander Newcomb then reported that he had seen several human torpedoes and that he was going to ram one of them. Just after 3:00 that afternoon, the crew of *PC-804* saw an enormous explosion rock the *Underhill.* The whole forward section of the ship, including the bridge, simply blew up, and what remained sank immediately. The captain, nine officers, and 102 men went down with that half of the ship. The after section, to the forward fireroom, remained afloat, sustained by its watertight compartments, but there were many wounded men in what was left of the ship. The patrol craft milled about, trying to find the submarine, but did not succeed. *PC-803* radioed in the flotilla and found a surgeon aboard one of the LSTs. The patrol craft went alongside and took the surgeon to the wreck of the *Underhill* to give assistance. As the small craft neared the hulk, the crew sighted another *kaiten* and gave chase, but did not claim a sinking. Then the crew of the *Underhill* was rescued by the patrol craft and the wreckage was sunk by gunfire.

Lieutenant Commander Oba left the scene, having expended at least three of his *kaiten.* Of the other three, two were found to be malfunctioning, and when he returned to Kure a month later, he had only this one sinking to announce. But it was success, and it reminded the American navy that there was still a very active war in progress, and that the Japanese could not be counted out until they really surrendered. Or it should have done so, but apparently the naval commands at Guam, Pearl Harbor, and the Philippines had grown somnolent in success, for the sinking of the *Underhill* did not bring about any renewed precautions in this vital communications area of the western Pacific. Halsey's ships continued their depradations along the

Japanese shore, but in midocean the American vessels were travelling at more than a little risk. Several of the Japanese I-boats were out, all armed with standard torpedoes and human torpedoes; as can be seen from the story of the *Underhill,* the contempt in which the U.S. navy seemed to hold the *kaiten* was not justified.

In these difficult months, the Japanese had also been working hard on their new aircraft-carrying submarines, and two more of these were ready on July 24. One, the *I-402,* was sent out that day to work up—undergo shakedown training for a month and then go into action. The *I-404* was fitted out and waiting at Kure harbor for orders, and final refinements before going out for her trials.

On July 25 Halsey wanted to strike the Japanese hard again in the Kure area. In spite of Admiral McCain's objections to leaving the airfields untended at this moment, Halsey was pre-occupied with the Japanese fleet. There were three reasons, listed by Halsey later in his autobiography, for this preoccupation.

First, there was the question of national morale, he said. The destruction of the Japanese fleet was the proper answer to Pearl Harbor. Many Americans felt that way, of course, but more important perhaps was Halsey's own promise to America that he was going to destroy the Japanese fleet personally. Now he was doing it.

Second, Halsey said, he had to knock out all enemy warships on behalf of the Russians, who were expected to enter the war momentarily. Even a dozen destroyers, working the run between Kamchatka and Hokkaido, could take an enormous toll of destruction. Halsey wanted to be sure that there was no cause for complaint from the Russians.

Third, Halsey said, was the matter of peace terms. He could not consider the situation in which Japan might use the existence of a fleet to bargain for terms. As a veteran destroyer commander of the First World War, Halsey was very much aware of the attitude of a government going down to defeat and the ploys it might attempt.

Fourth, and this reason was so overriding that Halsey did not even list it among his three, he had been ordered by Admiral Nimitz to knock out the Japanese fleet, and so he was going to do precisely that.

Actually, Admiral McCain's feeling that if the carriers concentrated on the air installations they could destroy Japan's ability to put planes in the air was not totally justified. The Japanese had so perfected the art of concealment that the Americans missed many of the planes on the airfields, particularly those moved even miles away from various fields and held in reserve for the final battle on the beaches. Certainly had Halsey dropped the attacks on the ships and concentrated on the planes, the carrier forces would have destroyed more planes, but probably not so many more as Admiral McCain hoped.

The politicization of the war in these last days of July was notable in almost every major decision. Nimitz and King had been most reluctant to bring the British fleet into play in the Pacific. They did not need it; that was the main factor. Since they did not need the British, they took the position that the British should not be allowed to take any action that would give them a claim on the winning of the Pacific struggle. That attitude permeated the fleet, and thus Halsey did not give the British task force any real responsibility. Admiral Rawlings was assigned secondary targets, such as Osaka, where there were a few ships but nothing important. As the Americans, British, and Russian leaders made political decisions about the war at Potsdam, so too were the American military leaders making political decisions.

On July 25, Halsey ordered up a strike on the Kure area of southern Honshu. The weather was foul and over the target port very little could be seen, so actually Admiral McCain had his way, with the pilots turning to airfields instead of the ships. The pilots, gaining experience in looking for planes on the ground, now began to find them hidden far from the airfields and destroyed a number of planes, several hangars, and other installations. They did not destroy any fuel dumps. So short were the Japanese of aviation gasoline that they took more precautions to protect it than they did the aircraft. Some of the planes struck Kyushu. Some concentrated on targets in Shikoku.

All during the war the problem of the downed aviator had dogged the fleet. During the battle of the Marianas, Admiral Mitscher had spent two days after the fighting trying to round up all his wet eagles, who were floating in rubber rafts in the Philippine Sea. But toward the end of the war, the navy took a leaf from the British book and began to employ small amphibious aircraft that could take off from a carrier's deck and land on the water, rescue a pilot and aircrew, and then fly back to the carrier. The impact on the pilots was the same as that of the submarine lifeguards on the B-29 fliers in the Marianas.

An example was the rescue of Lieutenant H. W. Harrison, who ditched after his fighter was hit by antiaircraft fire over one of the airfields. The PBM that was assigned to rescue in that area that day was low on gas, but Admiral McCain gave the order that the Dumbo was to rescue any downed pilots, and then if necessary to ditch in the vicinity of the task force. Ditching in that case meant a pleasant water cruise in a flying boat, unless something broke down. There was another difficulty: after the strikes took off from the task force the weather closed in behind them, and the Dumbo pilot had to fly through a solid front to get to the rescue area. He did, he picked up Harrison and one other pilot from the carrier *Shangri-la*, and brought the PBM back to make a water landing in the middle of the task force. The men were all picked up by a destroyer.

This sort of protection gave the pilots a new confidence.

On that night of July 25, Admiral Halsey was not pleased. His men had destroyed some sixty planes and damaged another seventy, but they were not getting at the remnants of the Japanese fleet. Only three aircraft of the whole task force had managed to find their way to Kure through the bad weather, and although they claimed to have damaged the big battleship in the harbor further, they made no claim about sinking it. And that was what Admiral Halsey wanted, a clean sweep of the Japanese navy to report back to the folks at home.

That day, as Halsey pondered his weather difficulties, President Truman made the final decision to use the atomic bomb against a Japanese city, fully knowing (or at least certain in his mind) that it would create more destruction to the civilian population in one blow than any other weapon any time anywhere. But in recent weeks, Truman's military advisors had laid out for him the bleak facts of the cost of an invasion of Japan, and he had decided that if this weapon could prevent that loss of American life, then it must be used.

That evening (7:00 Tokyo time) the Japanese finally realized they could not stand on the "no surrender" attitude that the military men were bent on pursuing. The cabinet cabled Ambassador Sato to offer to go anyplace the Russians wanted him to go to talk about peace, and to make sure that everyone knew Prince Konoye would come with the personal instructions of the Emperor. "Japan still cannot accept unconditional surrender under any circumstances, but we should like to communicate to the other party through appropriate channels that we have no objection to a peace based on the Atlantic Charter." (The charter was a declaration of principles issued in August 1941, before the war against Japan began, and thus had no specific demands.) But even now, surrounded, beleagured, half certain that the Russians were getting ready to enter the war, the Japanese government was still obdurate about unconditional surrender. "Should the United States and Britain remain insistent [on unconditional surrender] .... there is no solution to this situation other than for us to hold out until complete collapse because of this one point alone," the foreign minister instructed his ambassador to tell the Russians. "What they wanted," said the foreign minister, was "very reasonable terms in order to secure and maintain our nation's existence and honor."

These ideas were communicated to the Russians, but the Russians were not passing them along to the Western Allies, so President Truman had no inkling of the Japanese views other than what Radio Tokyo told him. The Russian foreign office was talking to the Japanese about "mediation," but the Russian military was talking to the Americans and the British at Potsdam about the specific details of Soviet entry into the war.

By this time, Admiral Halsey knew about the atomic bomb, although he did not know many of the details. Admiral William R. Purnell was sent to the Third Fleet by Admiral Nimitz, after Nimitz learned of the specific instructions from Washington. The atomic bomb was to be dropped, and it was to be dropped August 2 on a target on the island of Kyushu.

For several weeks Admiral Halsey had been puzzling over a directive from Nimitz that warned him away from a number of cities. He did not know that these cities were all the atomic bomb targets listed by General Groves. The high command did not want any mistakes: when the bomb was dropped, Japan was to feel the full impact, which might not have been the case if Halsey's planes had been knocking out parts of these cities earlier. Now Halsey knew why Hiroshima, a primary naval target, and Nagasaki, a naval base, were both on the proscribed list. Purnell then told him that he was to keep all his planes at least fifty miles from this area. It would be best, in fact, if he would stay away from Kyushu for the time being.

On July 26 the Third Fleet fuelled again, and the ships took on supplies. No matter how relatively effective the strikes of the past few days had been or not been, the resupply problem was the same: aviation gasoline, bombs, rockets, and napalm were expended and must be replaced if the fleet was to continue to operate.

The planes of the 20th Air Force were plastering Japan every day with bombs, and by July 26 millions of workers had been ordered to move out of Tokyo. The population of the capital city had been reduced almost by half, to about four million. The number represented a lot of people still, but when they moved about as half the number of past days, somehow they seemed to rattle around. A few of the returning crews to the island of Tinian in the Marianas noticed the arrival of a U.S. navy cruiser there that day. She was the *Indianapolis*, and she was carrying that first disassembled atomic bomb.

On July 26, the American and the Russian chiefs of staff met and discussed problems of combined operations against Japan. The political leaders prepared the Potsdam Declaration, which called upon the Japanese to surrender unconditionally and promised again "prompt and utter destruction" as the alternative. The question of the Emperor's status, as demanded by the Americans, was left for future discussion. The declaration also demanded that Japan give up all her territories except the home islands.

That day, Britain's conduct of negotiations was disturbed by the result of the British elections. The British Labour Party, led by Clement Attlee, defeated the Conservatives, and so Winston Churchill was out of office. Everything at Potsdam had to stop until Prime Minister Attlee could reach Germany. He did come over almost immediately, and the process of winding down the war went on. On that night of July 26 *I-58* surfaced and Commander Hashimoto took a star fix. He had nearly reached the Leyte-Guam shipping lane, where he had orders to patrol to the west. All was quiet. He saw no sign of ships or enemy aircraft.

On Tinian that day the usual B-29 raids set out for points in Japan, being careful not to fly over Hiroshima or Nagasaki, although none of the navigators knew quite why. The pilots of the 509th Group flew some more single missions. That day a number of engineers and scientists arrived on the island and went into long conferences with Colonel Tibbets, General Thomas Farrell, the senior military representative of the atomic project, and General LeMay. Captain McVay of the *Indianapolis* received his new orders: he was to go down to Guam for briefing and routing to Leyte, where he would be informed of the submarine situation in the waters of the Philippine Sea and given a route to follow to the Philippines. This word indicated no new caution developed in the Nimitz command following the sinking of the *Underhill*. The Japanese were still very much in the war, but U.S. ship captains had been lulled into forgetting it.

On the morning of July 27, Admiral Halsey's Third Fleet was still taking on supplies, preparing for another round of strikes against Kure and other ports where elements of the Japanese fleet were reported. Admiral McCain was of the same mind as before: this was all a waste of valuable time, when his planes should be hitting airfields and aircraft factories in preparation for the desperate battle coming with the invasion of Japan. But McCain was now keeping his mouth shut and would not complain until he wrote his operations report, much later.

Halsey was talking with Admiral Purnell, who gave him as much background as he could about the new weapon that was scheduled to be used against the Japanese the next month. Purnell did not know a great deal about the bomb, but he did know that it was reportedly the hottest weapon that had ever been developed. Halsey was impressed.

From Tinian and Saipan scores of B-29s took off on a different sort of mission this day. The Potsdam Declaration had been broadcast to the world, and the United States Office of War Information was trying to make sure that the Japanese people as well as the government knew what was happening. The "different" B-29 missions were leaflet missions; the planes carried millions of leaflets, and they were dropped widely over eleven major Japanese cities. They warned of the enormous air bombardment that would fall on Japan if the terms of the Allies were not accepted.

At Potsdam the Allied leaders waited expectantly for some signs from Tokyo. Some of them expected that the signs would be made clear to the Russians. Or perhaps a radio broadcast by the Japanese government would tell the story. The Russians were not pleased. They had not been consulted on the terms of the Potsdam Declaration because they were not at war with Japan, Secretary of State James Byrnes told Soviet Foreign Minister Vyacheslav Molotov. The Soviet foreign minister was not appeased. He had asked for a delay in the broadcast of this information just as soon as he had heard of the declaration—and that was two days earlier. True, said Byrnes, but the wheels were already in motion then, and the American press had been given advance notice with a release deadline of the twenty-seventh. This was no time for a detailed explanation of the difference between the American and Soviet approaches to public information and the press; besides, as a former ambassador to the U.S., Molotov knew all these matters very well. But the fact was that the American and British action had driven a new wedge between the Russians and their allies, and even as the war came toward its end, the Allied situation was deteriorating. Had the Russians been consulted and had they joined in the declaration, the results might have been far different in Tokyo.

For in Tokyo, early on the morning of July 27 the various arms of the government began getting the word of the Potsdam Declaration. They had all known of the big meeting in Germany, and they had been waiting for some announcement of the discussion. The military men expected the Russians to enter the war, and were surprised when they learned nothing of such a plan from the Potsdam Declaration. It took a little time to digest the foreign message and translate it into Japanese, and then the various translations had to be compared and fine meaning worked out. As this was happening, the military leaders pondered, and decided that the acceptance of the Allied terms would mean the absolute destruction of everything Japan held dear—and as far as they were concerned, this was quite true. The declaration made it quite clear that Japanese militarism was going to be destroyed one way or another.

When all translation was completed, Foreign Minister Shigenori Togo took a copy to the Imperial Palace. He had made an appointment to see the Emperor, and was ushered into the Imperial Presence immediately in the audience hall. Emperor Hirohito went over the document word by word, stopping occasionally to ask questions. It seemed strange that this had come to Japan by radio broadcast and not by a diplomatic message. It would have been simple enough for the Allies to have reached a Japanese diplomat in Bern or Stockholm or Moscow. The Emperor was puzzled by this behavior on the part of the Allies, and asked Togo what he thought about it. The foreign minister said bluntly that he felt the approach was most discouraging in terms of any sort of negotiations. It was not a message, it was an announcement of policy, and the Allies seemed to take the position that they did not care what the Japanese government thought about the terms. (This was certainly true. By this time neither Truman nor any other leader was willing to give the Japanese any concessions.) The puzzlement of the Japanese would continue for another ten days, until they learned the secret of the atomic bomb.

Surmounting that difficulty, Emperor Hirohito gave total attention to the details of the communiqué. It did promise humane treatment of the Japanese people in spite of what his generals had been telling him—that the Americans would do to Japan what they had done to Okinawa and the other islands; that nearly every soul would be massacred or forced to suicide. Hirohito now did not believe what the generals had told him. The terms were hard, but they were not inhumane. Neither the foreign minister nor the Emperor mentioned the most delicate question of all: what was to happen to the Emperor and to the imperial system? The communiqué did not mention it, and so every man was left to his own guess. The Emperor finished his reading, and observed that the terms were acceptable, for the war must be stopped. Japan was suffering too greatly and it was apparent that the Allies would not be diverted from invasion, and that would mean even more suffering by the civilian population.

With that remark, the audience was ended and Foreign Minister Togo stood up. The Emperor stood and left the room, Togo bowed after him in observance of protocol, and then he left.

But even as the foreign minister was waiting on the chief of state, back in the government offices of Tokyo the military was planning to continue the war. There could be no acceptance of these terms, the generals told Prime Minister Suzuki. Besides,

this was not an official act at all, but propaganda. Had the
Japanese government been consulted? Had an official message
from any of the Allies been received? No. Then the war must
go on until a reasonable and just peace could be assured, and that
meant maintenance of the imperial system, the military system,
the colonial system.

When the attitude of the generals had been made crystal
clear, the cabinet sought some means of meeting the situation.
Prime Minister Suzuki decided that the only thing to do was
ignore the declaration, as an unofficial matter and beneath
observance. So he told a reporter from Domei, the official
Japanese news agency. And that evening, in Potsdam, the Allies
had their answer: the Japanese were not going to accept the
surrender terms offered in the Potsdam Declaration.

Privately, Foreign Minister Togo told Prime Minister Suzuki
that there was a chance for some sort of Soviet mediation still.
Prince Konoye was poised, prepared to leave for Moscow on a
moment's notice, and the Soviet government had still not replied to the ambassador's request for an invitation to Konoye to
discuss peace terms. It would have been easy enough for the
Russians to say no and they had not said no. So the door was
still open, the foreign minister said. By ignoring the ultimatum,
the Japanese were still not rejecting it. A little more time might
bring some positive results to help the Japanese cause.

Prime Minister Suzuki ordered a bowdlerized version of the
communiqué published in the press, and made no comment for
the Allies to construe. He was, in fact, resisting a growing pressure by the military men to reject the terms absolutely. When the
generals saw the leaflets dropped on the cities, they came to the
conclusion that the Allies were making a great deal of noise about
nothing, and that the war would continue as it had. They saw no
reason to change the basic defense plan, which called for exacting
so high a price in American ships and lives that at some point the
Americans would back off and a peace could be obtained that
would let Japan keep her colonies and her old way of life.

So the war went on.

THE HUNTER
AND
THE HUNTED

Early on the morning of July 27 (U.S. time) Commander Hashimoto's *I-58* was cruising on the surface, heading westward along the sea-lane between Guam and Leyte. Since the establishment of Admiral Nimitz' headquarters at Guam, this sea region had become a prime target area for the Japanese. At 5:30 the newly installed radar of *I-58* picked up an unidentified aircraft. These days, with the Americans in control of the Marianas and the Philippines, the plane was certain to be enemy, so Commander Hashimoto ordered a crash dive. *I-58* remained below for many hours, which meant she was blind; since the radar did not function underwater, if Hashimoto wanted information that meant coming at least to periscope depth. At 2:00 he did so, and when he stood at the periscope and swung it around, he sighted a large ship. After a few minutes he recognized her as a tanker. For a moment Hashimoto was overjoyed, at last to be coming to grips with his enemies, but then another ship came into view and close inspection showed the second vessel was a destroyer. That made life more complicated. There was no possibility of coming up for a surface attack, which would have been by far the simplest and most effective.

Hashimoto had two alternatives. He could attack with conventional torpedoes, or he could use some of his six *kaiten.* For safety's sake, he chose the latter course. If he used torpedoes the destroyer would undoubtedly launch a counterattack, and if it were successful then all the *kaiten* would go to waste as well as the *I-58.* So the *kaiten* attack was by far the most suitable. He gave the order for the *kaiten* pilots to prepare for action. Just in case, he also ordered the torpedomen to prepare the tubes too. He decided to use *kaitens* No. 1 and No. 2, and ordered the pilots of those two small human torpedoes into their craft. They reached the *kaitens* by climbing up through a hatch on the deck, into the small craft, and then shutting the submarine hatch behind them. Once inside and locked into their suicide craft, the pilots were in touch with the submarine by telephone. They waited.

Commander Hashimoto estimated the enemy course and speed and gave the bearings to the *kaiten* pilots.

"Ready to start engines," he said.

Kaiten No. 2 started up easily enough, but the pilot of *kaiten* No. 1 was having difficulties and the engine would not turn over. No. 2, then, was to be launched first. At 2:30 the craft was ready to move, and the captain ordered the last straps released. The human torpedo was on its own.

Ten minutes later the pilot of *kaiten* No. 1 reported that he had gotten his engine going and was ready to take off. He too was released, and through the periscope Commander Hashimoto watched the craft launch their attack.

He could not watch for long, however, because the weather was growing sloppier and soon the *kaiten* and the tanker all disappeared from view in a squall. Not quite an hour after the launch of No. 2 the men in the submarine heard an explosion and about ten minutes later they heard another. Commander

Hashimoto was sure his *kaitens* had managed to sink the tanker, but he was too good a naval officer to claim a sinking without being able to verify it. He wrote in the log only that the two *kaitens* had made a "probable" sinking. In fact they had not, and the explosions that were heard aboard the submarine were the explosions of the *kaiten*, but not of the tanker.

The apparent sinking of an enemy ship gave Commander Hashimoto and his crew a decided lift of spirit. They needed it. That day the supply of fresh food gave out and from this point on they would be living on canned meat, canned and pickled fish and daikon, canned sweet potatoes that tasted like no sweet potato in the world, and other canned vegetables. The *I-58* had no freezing compartments, and so the fresh foods lasted just about the first ten days of any voyage, and this was the tenth day out. There was nothing to be done but bear it, and now they had something to grin about as well. Commander Hashimoto moved toward the point where the Leyte-Guam shipping lane crossed the lane that ran between the American-held Palau islands and Okinawa. With radar, he had found it possible to run on the surface most of the day, since there were few aircraft sightings. There was still the danger of encountering a submerged American submarine, which might not show up clearly on the radar, but in order to make best use of his fuel supply, Commander Hashimoto was willing to run this risk, as surface visibility was good. On the morning of July 28 the *I-58* was coming close to the junction.

Meanwhile, Captain McVay of the cruiser *Indianapolis* was preparing to take to sea again. He had just been briefed about the sea conditions in the area and given a general picture of the Guam command's assessment of the submarine situation in the war zone. The port director was aware of several submarine contacts along the projected route of the *Indianapolis* to Leyte. Nothing was said of the sinking of the *Underhill*, 250 miles east of Cape Engano. It seems that the word had not yet reached the

Guam Command though the event was four days old. So Captain McVay was not given any special warnings about Japanese submarine action, and the equanimity with which he viewed the sea-lanes was undisturbed. It had been a long time, barring the *Underhill* affair, since a Japanese submarine threat had seemed very real.

The *Indianapolis* left Guam at 9:00 on the morning of July 28 for her new task. It was a relief in a way to be getting back into action; the ferrying job from America to Tinian had not been the sort of work a cruiser was supposed to be doing. On arrival at Leyte, Captain McVay was to report to Rear Admiral Lynde D. McCormick, commander of the battle training unit there, for a workup before going back into action, this time with Admiral Oldendorf's new task force operating out of Okinawa. The run to Leyte was regarded by the Pacific command these days as a "milk run" with no apparent danger from enemy vessels. The Philippine Sea was now seen as an American lake, and no destroyers or destroyer escorts were available to take warships through. On paper it all seemed sound, but there was a serious deficiency: the *Indianapolis* did not have any sound gear, which meant her only protection from submarine attack was radar, which could locate a surfaced vessel, and the lookouts. But again, the deficiency did not seem to be a problem. This was a rear area, deemed safe, and as all knew, the Japanese fleet was virtually nonexistent. So many regulations enforced in the past had been changed or were disregarded. There was no requirement for the *Indianapolis* to take any special precautions. She was steaming ahead in a straight line, without zigzagging (which was a great nuisance to the navigation officer). Her ports and watertight bulkheads largely were opened up for ventilation, since she was an old-fashioned cruiser and did not have air conditioning. The voyage was a routine trip and it was regarded as just that.

Even at Okinawa, where suicide planes were still occasionally attacking, there was a feeling that the war was virtually over. It was true that a few Japanese continued to hide in caves and wreckage and come out to harry the base troops, but the real damage was caused by the kamikazes from Konoya airfield.

Lieutenant Morimasa Yunikawa was supervising the training of many of these young men at Kanoya Naval Air Base. He taught them how to fly less than twenty feet above the surface to avoid radar and so that the antiaircraft guns could not find them. Many of the larger guns could not depress to such an angle from shipboard. He also coached the young fliers in method: half a dozen pilots coming from different directions were almost certain to have results.

Lieutenant Yunikawa was despondent these days. Three times he had secured orders to fly a suicide mission, and on each occasion the mission was cancelled. It was very discouraging to build oneself up to the inevitable, and then be called back to earth.

Another young pilot was Lieutenant (j. g.) Hideo Suzuki, who was waiting impatiently for the call to action at Kanoya. He had trained under Yunikawa, learning to take off from the simulated deck of a carrier, flying a Zero to learn the Oka technique, and then a rocket plane. Just recently, as a part of the Imperial General Staff's disposition of suicide forces, he had been reassigned to Komatsu naval base at another point in Kyushu. The word had gone out that the kamikaze pilots would have only one day's notice when they got the "shutsujei meirei" —the order to make the last flight. One lived, then, from day to day. And from day to day others did get their orders, but not Suzuki.

On July 28, of his fellow suicide pilots a half dozen were selected for a mission against Okinawa. Despite Imperial Headquarters' orders that men and planes were to be retained for the last great battle, the commanders of the bases knew that if they did not send a few missions out, they would find themselves without effective pilots; the strain was enormous and most of these young men were living on their nerves.

There was the usual ceremony. The pilots lined up for inspection, wearing the white *hachimaki* (headband) of the

Divine Thunderbolt Corps. They downed the ritual cups of sake, and then they headed for their planes. In a few minutes they were in the air, flying by night to take the Americans by surprise.

Shortly after midnight on the morning of July 28 the ships at the U. S. picket station No. 9A off Okinawa were moving slowly in their pattern. So slight had the danger from kamikazes become in recent weeks that the number of pickets had been sharply reduced. The destroyers *Callaghan*, the *Cassin Young*, *Pritchett* and three landing craft were manning this picket station. Suddenly, the kamikazes appeared. One of them smashed into the *Callaghan* and sank her. So much for "safe" waters.

That morning Admiral Halsey's Third Fleet was back in action at a point ninety-six miles off the coast of Shikoku. From that point the American and British carriers began early in the morning to launch attacks against the ports of the Inland Sea, from Nagoya to northern Kyushu. Once again Halsey's word to the fleet was to "get the ships," and they were major targets. Fighters and bombers from the *Yorktown*, for example, began operating at 4:45 in the morning. The operations were continuous all day long, despite a weather front that blew up around noon over the Japanese islands. The pilots flew through squalls and found low visibility in the operating area, but they flew. At the end of the day, the photographs showed the *Hyuga* sitting on the bottom at Kure, with her deck half underwater. Two other battleships were smashed and one of them, identified as the *Haruna*, was beached and burning with a large hole in her stern. The proud cruisers *Aoba*, *Oyodo*, and *Tone*, which had fought against the Americans so many times, were smashed. So were all the other major vessels in the harbors, except the carriers *Amagi* and *Katsuragi*, which were still afloat but not operable. The Japanese lost some thirty warships that day, and another two dozen were badly damaged

Besides this, about fifty merchant ships of various sizes were sunk or damaged. At the end of the day, Admiral Halsey was content. He had promised to harry the remnants of the Japanese fleet out of their holes, and he was doing it. Admiral McCain was far more pleased with the score of enemy aircraft destroyed, about 150, with another 150 claimed as damaged. But there was the usual price. The *Yorktown* lost one fighter and one bomber, and other carriers suffered similar losses—light but still a price exacted by the enemy. The antiaircraft fire from the ships was strong and constant; the cruiser *Tone*, for example, was still firing her guns at the attackers as evening came, even though she was burning and on the beach.

On July 28 the B-29s continued their steady series of strikes against Japan, and almost unnoticed were the single-plane missions of the 509th Group. The Japanese were accustomed to seeing B-29s in the air over their cities. But the American pilots of the other B-29 groups were furious at the "special treatment" given the 509th, which did not seem to do anything at all. That day, also, army B-24s from Okinawa joined in the attacks on the Japanese ports and two of the planes, violating the orders to stay away from the stipulated cities, were shot down over Hiroshima.

That day the American submarine *Barb* was heading home-ward from her twelfth war patrol. The results indicated what was happening to Japan. Commander E. B. Fluckey had moved the *Barb* around the coasts of Hokkaido and the Sakhalin islands for a solid month without finding more than a handful of targets. She sank a small freighter and a destroyer escort, and a number of sampans and craft that a year before she would have passed by as far too insignificant to warrant even gunfire. By the twentieth of July the crew had grown so bored that Commander Fluckey organized a raid onto the shore, the crew sent volunteers to a point where the railroad neared the sea on Karafuto, one of the Sakhalin islands, and they mined the roadbed and blew up a train! It was hardly the work for which submarines had been fitted out, but there were no proper targets, and just before ending her patrol *Barb* used up most of the rest of her ammunition bombarding a shipyard on one of the Sakhalin islands.

In Japan, the Imperial General Staff continued preparations for the battle of Japan. Without stopping the flow of planes, the movement of troops, and the allocation of resupply, they argued the case with the politicians. General Korechika Anami, the minister of war, was determined that Japan should fight on. Admiral Soemu Toyoda, the Navy's chief of staff, met with Anami and they together pressed Prime Minister Suzuki to come out openly in disavowal of the Potsdam Declaration. The newspapers that morning published highly censored versions of the declaration with no mention of items the Japanese people might consider positive, such as the paragraph that stated the Allies had no intention of enslaving the Japanese people or destroying the nation. The propaganda line of the government these days was just the opposite: in the attempt to incite new war fervor into the people, the military were claiming that if the war was lost so would Japan be lost. That day Prime Minister Suzuki gave a press conference, at which he said he saw nothing of any importance or anything new in the Allied declaration. As he said the words he knew that he was committing Japan to fight on.

The Japanese declaration was in turn broadcast to the United States, and if there was any lingering doubt in the minds of President Truman and the war cabinet of the U.S. as to the need for using the atomic bomb, it was eliminated that day. The Japanese had rejected the warning—the Americans did not realize that the Japanese had no way of knowing that it was any different from the warnings issued many times before about the American position, including the Cairo Declaration that promised to defeat Japan utterly. Be that as it may, the American position on July 28 hardened. There was no slowdown in the preparations to drop the first bomb early in August. President Truman, still at Potsdam, met with Britain's new Prime Minister

Attlee and Stalin that evening in another session of the conference. Stalin discussed Japan's offer to send Prince Konoye to Moscow to negotiate a peace through the Russians as intermediaries, but said he intended to give a flat *No* answer. Truman, who knew all about it from intercepted messages, said nothing.

THE HUNTER STRIKES

On the morning of July 29 the flight crews of the 509th Bombardment Group set off on a mission against Japan. The planes flew alone to bomb various targets in Japan, each carrying a 10,000-pound bomb. All planes returned safely. None had even been hit by antiaircraft fire and none had been attacked by Japanese fighters over the target.

Admiral Halsey's Third Fleet was operating against Japan again on July 29, although under some difficulties. The weather had grown steadily worse in the past twenty-four hours, and it seemed that a typhoon might again be brewing.

After two disastrous experiences with such storms, the Halsey command was understandably edgy about the weather. As the bad weather grew worse, the emphasis was changed from the Tokyo plain and the Inland Sea to Maizuru, a base on the Sea of Japan on the northern coast of Honshu island. The big ships—battleships and cruisers—moved in close to bombard Japanese industrial installations at Hamamatsu. At the moment there was not a very effective assessment of any of the damage of that day; the weather was too poor for observation planes to operate. On the twenty-eighth there had been a little air opposition; apparently there were still some commanders who felt that the attacks on the fleet bases and nearby airfields must be met. But for the most part, in all these attacks the Japanese remained stubbornly on the ground, when McCain at least knew they still had plenty of air strength. To the pilots it was eerie to go in over a Japanese airfield and find nothing but flak to oppose them, but this was always serious enough to cause a few casualties in every day of operations.

At Potsdam, the meetings of the Allied leaders had taken on an almost defensive character. On July 29 Foreign Minister Molotov suggested that the United States ought to make a formal request to the Soviet Union to enter the war against Japan. Now, what did that mean? The Americans pondered, and decided it could be nothing but a ploy by the Soviets to shift responsibility for whatever happened to the shoulders of the Americans. Admiral Leahy, who had a strong feeling of distrust for the Russians anyhow, suggested that if President Truman accepted the ploy the U.S. would be under permanent obligation to the Russians and that it would cost dearly in the end. Secretary Byrnes, who was also distrustful of the Russians, did not want them to come into the war, and felt it was not at all necessary; that if the Soviets came in the results could not but hurt the U.S. position. The net result of all this concern was that the Americans and the British began hedging to avoid a definite commitment. It was not hard for the Russians to understand what was going on. An obscure message from Truman to Stalin was prepared, it took the whole day for the diplomats to worry over it, and it did not mean much when finished. Truman liked it, and so did Attlee. Byrnes did not like any part of it; he told Secretary of the Navy James Forrestal that he hoped anxiously that the Russians would not come into the war, because he saw nothing but trouble about Dairen and Port Arthur.

The Russian yen for Chinese territory was well known, and although it had been decided by the Allies that Manchuria would be returned to China, saying and doing were two different matters.

Potsdam, staged to increase Allied unity and chart a strong course of action to carry through the war, was turning into something quite different. The inherent mutual distrust of East and West, pushed into latency in the face of the greater German threat, was now beginning to emerge.

How far from all this was the military side of the Pacific war! On the evening of July 29 (U.S. and European time) Commander Hashimoto decided he had best submerge. The weather was acting up, and the I-boat was taking a heavy battering from the sea. They would be better off in the safety of the deep, and there was nothing to be gained by remaining on the surface because the clouds were hanging low over the water and the almost constant squalls made visibility virtually zero. The I-boat's engineering officer was eager to make some repairs that could be best done in the quiet of the depths. At 7:00, Commander Hashimoto raised the periscope of the submarine, took one last look around from a depth of about thirty feet, and saw nothing at all save the blackness of night. He took her down deeper then, and the engineers went to work. The captain left orders to be called at 10:30 that night and went to his bunk in the wardroom to take a nap. His orders had indicated a minimal state of readiness so most of the crew took the opportunity to sleep as well.

At 10:30 a petty officer awakened the captain and he prepared to go onto the bridge. First, however, he stopped to wash his face in cold water to wake up, and then lingered for a few moments at the ship's shrine, a tiny wooden box which contained some sacred mementos from the Ise grand shrine at home in Japan. But in less than fifteen minutes he was in the conning tower and took command of operations. He took the submarine up to periscope depth, and began to scan the horizon in a 360-degree swing of the periscope. He saw nothing. He ordered the radar antennae raised, and the radar operator announced that there were no signs of movement on the screens.

It was safe to surface then, and Commander Hashimoto brought the I-boat to the top, and the lookouts scampered up onto the conning tower to take their stations. As the last of the ballast was blown from the main tanks and the submarine came to the surface, the signalman on duty opened the hatch and climbed out. The navigator went out next, while Commander Hashimoto peered through the periscope so there would be no surprises. He was still looking through the 'scope when the navigator on the bridge shouted that there was a ship, bearing 90 degrees. Hashimoto lowered the periscope and pulled himself up the companionway to the outside. There between them and the horizon, clearly visible in the bright light of the moon, was a ship. He gave the order to dive and the lookouts hurried back to the conning tower. In a moment Hashimoto was back at his periscope and a few moments later water was rushing around the sinking boat.

Off on the horizon from the I-boat, the cruiser *Indianapolis* steamed along majestically. The day had been foul, which meant some of the compartments had been closed up against the sea and made the interior of the ship uncomfortable, but by evening the wind had freshened and a sixteen-knots breeze was blowing through the open ports and hatches. The sea was choppy and the lookouts strained their eyes as they looked around their horizon. But in the chop no one could see a periscope a little over five miles away. Steadily, at about fifteen knots, the cruiser headed on, a perfect target for her enemy. She was not zigzagging because no orders had been left to that effect, a matter that surprised no one on the bridge at watch-change time in these "safe" waters.

Commander Hashimoto saw this perfect target coming toward him. It was too perfect, the ship was approaching fast and would pass so close to the submarine that the long-lance torpedoes would not have time to arm. Hashimoto took the *I-58* into a long S-turn to increase the distance. But should he not use his *kaitens*? The pilots were clamoring for his attention and asking to be allowed to go. He preferred to use the regular torpedoes. The pilot of *kaiten* No. 6 was told to get into his machine as a backup, and the pilot of *kaiten* No. 5 was told to stand by. Hashimoto would fire six torpedoes, he decided, in a fan pattern.

Commander Hashimoto waited, still not quite certain of the nature of his target, except that she was a warship. She might be a destroyer. But as the *Indianapolis* closed to 4,000 yards (two-plus miles), the captain could see that the ship was bigger, with a tall mast. She was either a large cruiser or a battleship.

As Hashimoto made his calculations, the *kaiten* pilots kept coming up to ask wistfully if they could not go. But no, he looked at the moon and said it was too difficult for them to find their way. The ordinary torpedoes would do the job.

The waiting was sheer torture for everyone in the boat, and none but the captain knew what or why. He watched, he waited, and at 2,000 yards he was ready to fire. In a few moments six torpedoes were speeding out in the general direction of the American cruiser.

Two of the torpedoes struck the *Indianapolis* on the starboard side. The explosions tore enormous holes in the sides of the ship, and knocked out the communications system so that the officer of the deck could not tell the engineers to stop the engines. The *Indianapolis* kept running at over fifteen knots for nearly a minute before the word could be passed by hand. By that time it was apparent everywhere in the ship that something was dreadfully wrong: the cruiser was listing strongly to starboard.

A radioman sent out a distress message, giving the ship's position. Several more calls were made later.

The captain was thoroughly aroused by this time, and on the bridge. When he saw the extent of the list and learned of the extent of the damage, he ordered the ship abandoned. The word had to be carried throughout the ship by messengers. By the time it got to some stations it was no longer necessary; the men had seen that the ship was sinking and had gone over the side into the sea. Less than fifteen minutes after the torpedoes struck, the *Indianapolis* capsized and sank, taking down some 400 of the 1,200-man crew, either dead from the explosion and its results or trapped and drowned.

But 800 men were in the water, struggling to board a dozen life rafts and half a dozen floating nets that had been freed before the sinking. Most of them had life jackets, but about 100 did not, and they soon died in the water.

Aboard the *I-58* the captain's announcement that he had torpedoed a ship was not needed: the concussion was announcement enough, but Hashimoto danced around his periscope, shouting "A hit, a hit," and the men responded with shouts and laughter. Hashimoto had served in five submarines, and this was the first time he had ever fired a torpedo. The same sort of frustration shared by the men of the I-boat was suddenly released.

Commander Hashimoto watched through the periscope as his enemy sank. He ordered the torpedo tubes reloaded and brought the I-boat to the surface, looking around for the destroyer that should be there. But there was nothing, and after a few minutes, he set course for the northeast, hoping to find another target on the sea-lane.

THE HALSEY
FURY

Back at Kanoya naval air base, the surviving escorts of the planes that had attacked and sunk the *Callaghan* made their report. The technique of attacking at night was a good one, and it was decided that another flight would be sent off on July 29 to strike shortly after midnight on the thirtieth. The preparations were made.

That day, the kamikazes were flying as Commander Hashimoto made his attack on the *Indianapolis,* and four hours later one of the kamikazes smashed into the *Cassin Young* at the same picket station off Okinawa. The *Cassin Young* did not sink, but she lost twenty-two men killed and forty-five men wounded.

Had the reports of the success of the *I-58* and of the kamikazes around Okinawa been tallied, they might have brought a renewed concern to the American naval command. But the fact was that no one in authority knew on the morning of July 30 that the *Indianapolis* had been sunk. Apparently the power failure that had knocked out communications in the ship had also prevented the transmissions of the radio operators from ever getting out into the ether. The *Indianapolis* was sunk. As the dawn came up, some 700 men struggled in the water, waiting for rescue.

All sorts of normal safeguards protected a warship at sea. On July 28, when she was ready to sail from Guam for Leyte, the port director at Guam had sent off messages giving her course, speed and estimated time of arrival to all concerned. The concerned commands were the Philippine Sea Frontier, which had charge of the general area, the Port Director of Tacloban, where she was immediately headed, and Admiral McCormick, whose command she was to join for training before going off to Okinawa.

But at Philippine Sea Frontier headquarters, Admiral James Kauffman was absent on other duty. Besides, both MacArthur's Seventh Fleet and Admiral Nimitz' Pacific Fleet had sent out orders that port directors were not to report on the arrivals and departures of combatant ships. The move was supposed to assist security and cut down red tape. The result was that neither Philippine Sea Frontier nor Tacloban port officials paid any attention to the movement of the *Indianapolis,* and of course she had kept the usual radio silence until hit by the torpedoes.

Actually it was far too early for Captain McVay to expect the wheels of administration to begin moving in his behalf. He was not expected at Leyte until 11:00 on July 31. What he and his men must rely upon was the efficacy of the messages they had sent.

As dawn broke on the morning of July 30, McVay organized his officers and they rounded up the men and assigned them to groups around the lifesaving equipment. The men who had kapok life jackets were in good shape, but some had a more experimental rubber life belt, and many of these began to leak. The indications were ominous, but there was the message, and the men comforted themselves that rescue was just a matter of hours away.

Their spirits rose at 1:00 in the afternoon when a plane was spotted high in the air above them. But the plane soon passed over with no sign that it had seen the groups of men in the water. It seemed very strange.

That morning, as Captain McVay was pulling his men together, Admiral Halsey's fleet was taking another swipe at Japan's naval and air forces. The weather was growing steadily worse, but Halsey was in a hurry. The sweeps against the airfields on the Tokyo plain went ahead as scheduled. Tokyo and Nagoya targets were the main object. The carrier men had learned some new techniques: the most recent air photos were studied carefully before a mission was briefed and the hidden aircraft that could be found were carefully pointed out to the pilots. On the return, the photographs taken by observers were speedily developed so that any misses might be corrected on the next mission. That day, for example, the pilots of *Yorktown* claimed eight planes destroyed on the three airfields on their list, plus four planes damaged and several hangars and other installations destroyed. The claims were not so high these days; Halsey had made it clear that he was more interested in accuracy than in big numbers. The numbers were not large: the whole fleet's nest of carriers destroyed only 119 planes and damaged 142.

In the afternoon the pilots of *Yorktown* and other carriers went after shipping, particularly the naval vessels at the Maizuru naval base. They found a submarine pen near Taga and claimed a small coastal submarine as sunk. They also said they damaged one large I-boat and two other small submarines.

The fleet's rescue units were becoming extremely daring. Lieutenant Donald E. Penn, a *Yorktown* pilot, was forced to ditch after having been hit by antiaircraft fire, and he came down almost inside Maizuru Harbor. A Dumbo (flying amphibian) was dispatched, escorted by four fighters, and came in to pick up Penn. The antiaircraft guns opened up on the rescuers and forced Lieutenant (j. g.) Henry Camara to ditch also. Then a Japanese destroyer escort appeared from within the harbor, bent on capturing the two downed pilots, but the three other fighters buzzed around the warship like bees and drove it off while the Dumbo came down and picked up both men.

That same night Destroyer Squadron 25 moved into Suruga Gulf and attacked various installations. Captain J. W. Ludewig, the commander of the squadron, was looking for shipping, but he did not find any. That was the trouble—nobody was finding many targets. Since spring even the submarine commanders had been coming home to complain that they practically never saw anything larger than 200 tons—small coastal craft that during the early years of the war were beneath notice. Frustrated by inactivity and emboldened by experience, Captain Ludewig led the destroyers in within three miles of the inner point of the bay and bombarded factories. The destroyers started at least one big fire, but they did not know what it was. As for the factories, they did not know it, but the earlier submarine raiding and the B-29s had so diminished Japan's industrial capacities that the aluminum plant at Shimizu, the major industry, was not functioning at all becuase no raw materials were available.

On July 30 at General LeMay's headquarters, officers scurried in and out and orderlies bustled among the tents. The 20th Air Force was getting ready to stage the largest B-29 raid yet. A thousand bombers, it was said, would hit the Japanese cities to give the enemy a taste of what was going to happen to them, now that they had rejected the surrender terms. In a heavily guarded shop in the technical area of the Tinian base, a strange ten-foot-long bomb lay on a cradle. Except for the normal fins on the back of the bomb, one guard who had a look at it said it resembled a trash can on its side more than anything else. The men who guarded the bomb did not know what it was, but its strange appearance was unnerving. From the atmosphere around the secret installation they knew it was something very, very special.

That day, Colonel Tibbets was at Iwo Jima checking over the facilities there. He was the man who would fly the bomb to its destination, and Iwo Jima was the emergency landing spot. If something happened on the way to Japan the plane and its bomb would come down on Iwo, chosen for its isolation. If the bomb blew up there, only a relatively few thousand men would be affected.

In Washington, Secretary of War Stimson was trying to put together the known facts about the atomic bomb and what could be expected from it. It would be devastating, he knew that, but he also was led to believe that there would be no damage from radioactive materials on the ground, and he so informed Truman. Marshall believed that because he had been told by General Groves and Groves believed it because he had been told by the scientists. The atomic bomb would blow up all structures within two miles of its blast point and those within seven miles would be damaged, but that was that—they thought.

In Potsdam, President Truman continued the desultory talks with the Russians. In Moscow, Japanese Ambassador Sato tried to get assurances from the Soviets that they would accept a mission from Prince Konoye and work with him to end the war.

In Tokyo, the civil and military leaders broke into two groups, the civilians who wanted to end the war, and the military men who insisted that it be continued until a "just" peace could be obtained. They talked of "victory" of course, but no one really believed that. Victory in the last hours of July 1945 meant a victory in wresting the nation back from the edge of dissolution. The Emperor, who had told Foreign Minister Togo that the terms of surrender were acceptable to him, now said nothing. Whatever influence he might have exercised to end the war was not used.

Late in the day, Captain Hashimoto ordained a feast aboard *I-58*, or at least as much of a feast as could be arranged with only canned foods. The crew had boiled eels, a favorite dish, and corned beef and beans, all out of cans, to add to the usual rice and pickled daikon. That night Hashimoto sent a signal to Tokyo to announce his victory.

At dawn on July 31 Halsey's Third Fleet was retiring to deep water to refuel again. For three days planes of the fleet had been scouting a weather front that had all the earmarks of a typhoon. Everyone had learned from the two "Halsey typhoons," it seemed, and this time there was no hesitation. The weather station in Guam was alert and sending frequent messages about the progress of the storm as scouted by its big patrol bombers. Those reports came every six hours.

Halsey knew precisely where he was in relation to the storm and where it was going. That morning the fleet began to skirt the edge of the disturbance. The wind whipped up to twenty-five knots and a ten-foot swell came in from the southeast. Halsey turned south to clear the area and, when well away from the influence of the typhoon, began the fuelling and re-provisioning process. The men of the ships did not even know there was a storm about, but it was heading upward through the chain of Japanese islands.

Around noon the big B-29 raid started off. Not quite—but nearly—a thousand bombers made the trip, a staggering indication of the might the United States was now able to thrust against the Japanese homeland. Those thousand bombers could carry 5,000 *tons* of bombs. It seemed an enormous explosive power, and it was—but the atomic bomb sitting on its cradle in its innocent-looking way contained the equivalent of some 17,000 tons of explosive, or the power of more than three thousand of these big aircraft. In fact the explosive force was much greater because it was concentrated. The scientists knew much of this and suspected the rest; the airmen knew virtually nothing about it, and the Japanese knew nothing at all. After the big raid of the thirty-first in Tokyo the military men were still of the same mind; the Americans had huge numbers of conventional weapons, but the Japanese were prepared to resist with their unconventional weapons, and the Americans had not seen some of them yet.

Scores, hundreds of *kaiten* were being moved into the bays of Kyushu, Shikoku, and Honshu islands. Half a dozen were sent to the little island of Hachijojima, 200 miles south of Tokyo. The Americans would have to bring their ships past this island.

The *kaiten* force would be increased. There would be many *kaiten* to meet the Americans. Admiral Toyoda estimated that he and the army had at least 10,000 planes ready for the final battle. The navy was developing a new small five-man submarine called the *koryu,* and the *koryu* may have been what the planes of the *Yorktown* found that day before when they struck that submarine pen. But there were hundreds of *koryu* and other hundreds of two-man submarines called *kairyu.* Both types carried two torpedoes each, and the *kairyu* could be fitted out with a warhead as well and crash into a ship as the *kaiten* did.

Another suicide weapon, which the Americans had first encountered at Okinawa, was the *shinyo,* or motor torpedo boat. The shinyo was a fifteen-foot boat with an engine powerful enough to send it along at twenty knots. It carried a 330-pound explosive charge in the bow, and was intended to crash into ships, delivering the force of a torpedo. At least 2,000 of these boats were scattered around the bays of the Japanese islands, and more were in production.

Since early spring, the militant officers had led a campaign to bring the war to the enemy at every level. The *tokko* spirit, they called it, or special attack. Even the peasants were exhorted to reveal their true samurai spirit by accomplishing great feats and defying death to combat the enemy. Leaflets were distributed around the countryside showing the people how to make bamboo spears and antipersonnel traps with bamboo stakes. The railroad stations, the public buildings, even such places as public urinals were plastered with patriotic slogans.

There was no way that Admiral Halsey could counteract that sort of weaponry effectively. And in the final analysis although Admiral McCain was correct in his belief that the enemy retained many thousands of planes, they were so secured for the most part that no number of American attacks on the airfields and environs would have destroyed the Japanese capacity to launch that last attack by suicidecraft.

As Halsey waited out this third typhoon with extreme care, the men of the cruiser *Indianapolis* awaited the rescue that certainly should be coming on the second day. Very early on the morning of July 31, well before dawn, a plane was heard overhead. Believing it must be a search plane, the men fired off most of their emergency flares, but there was no reassuring return of the aircraft to look them over. In fact, Captain Richard LeFrancis of the army air forces was flying a C-54 (four-engine passenger-cargo plane) from Manila to Guam and passed over the men. He saw the pyrotechnics, and mistakenly took them to be an indication of a night naval engagement between American and Japanese vessels. When he landed at Guam and reported to the operations office there, he was told that it was none of his business; if it was a naval action the navy certainly knew all about it, and thus put down, he went away and said no more officially about what he had seen.

As dawn came on July 31, Captain McVay scanned the skies. They were blue and empty. The men of the *Indianapolis* were beginning to suffer. The effect of immersion in salt water exacerbated the burns and wounds of the injured, and many of them died.

Some men began to drink seawater despite the watch their officers kept. Soon they became delirious; some saw mirages and swam out to sea to disappear. Some rafts had water, the nets had none, and what water was available was diminishing rapidly. The sun was hot and sea salty. But worse than all these difficulties was the feeling of abandonment. Men began to lose heart. Captain McVay's best efforts could not prevent that as the hours passed and no rescue came.

At 11:00 on July 31, someone at Tacloban should have been looking for the *Indianapolis* and, when she did not appear by dusk, someone should have sent out the general alarm to the fleet. But no one took the slightest interest. The message to Admiral McCormick's flagship, the battleship *Idaho*, had been garbled in transmission and was unreadable. Since it was a routine message, the communications officer never bothered to demand a repeat of the message from Guam. He had so many routine messages, so much red tape, that this one seemed like all the rest. So Admiral McCormick did not know that the *Indianapolis* was on its way, and so it never occurred to him to worry about her. The port officials, who had the message, had filed it long ago in the bottom of the pile.

That afternoon Colonel Tibbets returned from Iwo Jima to Tinian. The air crew complained that they were dodging planes from the B-29 armada all the way home.

That day at Potsdam, President Truman and Premier Stalin fiddled with diplomatic niceties. Stalin wanted that letter from Truman inviting him into the war, and Truman had written his hedging letter. They talked about it and came to no particular conclusions. What Truman and his advisors were really concerned about was the coming drop of the atomic weapon and the results it might have. General Arnold of the U.S. army air forces was preparing a speech for Air Force Day in which he intended to make a new, even sterner warning to Japan, and since this would come just at the time of the A-bomb, others around Truman did not want him to make it.

Actually, no timing had been set for the drop of the A-bomb. It had simply been authorized by President Truman, and all the rest was being left up to the specialists. General Farrell had been at Guam, where General LeMay had established headquarters of the 20th Air Force. They had agreed that the bomb could be dropped on August 1, and Farrell had hurried to Tinian to consult with Colonel Tibbets. But when they checked the weather station they discovered that the typhoon would be passing over Japan that day, and that it could hang around for days. The plans were all put in abeyance.

Admiral Halsey, in his cabin aboard the *Missouri*, fretted in the inactivity of waiting. Since the earliest days of the war he had attacked the Japanese with an unusual fury and personal animosity. He wanted another shot at the Japanese in their

A B-29.

Until the last day, the sight of a kamikaze coming in was enough to frighten everyone.

The commander of the carriers,
Vice Admiral J. S. McCain.

Field Marshal Shunroku Hata.
He was chief of home ground defense
and a former minister of war.

The destruction of Japan.

Premier Stalin and President Truman at Potsdam. At Truman's right are Secretary of State Byrnes and Soviet Foreign Minister Molotov. Just over Truman's shoulder is Soviet Ambassador to the United States Gromyko.

oviet Foreign Minister Molotov.
t right is Andrei Vyshinsky,
ngtime Soviet bureaucrat.

Emperor Hirohito aboard his favorite steed. This is the horse that Admiral Halsey promised to ride through Tokyo.

Admiral Halsey as a captain just after he had won his golden wings. He was probably the worst flier in the naval air force.

Field Marshal General Sugiyama (left) with Prince Konoye in morning dress and Admiral Mitsumasa Yonai in April, 1938.

Japanese Field Marshal General Sugiyama in all his splendor.

Admiral J. S. McCain (left) plots trouble for the Japanese with an intelligence officer.

Rear Admiral John F. Shafroth, the battleship fleet commander, with Admiral Robert B. Carney, Halsey's chief of staff.

The old sea dog, Halsey.

Last minute plans for the naval landing on Japan are being made by Rear Admiral Oscar C. Badger, USN, and Brigadier General William T. Clement, USMC.

General Yoshijiro Umezu, signer of the instrument of Japanese surrender on behalf of the Imperial General Staff. He wanted to commit suicide, but he went to the surrender to represent the Emperor.

Rear Admiral Robert B. Carney, chief of staff to Admiral Halsey.

Fighters sit with their wings folded like big moths. What is apparently rubbish on the deck is material for barriers.

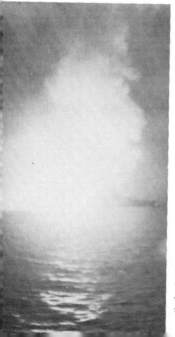

Halsey's planes struck Kure and other ports, and Japan's meager gasoline supply diminished.

When the guns of Halsey's battleships went off along the Japanese coast, one would think the ships had exploded.

Battleships at sea.

The fighter bombers hit everything that moved on the sea.

When the kamikaze hit, the result was a flare and a cloud of smoke which meant that more Americans were dead.

homeland, although he had planned to move the fleet back to Ulithi for base reprovisioning and repairs that could not easily be done at sea. He delayed the orders until after the storm ended so he could take another swipe.

10

THE TRAGEDY
OF DELAY

As dawn broke on August 1, the men of the *Indianapolis* had dwindled noticeably in number. The fresh water had run out. Men were dozing, slipping off the life nets, and their companions were too exhausted to save them. More planes came over, but none paid the slightest bit of attention to the men in the water, despite the sending up of flares. It was becoming clear that the duly constituted authorities were not looking for them.

One dismal fact would emerge from this drama: the naval command in the Pacific was seriously fragmented by political events. Nimitz had moved up from Pearl Harbor to Guam to be nearer the scene of action, to be sure, but he was not unmindful of the need to keep close to the center of affairs because of the competition for leadership now pressed by General MacArthur. It would have been proper and reasonable for Nimitz and MacArthur to place their commands in the same area, but neither man would come under the shadow of the other. So Nimitz operated from Guam and MacArthur from the Philippines, and there were in effect two naval headquarters in the Pacific, not always in synchronization. The affair of the *Indianapolis* was a tragic illustration of that fact.

Just at this point, Nimitz and MacArthur were trying to sort it out. MacArthur wanted to take over all army forces, including air forces in the Pacific, and give Nimitz back his Seventh Fleet and all naval forces. But Nimitz was commander of the Pacific Ocean Areas, which meant just about everything except the Philippines, and he would not relinquish that position. Before August 1, Nimitz and King were of the firm opinion that MacArthur was trying to take over control of all operations against Japan. He had already carved out a role for himself as supreme army commander of the invasion of Japan. Despite this, back in Washington, King still talked about the possibility of taking what to him was the more sensible route: invading the China coast rather than the Tokyo plain and Kyushu. But the plans were laid for the Japanese invasion and the chiefs of staff as a group were all acting that way, no matter how wistful King was.

On August 1, Colonel Tibbets wrote his operational order for the atomic attack on Hiroshima. Why Hiroshima, among all the cities on the list for possible destruction? That city was chosen over Kyoto, Yokohama, Nagasaki, and Kokura almost by accident, on a faulty premise. Kyoto, General Groves' favorite target, had been eliminated because Secretary Stimson had learned that it was the old capital of Japan and an historic shrine. Nagasaki had been chosen at the top of the list to replace Kyoto, but late in July intelligence reports indicated an Allied prisoner of war camp was located one mile north of the center of the city, and according to the best information if the bomb were dropped there the camp would be pulverized. So Hiroshima was moved up to number one target because intelligence said it was the only big Japanese city under consideration that had no prisoner camps. Strictly speaking that was true, but actually a handful of downed American airmen were being held in the city at that moment. The 20th Air Force and A-bomb special units had no way of knowing that.

The weather being questionable, Tibbets' operation order stipulated that the A-bomb mission would be flown on or after August 3. Everything was ready; from Washington to Guam to Tinian all had been checked and rechecked. In recent days Admiral Nimitz and General MacArthur had been informed about the bomb but not in detail. In the words of a later generation, the situation was *Go*.

By August 1, Japan was in the direst of straits. The enormous bombing raid of July 31 had emphasized what the Americans could do and were doing. The Tokyo-Yokohama industrial complex was smashed. Kawasaki, Nagoya, Osaka, Kobe were in ruins. Many of the industrial plants in the smaller towns of Japan were destroyed. Many others had been hit by bombers or by shore bombardment and their production facilities knocked out. The supply of raw materials had virtually stopped. The stock of petroleum was 7 percent of what it had been prewar. The harbors along the Inland Sea and the Japan Sea were closed by mines dropped by the B-29s. So were the waters around the Korean coast, and only a handful of coastal vessels moved between Korea, the Japanese "rice bowl," and the Japanese ports. Thus the dwindling supply of rice—most of it reserved for the military—meant the Japanese were reduced to a diet of about 1,500 calories per day.

A million and a half men of the Japanese army were assembled in the islands, mostly on Honshu and Kyushu. Seventeen divisions were training on Kyushu, but they had so little oil and ammunition that they might fight one major engagement and that was all. The aircraft that so worried Admiral McCain were not, for the most part, on the airstrips he was watching but on hundreds of small new secret airstrips in the interior of the country. At the proper time they would be moved on up to the coasts. That was one of the major Japanese secrets that had completely escaped the Americans.

At Potsdam, President Truman and Prime Minister Attlee met to discuss the effects the atomic bomb was likely to make on the war effort. What became apparent during the day was the fact that the bomb was still an unknown quantity and no one was quite sure what effect it *would* have, either as a weapon or on the earth. Some scientists were already talking about the chain effect of nuclear explosion and conjuring visions of a bomb that started a reaction that blew up the whole planet. The government scientists belittled the idea, but they were sufficiently worried about it to prepare official statements about the history of the Manhattan Project and the expected results.

Early on August 1 Combined Fleet Headquarters, or what now passed for it, ordered Commander Hashimoto to move north and hunt for American shipping closer to home. He headed for the Okinawa area, and intended to search the Okinawa-Ulithi sea-lane and the Okinawa-Leyte lane. Alternately surfacing and travelling under water to avoid any long-range detection by the Americans, Hashimoto went on. At around 3:00 in the afternoon, while travelling at cruising speed on the surface, the *I-58* lookouts sighted a westbound mast, then the hull, bridge, and funnels. Hashimoto estimated her size at 10,000 tons (Liberty ship). She was travelling alone and the range was 20,000 yards. Hashimoto increased his speed, but the angle was wrong, and the enemy merchantman kept pulling away from him. He cursed the naval engineers then, because *I-58* had been completed in the spring of 1944, and when it came to put the engines in her, the bureau of ships had suggested that the normal diesel engines with which the new I-class boats were fitted were heavy and scarce, and the engineers had agreed to installation of much smaller engines. As a result *I-58* could achieve only about two thirds the speed of the earlier I-boats, because of the smaller engines and because to compensate for the loss of weight in design, she had to carry useless ballast. This day, if Hashimoto had had the twenty-three knots of which the older I-boats were capable, he might have caught the American ship. As it was, with his top speed of fifteen knots, there was no chance.

Admiral Halsey was still moving the fleet slowly around in circles almost due east of Okinawa, waiting out the typhoon. There was no indication on August 2 that it was ready to pass over the target area. The storm was lingering maddeningly over Japan. The plans were made and made over—Halsey had decided to take a crack at the Sasebo-Fusan area—the lifeline between Japan and her Korean colony. But McCain was still arguing in favor of hitting more airfields and the aircraft production facilities. There was plenty of time to talk and plan. There was nothing else to be done at the moment.

On August 2 General LeMay arrived on Tinian with the orders for the atomic-bomb mission. The orders were essentially the same as the draft Colonel Tibbets had sent off earlier. Hiroshima was the target. Of course, Hiroshima might be blocked out by storm—the weathermen were as much worried about flying conditions as Halsey was about sea conditions, and in the case of the atomic bomb there was no margin for error; the bombardier had to see that target down below him. Actually, whether or not the target was Hiroshima or some other place was not terribly important. The important matter was to deliver the bomb properly to some target so that the Japanese would have full impact of this new weapon. If Hiroshima turned out to be an impossible mission for the day, August 6, then the crew was to deliver the bomb to the military center of Kokura, where an enormous army arsenal was located. If Kokura, too, was impossible, then the bomb was to be dropped on Nagasaki.

General LeMay gave Colonel Tibbets his copy of the order. Other copies were delivered by hand to various commands in the area. Thus a handful of top officers learned of a new weapon of such significance that the delivery of a single one of them was worth so much trouble. Except for Tibbets' B-29s, several of which would be required on various aspects of the mission, no other American planes would even fly within fifty miles of all these targets on the day of delivery.

At Okinawa and elsewhere in the Ryukyus, the army engineers were busily building airfields. Capture of these islands put Japan within striking distance of land-based fighter planes, and for a month the P-51 fighters of the 35th Air Group had been conducting sweeps over Japan.

They were meeting some enemy opposition, and on August 2 they saw over twenty planes over Kyushu. But as it was with the navy pilots these days, the army pilots found that the Japanese were operating under some unknown constraint. The encounters were brief; if the Americans did not shoot down their enemies quickly, they looked around and the Japanese were gone. The Japanese pilots were obeying the orders to try at all costs to preserve themselves and their aircraft for the coming final battle. Only because of the feeling by some air commanders that to give no opposition at all was intolerable and could bring nothing but disaster, were these Japanese fighter missions flown.

But the Japanese aircraft engineers were continuing to develop new designs. At the Oppama air field, a part of the Yokosuka naval base complex, Saburo Sakai, Japan's leading fighter pilot, spent weeks testing a new fighter, the *Reppu*. It was the most powerful fighter plane ever produced in Japan, with a four-bladed propeller and superchargers. Sakai felt that it was to the American planes what the old Zero had been at the outbreak of war, and that it could reestablish the air superiority of Japan. Technically perhaps, but actually there was no chance. The production of the *Reppu* was assigned to the Mitsubishi aircraft company, as Sakai was testing the plane. But shortage of materials was creating all sorts of difficulty. By the early days of August, the factory had produced half a dozen planes, almost handmade. But the materials for the tools and dies that would make it possible to bring the plane to mass production were not available.

On August 2 at Hiroshima and Kokura and Nagasaki, the people were engaged in their usual activities with the new development that had come in recent months: the search for food was the dominating factor in their lives. Saburo Sakai and the others of the armed services were still allocated food supplies, although the post exchanges and commissaries of the military were boarded up. But the civilian population was virtually starving, or would have been had it not been for the indomitability of the spirit. Doctors, lawyers, industrialists, sent their families to the countryside, where they could find more to eat, and those who had to live in the cities spent much of each day searching for and bartering for food.

At Nagasaki, nearly everyone who had anything of value spent the weekends in the country, finding food and trading. Men and women who had never done manual labor found themselves trudging out into the farmlands, and bringing back what they could carry in knapsacks. It was the same at Kokura. Somehow the newspapers managed to publish every day and the mail was delivered. Charcoal-driven automobiles chugged around the city, and sometimes a tram or a bus came along. Life was still almost as it had been, on the surface. But beneath, civil life was not like it had ever been before.

At Potsdam on August 2, the drawn-out conference of Allied leaders came to an end. From the standpoint of progress, the last week had been a waste of time. It was true that the stage had been set for the Russians to enter the Pacific war, but within the Allied circle not all believed the Russian entry was either necessary or useful. Some predicted it would cause more trouble than it could possibly be worth.

What had emerged in the last week of meetings was a deep aura of suspicion among the Allied leaders. Stalin knew enough about the atomic bomb to know that he was being kept out in the cold. The Allies suspected that the Soviets were planning to rape Manchuria of every bit of industrial material they could find. Even before the end of the war, some military experts were wondering how the division of the Korean peninsula at the 38th parallel was going to work out. The Potsdam talks had been arranged to establish a working peace among the wartime partners, but there was deep feeling on both sides as the talks broke up that the reverse had somehow happened.

On August 2, after packing up, President Truman flew to Plymouth, England, and then was taken out to the battleship HMS *Renown*, where he had lunch with King George VI. After lunch, the President moved to the cruiser *Augusta* with Secretary Byrnes and Admiral Leahy, and that day the warship headed for the United States.

Premier Stalin and Foreign Minister Molotov boarded a train for the long trip back to Moscow. None of the Allied leaders would fly homeward, the dangers were still too great.

In Tokyo, Foreign Minister Togo was having serious second thoughts about his dismissal of the American-British-Chinese statement out of Potsdam. The peace party was exerting serious pressure, although the military was still firmly in control of the government. Emperor Hirohito, no matter how concerned he showed himself to be in private talks, still refused to come out boldly in favor of a peace program. Togo sensed that at any moment something dreadful was going to emerge from the results of the Allied meetings at Potsdam. It seemed reasonable to believe that the Soviet stalling—for the Japanese were not stupid enough to fail to see that the Soviets were stalling them—would mean Soviet intent to enter the war. Togo and his associates were pragmatic enough to realize what the Soviets would want, and how easy it would be for them to get it. The foreign minister asked Ambassador Sato in Moscow to make every effort to speed the processes, and somehow create enthusiasm among the Soviets for the peace mission of Prince Konoye. Togo did not know, nor did Sato, that Stalin and Molotov, the only two men who might have made any decisions that could help them, were incommunicado as it were—available only for consultation on the most important matters, as they made the long journey home.

In the water off Leyte, the third day had passed and it had become painfully apparent that the men of the *Indianapolis* were a long way from rescue. After three days, no one knew they were missing. All the orders were safely tucked away in the files. At 10:00 on the morning of August 2, Lieutenant (j.g.) Wilbur Gwinn was flying a routine search mission from the base at Peleliu. His plane was a land-based two-engined medium bomber. Looking down at a point about 300 miles off Leyte, there in the water with nothing else around, he saw an oil slick. It seemed odd, so he circled around, losing altitude, until he came down below 1,000 feet, and then he saw dots in the oil slick and realized that they were heads. He told his radioman to begin sending a message. At first, as he gave the radioman the message, he counted thirty heads in the water, but as he circled, and the radioman tapped on the key, Lieutenant Gwinn counted more. Finally he estimated that there were 150 men down there. He dropped his life rafts, but that and waggling his wings as he circled and went off was the best he could do with his land-based plane. When the message reached the base at Peleliu, a flying boat was dispatched. Lieutenant Adrian Marks found the spot at about 3:30 in the afternoon, and dropped life rafts to those who did not seem to have any, and then landed his plane to pick up as many men as he could. He rescued fifty-six men before he took off and headed back to base. He also sent out a message saying he needed help because he could not bring them all in.

An army flying boat then arrived, piloted by Lieutenant R. C. Alcorn, but the sea was running very high by this time and Lieutenant Alcorn found that when he got down the plane began to take a beating. He taxied to one swimmer and got him aboard, then decided he had best take off and left the scene.

When Lieutenant Gwinn's original message had reached Tacloban, the navy finally launched a sea search. Even at this late date no one at Tacloban knew what the ships were going to search for; the men might even be Japanese. But with the news that there had been a sinking, ships moved. The destroyer escort *Cecil J. Doyle* was then discovered east of the island of

Babelthuap, and she was closest ship at sea to the coordinates mentioned in Gwinn's message. She was told to turn and go to the scene. The destroyer transport *Bassett* and the destroyer escort *Dufilho* were also at sea east of Leyte and they were ordered to find the oil slick.

The *Cecil J. Doyle* arrived first, at about midnight, and recovered the first survivors. Lieutenant Commander M. G. Claytor asked them who they were, and they said they were men of the *Indianapolis*. Claytor radioed the information back to base, and thus, four days after the sinking of this cruiser, the American navy finally discovered that she was lost. Back in Washington, Admiral King was not pleased, nor was Admiral Nimitz when the word got to him at Guam. Someone was going to be in serious trouble, but how serious was not then known, for the full extent of the tragedy was yet to be unveiled.

11

ALARUMS AND EXCURSIONS

On August 3, the typhoon was still lingering over Japan, so the Third Fleet milled about east of Okinawa, waiting. Even moving slowly through friendly seas cost heavily in fuel, and whether men fought or not each day, they ate, so Halsey had to begin worrying about logistics again. If he could get into action immediately, he could make several strikes before moving back to fuel and take on supplies. The next day's weather would tell the tale.

The B-29s flew their missions as scheduled on August 3. The pilots had half expected that the typhoon would cause a letup in air activity, but no, General LeMay did not believe in letting a small matter like the weather interfere with the war. The B-29 missions were routed around the typhoons and the targets were chosen where the weather was good—the aerographers hoped.

On August 3 in the very early minutes, the rescue of the *Indianapolis* survivors was in full swing. The *Cecil J. Doyle* kept picking up men. By 4:30 in the morning the destroyers *Madison* and *Ralph Talbot* arrived and so did the *Bassett* and

Dufilho. By this time the groups of survivors had spread out over a considerable distance, and the last group was not picked up until around noon on August 3. That last group included Captain McVay.

"Last group" referred to the last group of the living. For the dead, and that meant more than half of the 800 men who had gone into the water when the ship sank, there was no particular hurry, but the ships kept combing the area, searching for bodies all day long. Who knew but that one of them at least might still have a spark of life?

Captain Hashimoto, operating near Okinawa, was warned by radio to stay away from the Leyte area because many American warships were there, searching. He wondered what they were searching for. It did not occur to him that the Americans might be so careless as to have lost track of one of their major warships.

On Guam and at Leyte, a large number of officers suddenly became very much concerned by the manner in which they had handled the reports of the *Indianapolis*. The Philippine Sea Frontier's failure to note the nonarrival of an expected ship suddenly appeared to be important. Someone recalled that Admiral McCormick had been told personally that the *Indianapolis* was coming. But the admiral had seen ships come and go and ships detained by higher authority for purposes of their own, and there had seemed no reason to become upset in what was turning into an almost peaceful training command.

At Admiral Nimitz' headquarters there was a great deal of concern, once it was learned that the *Indianapolis* had been torpedoed and that the men had spent four days in the water. Nimitz wanted to know why, and he wanted to know in a hurry. Not even Nimitz' highly regarded radio intelligence organization was above criticism in this matter. After Commander Hashimoto had sunk the *Indianapolis*, he had radioed Tokyo. In Hashimoto's report he had mentioned a battleship of the *Idaho* class, but his enthusiasm and his poor estimate of the target was understandable

since it was all through the end of a periscope. Radio Tokyo
had the report and broadcast it back toward America, but the
radio monitors did not believe it. They charged that the Japanese had made far too many false claims. And of course this
was true; from the first days of the war the Japanese high
command had taken the position that war reporting was an arm
of the war itself and any fabrication was allowable if it served
the apparent aims of the government. Admiral Yamamoto had
been first to object to false claims and exaggeration. He had
warned that the greatest danger of these claims was to hood-
wink the officials themselves into believing the false propaganda.
But Yamamoto was long gone, killed early in 1943, and there
were none to complain these days.

Even so, there was a major difference between the radio
reports sent out for public and enemy consumption, and those
sent within the naval service for information. The radio intelligence group had picked up a coded Japanese transmission, which
gave the details of the sinking as truthfully as Commander
Hashimoto had reported them. But the fleet intelligence men
did not believe, even though the latitude and longitude of the
sinking would have checked out with the course of the *Indianapolis*, had any one in authority thought to check. So the
fact was that Seventh Fleet in the Philippines and Nimitz' own
headquarters had independent reports of the sinkings sixteen
hours after the event and did nothing. The war was so quiet
that many officers were that much asleep.

With the amount of paperwork that had begun to accumulate
in Nimitz' headquarters it seems less remarkable that this sort of
mistake was made. For example, the Joint Intelligence Center
of the Pacific Ocean Areas, which had begun in 1942 with a
couple of dozen people, employed 1,800 in 1945, and its presses
spewed out two million printed sheets of intelligence and 150,000
photographs every week. The reports of the Fleet Radio Unit
(FRUPAC) obtained by decryption of the Japanese naval codes
were restricted to a very small list of officers; the rule was that
it was not to be used except in conditions where action might

result in major advantage in important strategic situations. Obviously, the loss of the *Indianapolis* did not qualify in that regard. So in a sense, the failures in the *Indianapolis* affair were an indication of what happens when a war becomes "too big." The individual, and then the individual ship are lost in the shuffle of paperwork. It took the sudden shock of a pilot confronted by hundreds of heads bobbing in the sea to restore reality to that situation.

On August 3 Colonel Tibbets was picking the crew that would accompany him on the mission. Now, coming down to the moment for which the 509th Air Group had spent months in preparation, Tibbets faced all sorts of delicate problems. Several pilots had anticipated that they would fly the mission, although Tibbets had always known that he would do it himself. Resentments flared in the tents, but he had to expect that reaction. Another problem would develop soon. The British would have to be told that their request to send two officers on the mission had been denied. The U.S. was not going to share the glory of the atomic bomb attack with anyone.

In Moscow, Japanese Ambassador Sato called at the foreign ministry, but got no satisfaction whatsoever. He was not told the whereabouts of Secretary Molotov—that was a state secret. All he could learn was that his request for an invitation to Prince Konoye was still under advisement, and he could but suspect that this statement was true only in the loosest diplomatic use of the word. Stalin had already promised Soviet entry into the Pacific war. All that remained to be decided was the day of march.

In Manchuria, General Otozo Yamada was preparing his Kwantung army for the long-awaited war with the U.S.S.R. From his headquarters at Hsinking he sent orders to eight different army commands, headed by no less than lieutenant generals. More than a million officers and men in Manchuria and Korea were under orders to redeploy to meet the threat as

General Yamada saw it. The Kwantung army's mission, as decreed by Imperial General Headquarters, was to defeat the Soviet army, secure the strategic region south of the Hsinking-Tumen railroad and east of the Dairen-Hsinking rail line. The reason Yamada had to move his troops about was that this plan involved a major change in strategy. Earlier, Imperial General Headquarters had called on the Kwantung army to take aggressive action, which meant fight the war in Siberia and further west if possible. So all along the line, General Yamada's troops were pulling back from the broad plain to points where they could defend the industrial centers of southern and western Manchuria.

On August 4 Admiral Halsey was fretting more than usual after these days of inactivity. This was the day his planes were to have hit the ports of Sasebo and Pusan and any shipping in between. But bad weather forced him to cancel the strikes, after the fleet was moving east to make them. The difficulty was more than weather, however. General LeMay's B-29s had preempted the area, and when Admiral Nimitz learned they were going to be hitting there in force, he withdrew the fleet for its own protection. For the first time the American forces were beginning to find the skies around Japan crowded with their own activity. Nimitz told Halsey he had best get away from that part of Japan and move to a position to command the northern Honshu and Hokkaido areas, where there should be no conflict with LeMay's B-29s. Halsey issued orders that the fleet was to move to a point (38°5′ N 149° E) and refuel to undertake a whole series of air strikes against Honshu and Hokkaido. He was impatient with the delay, but there was nothing to be done about it. The steaming to get into position to strike Sasebo had made it necessary to replenish one more time before going back into action.

Off Leyte ships and planes were continuing to comb the waters, moving in concentric circles out from the oil slick. Now that the truth about the *Indianapolis* was known, the Pacific Fleet would spare no effort to make sure that the last survivor was found.

On the afternoon of August 4, as the planes from Saipan and Tinian buzzed overhead on their way home from Japan, the pilots and aircrews of the 509th Air Group who would be directly involved in the drop of the atomic bomb were gathered in the technical area at Tinian for a briefing. Just before, General LeMay called the two British officers who were expecting to go on the mission. He gave them the bad news. Higher authority —that meant the Joint Chiefs of Staff—had denied the request. There was no appeal at this point. The Britons asked him to make one final try and then went to the briefing, hoping against hope.

The briefing indicated how much there was to be done and how imperfect the plans were for the dropping of this first atomic bomb in combat. Three B-29s would fly off first as weather scouts, to make sure that the bomb-carrying plane did not get into trouble before it reached the target. The target was one of the three, Hiroshima, Kokura, and Nagasaki, and one plane would fly to each area to send back a series of reports. On the basis of their information the final target would be chosen. If all targets were impossible, the bomb-carrying plane would fly back to Iwo Jima, not Tinian. The aircrew would arm the bomb in the air en route to the general target area, and be prepared to disarm it in the air if the mission was aborted. But in all this there were real and suspected dangers; the arming and disarming of A-bombs had not yet been perfected as a military art. No one knew what might happen; thus, if the bomb was going to blow, it was going to blow up Iwo Jima.

Two B-29s were selected to accompany the bomb-carrying plane to the target and record the moment for history. One other plane was assigned to the mission, with the most unenviable task of flying to Iwo Jima and waiting next to the place where the bombing plane would land if the mission was aborted. In that task there was nothing but danger.

Navy Captain William Parsons, who had been involved in the Manhattan Project from the beginning, gave a brief explanation of the processes to these men who knew nothing at all about the A-bomb. When they were told that the scientists expected the bomb to destroy everything within a three-mile area, the airmen could scarcely believe it. Their whole concept of bombing ended with the 10,000-pound blockbuster, and what the scientists were talking about was a city buster.

The briefing was filled with ifs. No one knew quite what would happen, Parsons said, although he predicted an enormous flash of blinding light, and then the formation of a mushroom cloud. As others brought forth protective goggles of a new sort and showed the airmen how to use them, the enormity of the change that was coming began to strike home.

On August 5 General MacArthur's headquarters had intelligence that indicated a buildup of Japanese aircraft on fields in the very northern area of Honshu and in southern Hokkaido. The army feared that some special attempt was under way to attack Okinawa. But the fact was the Japanese were planning a suicide attack against Saipan and Tinian in the hope of relieving the pressure of the B-29s against Japan. The plan called for over 200 Betty bombers and other craft to fly picked volunteer troops to the airfields in the dead of night, land by any means conventional or crash, and turn the troops loose to destroy every plane and installation possible. There was no question of anyone coming back to Japan from this mission. It was to be an enormous *banzai* attack.

On the basis of this information, MacArthur asked Admiral Nimitz to use the carriers to make a preemptive strike on several airfields, where the concentrations had been reported. Nimitz prepared to send a message to Admiral Halsey ordering the change in operations.

At 8:00 on the morning of August 5, the Third Fleet was steaming northeast to the refuelling rendezvous. The ships were to meet the tankers and ammunition and supply ships on August 7 about 500 miles further out from Japan. On August 5 the carriers sent off fighters and bombers for practice missions and the antiaircraft gunners practiced firing. The British Pacific Fleet Task Force was with the American ships until late in the day, when the British turned off to make a rendezvous with their own set of supply ships.

East of Leyte the destroyers and escorts continued to comb the waters, checking every bit of debris for human survivors. The results were negative and often grim. Bodies immersed in salt water for a week are not a pretty sight.

The *I-58* continued to cruise off Okinawa, searching for another American target. But the weather was rough and visibility difficult. Commander Hashimoto found nothing. The *I-58*'s war patrol had lasted 18 days so far and conditions in the boat were beginning to grow difficult. A shortage of fresh water made it impossible to wash clothes, and if the washing could have been somehow accomplished, there was no way to dry them in the steamy interior of the submarine. To surface for three or four hours was unthinkable in this enemy-dominated water. The men wore the same clothes day after day, and some of them began to develop skin irritations.

Aboard the USS *Augusta*, heading west, President Truman awaited the word that the atomic bomb had been dropped. Having made the difficult decision back at Potsdam with his characteristic firmness, Truman put the matter aside and turned to other problems of government. The *Augusta* sped along through waters that were now safe, but even a year earlier would have been dangerous for any vessel.

In Manchuria, General Yamada pulled the Third Area Army back from Tsitsihar in northern Manchuria to Mukden. The Fourth Army was given the additional duty of defending the

northern front. The Thirtieth Army was moved down to southern Manchuria and ordered to dig in. A new Forty-fourth Army
was created from various units, and moved to defend western
Manchuria. Last-ditch positions were fixed (on the map) at a
line that ran from Hoeryong to Yingkou, past Antu, Tunghua,
and Liaoyang. In Korea, seven infantry divisions were moved
about by Lieutenant General Senichi Kushibuchi from his headquarters at Hamhung.

On August 5, the 509th decided to make one last prebombing
test to check the type of fuse employed on the strange-looking
atomic bomb. Again, no one was sure that the bomb would
work at all; the previous test at Alamogordo had been conducted
by an atomic device fixed atop a 100-foot high scaffold. One
B-29 took a bomb like the A-bomb but filled with concrete instead of plutonium, and after it reached 30,000 feet the pilot
was told to drop the bomb. He did. The wires pulled out of
the sockets in the aircraft. Next sound the monitors should
have heard was a click as the final switch closed, or, barring that,
see a puff of smoke at 1,850 feet altitude. If it had been the
bomb that would have been the point of explosion. The
scientists on the gound watched through binoculars. They saw
the bomb drop and followed its course down. There was no
puff of smoke. The bomb dropped into the sea. Some of them
predicted that the bomb that would be dropped over Japan the
next day would never go off.

Captain Parsons that day practiced inserting the explosive
charge and detonator into the atomic bomb. For several months
higher authorities, and this meant General Groves, had assumed
that the bomb would be armed before the B-29 took off. But
Captain Parsons was afraid that some mishap might cause a
premature explosion, so he had decided to arm the bomb after
takeoff. Only late that day, when it was too late for General
Groves to stop him, did Parsons inform Groves back in America
that he had changed the plan.

On the evening of August 5, 600 of General LeMay's big bombers were over Japan, dropping mines in the Inland Sea, high explosives on factories, and incendiaries on the cities. Another night of terror was in store for Japan.

Just before midnight, the crews of the B-29s scheduled for the A-bomb mission assembled for a final briefing. A chaplain appeared to bless the mission in the Name of Jesus Christ on the basis that God was on the American side. The mission that would cause more destruction and cost more lives than any single act committed by any military force in history, was blessed and about to begin.

12

THE DAY OF
THE BIG BANG

On the morning of August 6, the Third Fleet was steaming toward the fuel rendezvous point. But that did not prevent the destroyers and destroyer escorts from pulling alongside the bigger ships and taking on oil. One of the secrets of U.S. task force operation in the last half of the Pacific war was this ability to handle the needs of the small ships without slowing down the force appreciably. Earlier the task force had been hampered by the lesser fuel capacities of the destroyers. This morning in the early calm the destroyers came alongside as they needed to and topped off.

By 8:15 the task was completed, and the ships set about the usual training programs carried out when they were not in action.

Just after 1:00 on the morning of August 6, the air crews of the seven B-29s involved in the atomic bomb mission began loading aboard their planes. The first planes off were the three weather planes, and they were followed by the plane that would stand by at Iwo Jima. The crew of the plane Colonel Tibbets had named *Enola Gay* (after his mother) was delayed. General

LeMay had decided publicity would be the watchword after this mission and had arranged for still and motion picture cameras to film the departure and return of the flight. William Laurence of *The New York Times,* who had been covering the atomic project from the beginning, had come to Tinian and he was on hand to interview the crew before the flight. It was 2:45 in the morning before the atomic bomb plane got off the ground. It was followed by the two photographic aircraft.

The flight took the three aircraft over Iwo Jima. As the plane headed in that direction for the three-hour leg that would put them above their "safe" position, Captain Parsons armed the atomic bomb. Just before 5:00 in the morning, they were over Iwo Jima. All was well, and the three planes turned toward Shikoku, the nearest Japanese island.

Just before 7:30 in the morning, the weather planes began arriving over their target cities. Major Claude Eatherly reported that the weather over Hiroshima was clear, so Colonel Tibbets opted to bomb that target. Just a few clouds might have made all the difference in the world to the people of Hiroshima.

Hiroshima was a name unknown to most Americans, but it was an important Japanese city, and particularly important to the army and the navy. The Second Area Army headquarters was located here, and it was also the site of several important naval training schools. The Mitsubishi aircraft company had a factory here. Toyo Industries built naval guns. Equally important, Hiroshima was the communications center for the defense of Kyushu, and the Japanese by this time expected that the first American landings would be aimed (as was the fact) at Kyushu. So Hiroshima had an importance in the Japanese scheme of defense out of all proportion to its size or previous position. One indication: the local airfields and hidden hangars housed 5,000 aircraft for use as suicide planes in the coming final battle for Japan. The atomic bomb flying team knew nothing of these matters. To them, Hiroshima was just a target, picked by higher authority.

The bombing plane flew toward the city at 31,000 feet. Just after 8:00 the plane reached the point where the bombardier began his calculations. At that time the Japanese air observers reported the coming of three B-29s. There was nothing particularly unusual about that; the Japanese had been tracking this mission, as they did others, from the time they first came into radio range.

At 8:15, the *Enola Gay* was over the Aioi Bridge in the center of Hiroshima, the point of aim, and the atomic bomb was dropped. It missed the bridge by a good wide margin, but for once the miss made no difference. The bomb exploded in the air, as planned.

The people of Hiroshima had been worrying for several months about a strange phenomenon connected with their city: Hiroshima was not getting bombed the way other major Japanese cities—and some smaller ones—were taking attack from the B-29s. Everyone knew what had happened to Kure, on the east, and Shimonoseki, on the west. The most recent strikes by the carrier planes on Kure caused the navy men in particular to wonder why Hiroshima was spared. So did the managers of the factories; the Americans must know what was being made a Hiroshima.

In the absence of any real information, all sorts of theorie sprang up, from the most ridiculous (that President Truman had a relative who was held captive here) to the totally accurat (that Hiroshima was being saved for some very special, horribl fate).

But people cannot exist on fear and wonder, and as the month had gone by and the people of Hiroshima had seen B-29s com very near their city, then turn and head for other points, the began to accept *B-san* (Mr. B), as they called the B-29s, an more or less to disregard the big bombers. That is not to sa the people of Hiroshima were not aware of the bombers or the destructive potential. The war had brought Hiroshima's popula tion down from about 350,000 (the size of Portland, Oregor to 280,000 civilians. The number of military had increase enormously in recent weeks as the army built the defenses. Or defense under construction by the citizens was a firebreak. The Ota River and its three tributaries ran through the city on a general north-south line. One reason Hiroshima had been built here was because of the easy transportation provided by the four arms of the delta in the days before big roads and superhighways. But the city had been densely built, and drawing on the experience of Tokyo in the dreadful fire raids, Field Marshal Shunroku Hata, commander of the Kyushu armies, had decreed that the citizens must build firebreaks. For months some 40,000 young and old residents of Hiroshima had been put to work demolishing houses and creating wide lanes across which (it was hoped) fires would not jump.

The Fifty-ninth Army was entrusted with the defense of Hiroshima proper; Marshal Hata's headquarters was not in the center of the city but northeast of it, above Hiroshima railroad station on the slope of Mt. Futaba. Fifty-ninth Army headquarters was located in Hiroshima Castle, which stood above the Ota River bank.

Hiroshima's army headquarters, far more than those of most places, was aware of almost every American movement toward Japan. Since Marshal Hata was entrusted with the task of repelling the coming American landings, he had to be sure of early warning, and so a complex communications establishment was built in a former middle school near Second Area Army Headquarters. Admiral Halsey and General LeMay would have been surprised to learn that English-speaking officers were monitoring radio transmissions with such expertise that almost every approach to the Japanese homeland was telegraphed to Tokyo long before it appeared. At 7:09 that morning, the army communications headquarters reported three B-29s heading toward Hiroshima, and the air raid precautions began. The planes were then passing over Hiroshima Bay. At 7:25 the planes turned, over the middle of Hiroshima prefecture. At 7:31 the air raid warning began to sound, as the planes moved in succession toward the city. The following account is my translation of the official Japanese history of the event:

"That morning the air over Hiroshima was clear, the skies bright, the temperature was about twenty-six degrees Centigrade, and the wind was scarcely moving at all. At 8:06 a lookout at Matsunaga, eighty kilometers east of Hiroshima, reported three B-29s. A few moments later two of them appeared east of the city center. At this point the antiaircraft guns began firing. Five hundred meters behind the other two bombers came a third, heading south. It dropped some object and then turned sharply north. From one of the aircraft, parachutes were seen to fall. [These were blast gauges dropped by one of the accompanying B-29s to measure the effect of the atomic bomb—Au.] It was now a little after 8:00.

"Then there came a blue-white flash of violent light. Immediately this produced a huge red smoke cloud. At the same time on the ground a yellowish pillar of smoke appeared. It rose gradually until it reached a height of 20,000 meters. It was now around 8:00 in the morning. Hiroshima city had been changed into an incandescent peak of fire. As to what happened at the military camp, one can only conjecture."

From the accounts pieced together later by Americans and others, it was probable that the bomb's center was just above a medical clinic not far from the Aioi Bridge. The entire clinic was simply vaporized. Two thirds of the city's 90,000 buildings were destroyed, all utilities were wrecked immediately. The worst effect was the total destruction of the water system, with 70,000 breaks in the lines. There was no way the Hiroshima firemen could get water to the fires. Hiroshima Castle, the military headquarters, was completely destroyed. A number of American prisoners of war were held there, and most of them were killed.

From above, the firestorm was far more impressive than on the ground. In a moment it had spread to a circumference of more than a mile. (Second Area Army headquarters, on the shoulder of Mt. Futaba, was wrecked but not pulverized. It was far enough from the center of the explosion to be more or less conventionally destroyed.) Up in the plane first came the shock wave, and then the occupants saw the smoke cloud rising in its peculiar mushroom shape. In a minute the city was blotted out, but not before the fliers had a vision of a red hot core below, and fires spreading out everywhere.

The *Enola Gay* circled the city while Captain Parsons sent a message back to Tinian that the mission had been every bit as successful as anyone could hope. Flying back to the base at Tinian, the crew of the B-29 could see the smoke cloud behind them until they were nearly 375 miles out at sea.

Within a matter of minutes after Captain Parsons reported the success of the atomic bomb explosion, the word was travelling across the Pacific to Washington. From there it was immediately forwarded by radio to President Truman aboard the USS *Augusta*, steaming home across the Atlantic. The President had decided to lunch with the enlisted men of the ship that day, and he was on the messdeck when the word arrived. First came a quick message about the success. Then came a series of messages with details of the explosion. Truman read these to himself, and then to Secretary of State Byrnes who was with him at lunch. Then he stood up and read the messages to the enlisted men of the cruiser, who began clapping and cheering. In a few minutes Mr. Truman left the messdeck for the wardroom to tell the officers the big news.

Back in Washington General Marshall had the word and telephoned Secretary of War Stimson. By prearrangement, statements were then issued to the American press and to the Office of War Information for dissemination abroad. The official message from President Truman carried a grim warning to Japan. He reminded the Japanese and the world that the Potsdam Declaration of July 26 had been made "to spare the Japanese people from utter destruction" and that if Japan did not accept the terms of the American offer "they may expect a rain of ruin from the air, the like of which has never been seen on this earth."

In a way that would never be forgotten, science had changed the world for the worse.

DAYS OF AUGUST

On the morning of August 7, Admiral Halsey was riding in the *Missouri* as she made a rendezvous with the British Pacific Fleet task force. Through navy channels Admiral Halsey had the word from headquarters that the bomb had been dropped and some indication of its enormous striking power. But far more questions were unanswered. What effect would this new weapon have on the war? Halsey did not know, nor did Admiral Rawlings. All they could do was conjecture together. Halsey considered the matter and then put it aside. There was still a war to be fought. From Cincpac came new orders to strike those Hokkaido and Honshu airfields where the suicide attack against the Marianas was being readied.

On the morning of August 7, General LeMay ordered heavy raids on Japan by conventional B-29s carrying conventional weapons. The Toyakawa Arsenal was destroyed that day and so was the Nakajima Aircraft Factory. The city of Yawata was subjected to a rain of fire bombs. Planes from the 509th Air Group joined other units.

Several aircraft had come into or out of Hiroshima's blasted airfield on the afternoon of August 6, and from nearby cities survivors and visitors carried the word of what had happened. The story was of total disaster. What was not then known in Hiroshima was the cause of it.

On the afternoon of August 6, surviving officials had begun to make inspections and try to create some order in the waste-land that had been their city. Refugees were streaming along the roads trying to find shelter in some cases, just moving in others. Marshal Hata picked himself up after the shock of the bomb had worn off and found that he was relatively uninjured. But the same could hardly be said of his staff. All the generals were dead, and his highest-ranking officer was a colonel. Using the colonel as chief of staff, Field Marshal Hata began to investi-gate the situation of the city. That evening as the men of the 509th Air Group celebrated their "victory" with a feast and beer party in the tent city on Tinian, Japanese soldiers and sailors were trying to bring order to the shattered city. The mayor and most of the civil officers were dead. There were virtually no resources for survival. What remained was the land and the river with its four branches. The houses that stood were mostly blasted in one way or another. The market and the stores had dissolved in the heat of the bomb. People wandered the streets in states of shock and disbelief, some of them horribly wounded. The doctors who were assembled tried to treat those who seemed to have a chance of survival. They came upon strange injuries; many people had their clothing blown off, and in some cases the imprint of the design of the cloth was etched into their skin but they had survived.

That afternoon of August 6 help began to filter into the city from army and navy units. Scientists from Tokyo arrived the next day, and on August 8, after thorough investigation, they finally issued a communiqué announcing that the blast had been caused by an atomic bomb.

On the morning of August 7, when no one in Tokyo was yet quite certain what had happened—except that there had been an enormous, almost unbelieveable disaster at Hiroshima—the cabinet began to meet. By noon the authorities had enough reports to be fairly certain that an atomic device had been employed, but they had no intention at this stage of informing the Japanese people of that fact. In the afternoon Foreign Minister Togo received the translations of the statements made by President Truman and other officials, which confirmed what their own scientists were finding, and he renewed the demand for Japanese surrender.

Most of Japan's civil population relied entirely on their newspapers and radio broadcasts for information. Beginning at 6:00 P.M. on August 6 the Japanese home radio service of Radio Tokyo had announced a bombing raid on Hiroshima in bored tones. "A few B-29s hit Hiroshima City at 7:20 A.M.," the report said, "and fled after dropping incendiaries and bombs. The extent of the damage is now under survey." That night a special broadcast announced changes in the routing of trains in southern Japan. Trains from the town of Asaki would turn and take another route at Mihara, said the order. Trains from Mihara to Kaitachi would take the line that ran around Kure. Hiroshima was not mentioned, but anyone with a railroad map of Kyushu island could see that for some reason trains were being routed away from that city.

By the morning of August 7 the radio was still persisting with the story, but in such odd terms that any curious person would wonder if so little damage was done, why would so much talk be continued about it? *Asahi Shimbun,* Japan's largest morning newspaper, announced that about 400 B-29s had hit Japanese cities on August 6. Special mention was made of "two B-29s which dropped incendiary bombs" on Hiroshima. "It seems that some damage was caused to the city."

The Japanese journalists were operating under the strictest of censorship controls, and none of them were among those invited by the military to go to Hiroshima. Even so, by the afternoon of the seventh, foreign broadcasts were battering Japan so heavily that even the censors knew something more must be said. From Hiroshima, Field Marshal Hata's investigation showed that the bomb had been atomic, and reluctantly on the afternoon of August 7 Imperial General Headquarters issued a communiqué announcing that "a considerable amount of damage was caused by a few B-29s that attacked Hiroshima August 6. It seems that the enemy used a new type of bomb in the raid. Investigation is under way."

At sea the men of *I-58* knew no more than Japan about what had happened at Hiroshima, although they might have learned. They often received digests of American broadcasts, although by general orders this practice was forbidden to all but senior officers. The diving officer, Lieutenant Nishimura, was fluent in English and often turned the submarine's radio to the Voice of America. On August 7, he heard the broadcasts announcing the destruction of Hiroshima by an atomic bomb, and President Truman's statements. He took this information to Commander Hashimoto, but the captain of the submarine refused to listen. To admit what Nishimura had heard would be to destroy the morale of the men of the boat. He sent Nishimura away, but later when the news became general in Japan he would remember. Just now, his main job was to fight the war to a finish as ordered by the Emperor.

The Emperor, in the palace at Tokyo, had news of the early reports. On the afternoon of August 7 he had done nothing about it; in fact as far as official Japan was concerned, Hirohito did not even know that anything unusual had occurred.

On Guam on August 7, General LeMay's staff was already planning the second strike against Japan. This was to be aimed at Kokura, the arsenal city. Colonel Tibbets flew down to Guam on August 7 for a press conference to be held the next day. He could have dropped the second bomb, too, but he demurred in favor of Major Charles Sweeney. This time the British representatives would be taken along to satisfy British pride. The decision was made, and the orders were issued.

Early on August 7 Admiral Halsey's Task Force 38 joined the British Task Force 37 and prepared to move up against Japan once more. The existence of those Japanese suicide units on Honshu and Hokkaido had brought the order to move. During the day there was little to see but the rolling ocean, but that night at about 10:30 came reports from radar of enemy ships about seventy miles away. A task group of surface vessels was quickly formed and sent out to intercept. They found nothing.

On the morning of August 8 the ships had still found no enemy vessels, which seemed much more reasonable than to have discovered them, given the smashing Halsey had delivered to the remnants of the Japanese navy. By morning the staff had decided it was all a radar illusion caused by the strange weather they were experiencing. The typhoon had passed but the weather continued to change several times a day.

The changeable weather worsened as dawn came, and Halsey's strikes and those of the British carriers had to be cancelled. The fleet was running through fog at this time. Halsey turned southeast to clear the fog. He was growing impatient and frustrated; although by going south he made it impossible to hit the Hokkaido targets the next day, something had to be done to break the logjam.

For a change that day the Japanese sent out search planes, and two of them were shot down by pilots of the combat air patrol. But not at first. The weather was so foul that when the first Japanese plane was detected just before 6:00 in the morning, the fog was dense and no planes could be sent up. At a few minutes after six, another Japanese plane appeared, and again the carriers had to refrain from action. But at 11:45 when another "bogy" was detected the carrier *Wasp* managed to get patrol planes into the air, and one of them shot down the intruder.

In fact, during this day a number of Japanese flights were detected, and it seemed probable to Halsey that the enemy had sighted his force and was searching for it. Many bogies appeared on the screen. Planes from *Yorktown* and other carriers went up to try to meet these enemy flights, but the weather was so spotty that most of the American fighters missed the enemy.

But so too did the enemy planes fail to find the carrier force. Altogether no fewer than three Japanese air raids in some force were noted by the carriers. Halsey had to assume that these would be kamikaze units. The war seemed to be warming up again for the Third Fleet.

That day the truth was unavoidable in Tokyo. Radio Tokyo picked up the Truman message, which the Japanese regarded as a glorification of the dropping of the dreadful bomb. The army was all the more determined to resist to the bitter end. But Foreign Minister Togo and Prime Minister Suzuki, meeting privately, agreed that this destruction must not continue. Togo knew already that the Emperor had been inclined to accept the American surrender terms before the bomb was dropped. The two politicians decided that the Potsdam Declaration terms must be accepted, and Togo went to see the Emperor. He told him what he knew and advised that this new bomb had revolutionized warfare, and that it must be expected that the Americans had more of them or would be able to produce more soon. Japan was not even in the running in an atomic race. The Emperor agreed that the war must be ended as soon as possible. Togo returned to the government offices from the palace and told Suzuki what the Emperor had said. Prime Minister Suzuki ordered aides to begin calling members of the Supreme Council of Government for an immediate meeting. Most of the military men, suspecting what was coming, begged off and said they could not be present at a meeting on such short notice.

So nothing intervened to stop the plans for the dropping of the second atomic bomb.

That day in Washington, President Truman arose from his own bed in the White House for the first time in weeks. Secretary Stimson came to call that morning, and brought with him photographs of the destruction wrought at Hiroshima. Even from high level, the virtual annihilation of a city was quite apparent.

Stimson also had with him a detailed report on the damage, prepared by the Strategic Air Force. It was sobering to the President, who observed that this sort of destruction of life placed an enormous responsibility on himself and on the war department, but he did not move to stop the drop of the second bomb. Secretary Stimson indicated that it might be possible to secure the Japanese surrender at this point if the U.S. could make it easy to accept the terms of surrender. He was obviously referring to the big question mark: what was going to be the fate of the Emperor and the imperial system if the Japanese did surrender?

Stimson assured Truman that he was not dealing with the Germans here. The Japanese responded to courtesy. Truman was noncommittal. When Stimson left the White House and returned to the Pentagon, he repeated his remarks to General Marshall. The general agreed with him. But the plans to drop bomb number two went on.

In Moscow that day Ambassador Sato finally had the call he had been awaiting for weeks. Foreign Minister Molotov sent word to the Japanese embassy that he would see Sato at 5:00 in the afternoon. The ambassador prepared to make his best arguments for the reception in Moscow of Prince Konoye to carry out the delicate mission of seeking peace with the help of the Soviets.

But when the ambassador arrived at the foreign office he was greeted coldly by a series of flunkies and then brought to Foreign Minister Molotov, who immediately launched into a long statement of Soviet grievances against Japan. He concluded with the warning that as of the next day, August 9, the Soviet Union considered itself to be at war with Japan. By the time Ambassador Sato got back to the Japanese embassy, the Soviet troops were already marching.

THE SECOND BOMB

On the evening of August 8 several scientists gathered with the pilots and crew who would carry out the second mission of the new atomic era against Japan. They explained something about the second bomb; it was made of plutonium, which was more powerful than the uranium-235 that had comprised the explosive mass of the first bomb.

Winston Churchill may or may not have been amused to learn that the bomb was named for him and called "The Fat Man" because of its distinctive shape. This, said the scientists, was to become the standard bomb of the future. The briefing was much like that given the men of the first mission: it said three B-29s would fly. The only difference was that this time they would have passengers, the two British offical representatives and William L. Laurence of *The New York Times*. Two weather planes would go out ahead and report on cloud conditions over Kokura and Nagasaki. The bombing had to be visual, which meant that they could not hurry over target, take a radar fix, drop and run, the way the B-29s so often did with conventional weapons in heavy weather. Again the chaplain prayed for them to reassure any doubters that God was still on the American side.

At about 2:00 in the morning, the preliminaries were all over. The bomb was loaded aboard *Bock's Car*, the plane that Sweeney had preempted from Captain Fred Bock when his own aircraft developed mechanical difficulties. Pilot Sweeney gave his crew a little pep talk on the runway, speaking of the last mission (in which he had flown one of the instrument planes that accompanied *Enola Gay*). He promised the men that this too was going to be a "perfectly" executed mission. They would put the bomb right on target even if they had to fly it in.

That bit of hyperbole did not frighten his crew. Most of them were veterans of that first mission and had seen it done once. It was true that the weathermen were reporting a general cloud cover over southern Japan, but they would live with it. They had to, or turn the mission over to someone else. It was made quite plain to the crew of the second atomic mission that the second bomb must be delivered that day. President Truman, said the authorities on the field, wanted to shorten the war.

One minute after midnight on August 9 Soviet troops marched across the Manchurian border, as Foreign Secretary Molotov had warned Ambassador Sato they would. It was, said the Imperial General Headquarters, a "strategic surprise attack" because they did not expect it to come quite so soon. The Japanese timetable estimated the Soviet intervention to be coming at the end of September. But then, prescient as the Japanese intelligence experts were, they had not known of the existence of the atomic bomb, and now it was apparent that the Soviets wanted—insisted—on joining the war immediately to get in on the spoils. If they waited, Japan might surrender under those atomic blows, and then there could be no excuse for the Soviet troops to move in.

It was ironic in a sense that the Japanese military spoke of a surprise attack in connection with the Russian movement into Manchuria. Japan had attacked the Russian-held Port Arthur in Manchuria on February 8, 1904, thus precipitating the Russo-Japanese war. The Japanese had not declared war until two days later. *That* was a surprise attack; the Soviets had respected

Western conventions when they gave the Japanese formal warning the day before the August 9 invasion of Manchuria forty-one years later.

The Japanese immediately launched a counterattack. The Soviets were moving fast with armored armies, a technique they had perfected in the war against the Germans. The Japanese countered with kamikaze air attacks, low-flying planes coming in to do as much damage as possible. Even a heavy tank was not immune to a kamikaze flying bomb. The war was hardly even official this night, and the Japanese government, having been warned by the ambassador in Moscow, still had not made up its mind to declare war on the U.S.S.R. That night in Moscow, American Ambassador Averill Harriman and American diplomat George Kennan saw Stalin at the Kremlin. It was late, after midnight, and Stalin informed them with gusto that the Soviets had already entered Manchuria and that major units of the armies would be across the border before morning.

On the morning of August 9, Admiral Halsey's force was finally back in action, much to his satisfaction. At 4:00 A.M., operations began off the Honshu coast. Halsey also hoped to be able to hit Hokkaido, but there was no chance; fog had settled over that northern island and hung in all day. The Americans and the British hit hard at nine airfields on Honshu, and found a large number of planes. Together the American and British attacks destroyed or damaged about 400 planes, many of them twin-engined bombers, which gave credence to the report from MacArthur's headquarters that a major suicide attack of planes and troops was to be launched momentarily against the B-29 bases.

At 3:30 that morning two groups of surface ships also struck the Japanese. The light cruisers *Newfoundland* and *Gambia* of the British Pacific Fleet hit Kamaishi on Honshu, bombarding several military and industrial targets. They were accompanied by the American battleships *Indiana, South Dakota,* and *Massachusetts;* the cruisers *Quincy, Chicago, St. Paul,* and *Boston;*

and ten American destroyers. The destroyers *Erben* and *Stembel* sank three small enemy ships. No large ships were discovered.

The carrier attack on the northern Honshu fields completely wrecked the Japanese plan for the attack on the Marianas air bases, and this destruction so angered the Japanese that they responded with a real attack on the task force for the first time in many weeks. Several attack waves were launched against the carriers, but none succeeded in getting through. Late in the afternoon one attack of about twenty Japanese planes approached the fleet. It was disposed in a defensive pattern, with picket stations out at the sides. The attacking planes did not get to the carriers, but they did find the destroyer pickets southwest of the main force. They attacked. Four planes came in very close to the four picket ships and one kamikaze crashed into the center of the destroyer *Borie*. A hundred and fourteen men of the crew were killed or wounded, but the destroyer managed to survive the attack. She and her companion ships shot down three suicide planes and drove the others off. By the time the attack developed in midafternoon, the planes of the combat air patrol were rushing to the assistance of the ships. They shot down nine Japanese planes, and one, which very nearly got through to the carrier *Wasp*, was destroyed by that ship's antiaircraft gunners.

The *Borie* was sent off to the hospital ship *Rescue* to transfer her wounded. After that she was dispatched to Saipan.

August 9, as it turned out, was the day when the war heated up. Perhaps one reason for this was the intense struggle then going on among the Japanese leaders, with the diehard military and naval officers insisting that they would fight to the last man. The task force score for the day, besides the many airplanes destroyed, included ten small ships, the largest of them a destroyer, and many small vessels such as junks and luggers. When the observation planes appeared over the coastal targets that day and the next, they found that the destruction of the airfields had been thorough with a number of hangars burned, revealing planes inside. The surface ships had smashed parts of the Japan Ironworks factories at Kamaishi, the railroad yards there, and the port facilities. At the end of the day Halsey could be a bit more pleased with results than he had been for over a week.

The B-29 carrying the second American atomic bomb took off from Tinian at 3:00 on the morning of August 9, heading for Japan. It would be several hours before Major Sweeney would learn from the weather ships which of his two targets was to get the Fat Man, the plutonium bomb. With the success of the first atomic bomb three days earlier much of the tension that had built up among the men of the 509th Air Group had evaporated. But the tension had left its residue. Major Sweeney had not slept more than a few hours in the last seventy-two, and he found himself growing sleepy as the plane droned along. He turned the controls over to his copilot and crawled to the rear of the pilot's compartment. In a few moments he was fast asleep. Elsewhere in the plane, other members of the crew slept, too. Only the copilot and the flight engineer were fully alert. None other seemed to be needed. About three hours out, the warning lights began to flash, indicating something was amiss with the plutonium bomb. For a few minutes the two bomb experts aboard nearly panicked, but then they found the trouble—a switchover error in the wiring system had activated the warning lights. Nothing was really wrong, although the switch had been irregular and no one had been notified. But an error had been made, where there was little margin for error.

By 7:00, pilot Sweeney was awake and back at the controls. He began gaining altitude. He would go to 31,000.

Just before 9:00, Major Sweeney's plane received a message from the weather plane over Kokura, the primary target. All was clear. The sky was cloudless. A second message from the Nagasaki weather plane indicated that only a slight haze stood over that city and that a small group of clouds was dissipating.

Sweeney was upset, because one of the two instrument planes that was to meet him at this altitude had not appeared and he could not wait. He turned, moved across the coast of what the Japanese called *hondo* (the homeland). It was not long before the B-29 was approaching Kokura and the arsenal that was still producing a steady stream of weapons for Japan's armies. Captain Kermit Beahan, the bombardier, was looking down into his bombsight. He picked up the railroad station, which meant they were a mile from the arsenal, the aiming point for the plutonium bomb.

But as Major Sweeney flew toward the arsenal with bomb bay doors open, a cloud of smoke drifted across the target area. It came from the Yawata Steel Factory, which had been bombed during that big attack on Japan staged by General LeMay on August 7. Major Sweeney circled and made a new approach. Three times the B-29 tried to make the bombing run, and failed. The visibility was just too poor to make the run. Sweeney headed the plane toward Nagasaki. At 11:00 he was over Nagasaki, but the clouds had blown in by this time and 70 percent of the city was invisible. They had been told to make a visual drop, not a radar drop, but the visibility was so poor that Major Sweeney decided to make the radar drop if necessary— and it seemed likely that it would be necessary. At the last moment, Bombardier Beahan announced that he had a clear spot in the clouds, that he could see the Mitsubishi Arms Plant below, and he took command of the plane and dropped the bomb as was standard operating procedure.

In fact, the hasty bomb drop put the plutonium bomb in the wrong place. It was scheduled for drop on the center of Nagasaki, but it actually fell in the center of a triangle whose points were three separate Mitsubishi factories. All three were destroyed. The B-29, with its single instrument plane tagging along behind, headed for Okinawa. A malfunction in the fuel system made it imperative that they stop there rather than trying to make Tinian. They barely made it. One engine cut out as they bounced onto the landing strip.

At Nagasaki the damage was enormous, despite the fact that the bomb had not struck near the aiming point. From the center of the explosion the primary effect extended for more than half a mile in all directions. Everything within that large circle was pulverized. Steel beams lost their shape and turned to liquid. People were either vaporized or turned into carbon scarecrows. Nothing lived in that circle. Outside the circle the effects varied because so did the terrain. For example, one woman within 1,500 yards of the bomb fell into an eight-foot gulley as she ran to escape—and survived. A businessman who had an office near Nagasaki railroad station leaned over behind his desk to pick up some papers just as the bomb blew. He got up with two tiny scratches from flying glass. His secretary, sitting on the other side of the desk, was killed. Several boys were swimming in the Urakami River; one dived under the water just before the bomb blew; he came up to find all his companions lying dead on the riverbank. He was unhurt.

It was six hours before the authorities were able to make any organizational sense of the disaster. The utilities systems were destroyed, the trolley service knocked out, but limited railroad service to the north was soon restored. Unlike Hiroshima, the rugged configuration of Nagasaki (the name in Japanese means long, high cape) prevented the uniform destruction of the water system, so some buildings could be saved by firefighters. Actually about 20,000 of the 50,000 buildings in northwest Nagasaki were destroyed by the blast. The telephone company had its own emergency power system so some telephone service remained. At a meeting held late on the afternoon of August 9, the air defense officials estimated that they could have the city working again in three days, although the northwest area had suffered extreme damage.

Starting from the center, the defense workers began the grisly task of disposing of the bodies of the thousands of dead before they contaminated the entire area.

In Washington, President Truman had two separate bits of vital information. Early in the afternoon (Washington time) he called the press together and told the reporters that the U.S.S.R. had declared war on Japan. Later in the day he had the news that the second atomic bomb had been dropped and that the mission had apparently been successful, although no details were available because of the poor weather over the target.

As the word reached the United States, so did a message from General Carl Spaatz, chief of the Strategic Air Force. He wanted to make another atomic bomb attack on Tokyo. But the matter at the moment could not be resolved because no third atomic bomb was yet ready. It would be at least a week or so before such an attempt could be made under any conditions. Secretary Stimson opposed another drop. He felt certain that there would be no further need; the Japanese would simply have to understand the power of this weapon after the second bomb, and the war must come to an end.

That morning of August 9, the Supreme War Council of Japan was finally assembled in response to Prime Minister Suzuki's call. The meeting was to be held at the Imperial Palace. The Emperor, however, was not scheduled to appear at the conference until evening. The military and civil leaders of the Japanese government would have all day to discuss current events and try to agree on a policy.

For three days, General Korechika Anami, the minister of war, had refused to discuss the question of surrender. He had strong support from General Yoshijiro Umezu, his chief of staff of the army, and Admiral Soemu Toyoda, the chief of staff of the imperial navy. When the first reports indicated that the new bomb must be some sort of super-bomb, they had waved away the implications. Nothing was beyond the power of the Japanese people, they said. The fight must go on to the end, and in that end Japan would somehow be victorious. When the military men now talked about "victory" it had an entirely different meaning from the implication in their minds four years earlier. In the fall of 1941, as the generals and admirals planned the war against the U.S. and the Western colonial powers, they were thinking of absolute victory, after which Japan would control East Asia and much of the Pacific. But by 1944 "victory" had come to mean a peace with honor, and no more—the militarists would be satisfied to keep Japan free from occupation. They hoped to retain nearby Korea, Formosa, and Okinawa, and the islands north and south.

For two days after the drop of the Hiroshima bomb the military leaders had refused to accept reality. Finally, on the night of August 8, reality had caught up with them. Dr. Yoshio Nishina had hurried down to Hiroshima from Tokyo University. As Japan's leading expert on nuclear matters, even the military had to accept his word. And on the night of August 8, Dr. Nishina came back to Tokyo to report to Prime Minister Suzuki's office that the explosion had indeed been caused by an atomic bomb, just as President Truman had announced.

On the morning of August 9, then, the members of the Supreme War Council had that information to digest. From Hiroshima also had begun reports of secondary reactions to the atomic explosion. People who were apparently unhurt began to come down with various illnesses. It was an ominous sign.

Until this point the Japanese government had been talking about making protest through the International Red Cross about the American use of the atomic bomb, a devilish weapon, obviously far worse than poison gas, which had been outlawed by international convention. (The Japanese conveniently forgot that they had used poison gas against the Chinese, and that their treatment of Allied prisoners of war would never pass muster with the Red Cross and eventually would lead to a series of trials for individual acts of brutality under the name of "war crimes.")

The military, having denied on August 7 and 8 that the Americans could have an atomic bomb, had delayed the protest. Now it seemed less important than facing the facts. Prime Minister Suzuki, who had hemmed and hawed in the beginning, now came out forcefully for acceptance of the Potsdam surrender terms. On the morning of August 9, Prime Minister Suzuki was awakened with the word that the Soviets had attacked and that the Kwantung army was engaged in combat in Manchuria. General Yamada at Hsinking had ordered the Seventeenth Area Army in Korea to join the action, following a direct order from Imperial General Headquarters. The Fifth Area Army at Sapporo was also assigned to the anti-Soviet front in Manchuria, and although theoretically the Imperial General Staff could not act to start fighting against another country without the acquiescence of the cabinet, in fact the orders had gone out before Prime Minister Suzuki knew anything about the beginning of military action.

Prime Minister Suzuki on August 9 had decided that he must rely on the Emperor to resolve this weighty issue. He had made it quite clear earlier that Japan's road could lead to nothing but disaster. He sensed that the Emperor agreed with him, but what was needed was something new to Japan, something that was unknown since the days of the Emperor Meiji. Emperor Hirohito had always reigned, but not ruled. He had been consulted on all vital national matters, but he had always accepted the decisions of his government. If he had strong feelings on a subject, these were quietly communicated to the government before any meeting so they could be taken into consideration. When the actual confrontation of government and Emperor occurred, the Emperor had never argued. What the prime minister must have this time at the Imperial War Conference was actual participation by the Emperor and a statement that would break the power of the military.

Already there had been an inkling of this sort of rebellion against the militarists in the activity of the people. Men and women on the streets were snickering at the sight of grown soldiers training for action with long bamboo spears instead of rifles. What must happen now could only happen with the help of the Emperor. The problem was to be sure that the Emperor knew.

By the morning of August 9, the Emperor did know that there was serious conflict within his government. Days earlier he had told Prime Minister Suzuki that he was prepared to issue any imperial order just as soon as the government asked him to do so. But by that, the Emperor meant that he expected a consensus, or at least a majority vote. And the government was badly divided.

At 11:00 in the morning, as the B-29 carrying the plutonium bomb approached Nagasaki, the generals, admirals, and civilian members of the Supreme War Council met at the Imperial Palace. This body differed from the government in that it included a number of senior statesmen who were not part of the cabinet, and some of these men had enormous influence in Japan.

The military members began by arguing that if, as now seemed indicated, the bomb dropped on Hiroshima had been an atomic bomb, and if just one was dropped when everyone knew the Americans had thousands of B-29s, then there must simply have been that one bomb. Therefore, said War Minister Anami, one need have no further fear of an atomic attack. The destruction of Hiroshima was, quite to the reverse of the civilian way of thinking, really an asset to the government, because now it would be far easier to rally the people of Japan—who were admittedly growing restless in the shadow of constant defeat—to the last great struggle that should bring "victory." The enormity of the American crime in killing perhaps 100,000 people with one dreadful devilish weapon could be turned to world advantage. The struggle must go on.

What about the Soviet entry into the war? The civilians asked: Did that not mean certain defeat?

They had planned all along on a war against the Soviet Union, the militarists said. True, the timing had been chosen by the Russians, and that was perhaps unfortunate, but the principle was the same. The always-victorious forces of the Emperor would throw the Soviets back. But as for the atomic bomb, said the war minister, they must forget it . . . .

Just as he was pressing the argument, an aide entered the meeting room and whispered. There was silence. Then, in considerably less confident tones, the war minister announced that a second atomic bomb had just destroyed large parts of Nagasaki. The conference soon broke up in disarray.

The confusion came because the civilians had to digest the new information and the militarists had to find some new justification for continuing the war that could not end. And why could it not end? Because if it did end, the leaders of the military faction knew, all their power base would erode. Under the Allied policy they had seen operative in Germany, the army and navy had been disbanded, the whole country put under stringent military rule by foreigners, and the German empire completely dissolved. To Japan it would mean the end of an era that had begun in the 1920s, and the military leaders were quite willing to see the destruction of their country and the death of most of its people rather than to relinquish power.

Prime Minister Suzuki went back to his office. Early in the afternoon he sent word to all members of the Supreme Council that the meeting would be resumed at the Imperial Palace at 11:30 that night, and that this time the Emperor would be in attendance.

The moment of decision was fast approaching.

In the afternoon the prime minister met with the cabinet, which had much of the composition, but not all, of the Imperial War Council. In the cabinet meeting, when the prime minister again enunciated his belief that there was no alternative but surrender and that all they could expect from the Allies was the retention of the imperial system, the cabinet members indicated that the majority were against him. The home minister and the minister of justice sided with the military faction. General Anami, spokesman for that faction, said that Japan had not yet nearly reached the end of her tether, and that when the enemy tried to invade the Japanese homeland, and suffered the enormous casualties that could be inflicted, they would have to back off. At that moment, Japan should be able to secure an "honorable peace."

At Sasebo on the afternoon of August 9, Lieutenant Commander Yukio Inaba boarded the *I-373,* one of the new big I-boats equipped with radar. He had orders to carry out a patrol in the South China Sea, and work particularly around Formosa where American warships might be found.

The *I-373* sailed that day.

On the evening of August 9, Governor Nagano of Nagasaki's prefecture held a meeting of his various civil defense officers and businessmen who were trying to restore order to their shattered city. At the meeting, when an official of the Kyushu Electric Company asked for assignment of soldiers to help put up light poles and string wires to restore the city's electrical system, Commander Matsuura of the district military police began to shout. In the past, for years, the military did precisely as it pleased with the civil population, and when a military officer began to shout, the civilians had backed down without a word. But not this day. The electric company man shouted right back, and in the end shouted the soldier down. Moreover, the governor ordered the military commander to help restore the electricity of Nagasaki. The military commander left the meeting in a deep state of shock.

So the rising of the civilians against the military power that had kept Japan subjected for so long had begun. But such manifestations as that in Nagasaki, which were not even known to Prime Minister Suzuki, could have no effect on the fate of the nation in the next few days, or even weeks. The one power superior to that of the military was the power of the Emperor, unknown because never in this war had he exercised it, although in theory the word of the Son of Heaven had the authority of the word of God.

At 11:30 the conference began in the audience building of the Imperial Palace. War Minister Anami spoke for the militarists, and was supported by Army Chief of Staff Umezu and Navy Chief of Staff Toyoda. Against continuing the war were Prime Minister Suzuki, Foreign Minister Togo, and Admiral Mitsumasa Yonai, the navy minister. Although this group was known as the "civilians," the fact was that both Suzuki and Yonai were navy men. Yonai had commanded the first Japanese expeditionary fleet on the Yangtse River in 1928 when Japan had joined European nations in "controlling pirates," and then had never left the river. In 1936 Yonai had been named commander of the combined fleet; in 1937 he was navy minister in the cabinet, and so served under three successive prime ministers. Since 1939 he had been an imperial councillor, and since 1940 a *jushin* (elder statesman). He had even served as prime minister for a few months in 1940. As might be imagined, Admiral Yonai had enormous influence within Japan and the imperial circle, and not even the most pugnacious general could face him down. He had decided, after years of supporting the militarist position, that the war was lost and that it must be brought to an immediate end if Japan was to survive as a nation. The lesson of the Allied dismemberment of Germany was not unnoticed.

Prime Minister Suzuki's life had paralleled that of modern Japan. He was born in 1867 at the beginning of the Meiji restoration movement, he graduated from the Naval War College, commanded a torpedo boat during the Sino-Japanese war of 1894, a destroyer division during the Russo-Japanese war, and became an admiral in 1917. For years he had been a military councillor to the Emperor and grand chamberlain and privy councillor. One reason for his selection as prime minister was to try to woo many factions of a fragmenting Japan.

Since the war had grown hard for Japan, the meeting room at the palace had been transferred to an underground bomb shelter, and it was here that the councillors assembled in their heavy formal clothes. There was no air conditioning. By the time the Emperor entered the room just before midnight, all his council members were sweating.

The prime minister had set the stage with three documents. One was the translation of the Potsdam Declaration, which demanded unconditional surrender as a single term of peace. A second document, prepared by the prime minister's office, accepted the declaration, with the single stipulation that the imperial system be continued as it existed. The third plan, the only one that might be regarded as acceptable to the militarists, called for retention of the imperial system, punishment of "war criminals" in Japanese courts by Japanese procedure, disarmament of Japanese troops by themselves, and no occupation of the home islands. All these were lessons learned from the defeat and occupation of Germany.

Previously, of course, Foreign Minister Togo had conferred on the Potsdam Declaration and had secured the imperial assent to its acceptance. But until the Emperor said so in just that many words, there was no way the military men could be overwhelmed. Suzuki's purpose in calling this meeting was to overwhelm them this night.

The prime minister opened the meeting by reading the Potsdam Declaration, although every man in the room was familiar with it.

He then asked for discussion, turning first to Foreign Minister Togo. The foreign minister repeated his view, stated endlessly in recent meetings:

Hiroshima and now Nagasaki were still stunned by the shock of two enormously powerful bombs that could kill millions of civilians. The Red army was inside Manchuria, and only the employment of hundreds of suicide aircraft was slowing the Russians down as their armored armies drove forward. Thousands of American aircraft were swarming around the cities of Japan. Most recently, the long-range B-29s and the carrier aircraft of the American fleet had been joined by fighter planes and smaller bombers based on Okinawa and other islands close to Japan. The foreign minister did not know of the most recent debacle, the wiping out of the suicide force that was to stop the B-29s. But he did know that the Nagasaki bomb had virtually wiped out the Mitsubishi industrial complex at that port city, and he did know that Admiral Halsey's battleships and cruisers did not hesitate to come right up to the Japanese shoreline to bombard. Japan's industrial plant was in shatters: two miles of Osaka had been completely destroyed, and the U.S. Strategic Bombing Command estimated that of the 257 square miles of Japan's six largest cities, nearly half had been reduced to rubble. The Japanese did not put it that way, of course, but everyone in the room knew that a third of the population of most cities and half of some had left or died. *B-san* and *bei kaigun*—the American navy—were wreaking the total destruction of the cities. They must seek peace. They must accept the Potsdam Declaration, with the provision that the imperial system be retained.

Prime Minister Suzuki then asked Admiral Yonai for his views. They were already too well known to the military party, and because of them, Admiral Yonai had been forced out of politics almost at the beginning of the Pacific war. In 1937, when Yonai had been pulled from his post as chief of the combined fleet to become navy minister, he had remarked bitterly to a friend that "nothing could be worse than to leave the fleet merely to become an army dependent." Yonai had been closely associated with Admiral Isoroku Yamamoto, the chief of the combined fleet who executed the Pearl Harbor attack, but both were several times under death threat from the Black Dragon and other militarist societies because of their antiwar views. In the past three years, since the death of Yamamoto and the turn of the war's tide in the Allies' favor, Yonai had been virtually ostracized by the militarists for his criticisms. But in recent weeks he had been brought back into prominence.

Yonai said he agreed completely with Foreign Minister Togo.

Then, as he had to do, the prime minister asked General Anami for his views. In recent weeks the control of the army had been taken over by the military affairs bureau of that organization, and instead of the bureau responding to the war minister and the cabinet, the bureau was attempting to exercise control of the government through the army's power backed by the millions of troops in the homeland. The bureau had long been the center of army intrigue and the focal point of militarist policy. In 1935, for example, Major General Tetsuzan Nagata had been assassinated when he was chief of that bureau, because the militarists believed he had deserted their cause and was putting the army into the hands of civilians. Two of the more ardent militarists and bastions of the bureau were Colonel Okikatsu Arao and Major General Joichiro Sanada. In the past four days the bureau had been putting enormous pressure on General Anami. The Potsdam Declaration *must not* be accepted, said the military affairs bureau to the war minister. It would mean the death of the army as they knew it. If Minister Anami could not sway the cabinet to this view, then he had best commit suicide. Thus did the military affairs bureau of the army issue its ultimatum to the man who was theoretically its leader: conform to militarist policy or die.

At this meeting at midnight on August 10, General Anami stated the army position as demanded by the military affairs bureau: he opposed the acceptance of the Potsdam Declaration in any form. The Japanese people must fight, to the death if necessary, to preserve the national honor.

Prime Minister Suzuki asked him under what conditions he could support the surrender. Only in extremity could the army even countenance the second suggestion, that the Japanese agree to give up if the Americans let them handle all their own affairs and did not occupy the country. But even surrender under these conditions was anathema to the army, the general said.

Admiral Toyoda and General Umezu echoed the war minister's views. Baron Hiranuma, who was president of the privy council and a member (nonvoting) of the Supreme War Council, asked some pointed questions of the army minister and the prime minister about the nation's defense capability. General Anami was stubborn in his reiteration of the army's determination to kill everybody in Japan if necessary, on the beachheads and in the mountains, to continue the national destiny. As for preparedness, he cited the numbers of suicide craft of various sorts, and the continuing (though vastly diminished) flow of essential military supplies.

Baron Hiranuma was not much impressed and said so; he sided with Foreign Secretary Togo, for what good that would do. In terms of the meeting itself the position did not do any good at all, since he was voteless. But it did pave the way for Prime Minister Suzuki's next move, which had been well planned. The prime minister noted that the council had spent many days and many hours in fruitless argument since the Potsdam offer was made, but that agreement was not even in sight. Therefore, there was only one option: they must ask for imperial guidance and substitute the Emperor's wish for the decision that could not be reached.

The militarists were absolutely shocked. Never in the history of their power had a prime minister asked for the "Voice of the Sacred Crane"—an absolute command by the Emperor of Japan.

Without warning, Prime Minister Suzuki had done the unthinkable, and the military faction had not even had a chance to put its case privately to the Emperor before he was being called upon to make the most vital decision of his reign.

15

AGONY

The Emperor was ready. Prime Minister Suzuki had convinced him, even before the dropping of the Hiroshima bomb, that the war was lost and any attempt to perpetuate it could only result in the deaths of millions of Japanese. After the first bomb, Suzuki had also persuaded the Emperor that his government was at an impasse and only the royal word, the Voice of the Sacred Crane, could resolve the situation in favor of peace.

When the prime minister called on him, the Emperor sat forward on his throne and spoke slowly and clearly.

The generals said they could win the great battle of Japan, but he did not believe it, he said. The reason was that he had checked on several statements made by his ministers and found them not supported by the facts. He had sent representatives to the beaches to see the new fortifications the army was talking about, and they found none. He had sent emissaries to the military camps to see the new divisions of troops being organized and fitted out with the most modern weapons—according to his generals. He had found the troops to be a conglomeration of the unfit and their weapons to be wooden staves. He was now faced with the life or death of the Japanese nation, he was convinced, he said. To follow the generals' path would be to preside over the dissolution of Japan. If the nation were to remain one people, then the people and he must face the unthinkable. He agreed with Foreign Minister Togo that there was but one course open to Japan. She must surrender.

So saying, the Emperor paused, then added that as far as he was concerned what happened to him was not important. The nation must be preserved. He then walked out of the room.

There was no question about what would happen next. The prime minister suggested that the word of the emperor be accepted without further discussion, and it was. The meeting was over, and the councillors stepped out of the overheated bomb shelter and into the sultry Tokyo night. It was not much more than an hour before dawn on August 10.

Admiral Halsey's Third Fleet was at sea that morning of August 10, about 150 miles east of Kamaishi in northern Honshu. At 4:00 in the morning—some of the Japanese councillors had not yet reached their beds—the carriers began air strikes against Japan. As the Emperor had indicated, as far as the Americans were concerned there would be no surcease of grim warfare until Japan surrendered. Halsey had yielded to Admiral McCain's arguments, and the day's strikes were concentrated against airfields and air installations. The operations of the day before had convinced Halsey that there were far more aircraft available to the Japanese than his intelligence reports had previously indicated. McCain had pointed out that while the planes and fields of Kyushu had apparently been almost devoid of gasoline (aircraft attacked on the ground did not usually burn and virtually no planes had risen to meet the Kyushu strikes), the same could not be said of the planes they had destroyed or damaged on those Honshu fields on August 9. So the Japanese had gasoline, and they had airplanes, and they were saving them. The fleet could do no better service to the coming invasion of Kyushu and Honshu than to destroy all planes possible, particularly since these days every one of them was a potential flying bomb.

Thus shipping and industrial and transportation targets, which had been first on Halsey's priority list, moved down and the air installations moved up.

But the flurry of activity on August 9 in the air seemed to have evaporated. The carrier planes saw no enemy aircraft flying, but they did find several hundred on the ground at various fields. Admiral McCain had been preparing for the day when his advice would win out, and his intelligence officers had studied every centimeter of photos taken of Japanese airfields and their surrounding countryside on recent missions. They had circled little spots that seemed to be nothing but brush until one took a second or third look. They were, in fact, beautifully camouflaged aircraft parked in camouflaged revetments, many of them five or six miles from the airfields. The pilots of the American strike force were given copies of these marked maps and instructed to go in first at treetop level and spot targets, then come back to attack. In the absence of Japanese fighter activity, this low-level attack system was effective and relatively safe, although that day the Americans lost fifteen planes in combat and the British lost six. Eight of the Americans and four British pilots were rescued.

But together, the British and American fliers claimed to have destroyed 175 Japanese planes on the ground and to have damaged another 153. The figure was eminently satisfactory, partly because late in the day the pilots from the British task force found two new concentrations of Japanese planes at Mamurogawa airfield and Obanazawa. Most of the other results were achieved by reworking old "diggings" under the new intelligence reconaissance system.

Some of the planes, unable to find proper targets at the airfields, followed instructions to hit the secondary targets: shipping, rail lines, and industry. The British and American pilots sank about fifty small craft, ranging from patrol boats to ferries. They attacked two destroyer escorts and left them smoking. One, they suggested, later sank—at least a later patrol could find no evidence of it afloat—but it was still a probable. The

British and Americans also damaged another sixty small vessels,
ranging from a passenger ferry to an icebreaker in the port at
Aomori. Attacks on such craft as ferries, which would have
been ignored as wasteful six months earlier, indicated how true
were the words of the Emperor. No life was safe in Japan these
days, and it was obviously going to grow much worse.

Other British planes hit a freight yard at Onohama, and destroyed four locomotives and several passenger and freight cars.
The Americans struck the rail yards at Niigata, where they burned
up nineteen locomotives and thirty-two railroad cars. By August
10, Japanese living in the outlying areas found it almost impossible to travel. Not only were trains attacked in motion, but
also the constant destruction of locomotives and the damage to
tracks and rolling stock made train travel dangerous and unreli-
able. For example, west of Matsushima that day, British fighter
bombers swooped down on a moving train, derailed it, and left
the locomotive and cars burning furiously as they flew back to
their carrier unhindered. The losses came entirely from antiaircraft guns. The American and British had to brave a real hail
of fire around the airfields in particular. But that was a part of
the job, and at the end of the day Halsey was quite satisfied
with the low ratio of losses to damage inflicted.

Commander Hashimoto took the *I-58* steadily northward.
He had tried to put the report of the atomic bomb dropped on
Hiroshima out of his mind, but the news reports from Radio
Tokyo were beginning to confirm the gist of the forbidden
American broadcast monitored by Lieutenant Nishimura. Then,
on August 9, late in the afternoon, came a report that Nagasaki
too had been bombed with an atomic device. And Radio Tokyo
announced that the Soviet Union had entered the war. Moving
north, Commander Hashimoto would also have to begin watching for Soviet ships or submarines, and Soviet aircraft if he
reached the waters off Honshu.

On the morning of August 10, the *I-58* was moving slowly,
submerged. The sound detector picked up the pinging of an echo,

which meant some foreign object not far away. Commander Hashimoto raised the periscope and looked around, to see a destroyer. He recognized her silhouette as American, and prepared to attack by ordering the crews of *kaitens* No. 5 and No. 6 to stand by. The *kaiten* operators were exultant. For days they had been reproaching their commander for using conventional torpedoes to sink the "*Idaho*-class battleship" (*Indianapolis*). Now, it seemed, they were to have the chance to give their lives profitably for the Emperor and Japan. The destroyer was about five miles away, so there was time, if the ship did not suddenly put on speed and charge off; the *I-58* could never catch her then.

There was trouble with the *kaitens* again. No. 6 began to give off a foam of white bubbles that rose clearly to the surface. If the destroyermen were watching they might well see the disturbance and come to investigate. No. 5 was making an enormous amount of noise as her engines warmed up. Finally she was launched, but No. 6 could not be. The engine stopped and the bubbling continued, to Commander Hashimoto's dismay. He ordered the captains of *kaitens* No. 3 and No. 4 to embark and get ready. But No. 3 would not start.

By this time, Commander Hashimoto had visions of the destroyer charging down on him to attack. He raised the periscope very cautiously. The destroyer, far from attacking, was further off than before. And, as he watched, a convoy appeared past the destroyer. He ordered the launch of No. 4 *kaiten*.

He watched through the periscope as No. 4 moved into the middle of the convoy. Then he heard a loud explosion, and the convoy began to scatter. He looked again, and the destroyer had disappeared. He assumed she was sunk. (The fact is that no sinking or even damage of a U.S. ship by submarine was reported that day.)

That night as they reached the waters in which the Americans were operating, *I-58* picked up several ship noises. But there was no moon, and when Commander Hashimoto raised the periscope all he could see around him was the blackness of night.

There was no point in trying to attack under such circumstances. *I-58* remained below, and a few hours later, Commander Hashimoto was glad they had. A destroyer came by, quite close, and seemed to have them in its sound detectors. The crew braced for a depth charge attack, but it never came; the destroyer passed almost over the submarine, and then went on.

On the morning of August 10, General Yamada had the sort of orders that Imperial General Headquarters had been issuing for the past year. He was to defend the Manchurian border and Korea and drive the Russians back at all costs. He was not to lose. He was not to surrender. He must win victory. Under all the hyperbole was the usual instruction that he was to fight to the last man, not stated, but well understood in Japanese military language.

That day on the eastern borders of Manchuria the Soviets poured across in two areas, one against the Third Japanese Army and the other against the Fifth Army. The kamikaze planes stopped many tanks but others took their places, and like a file of army ants the Soviets moved on, into Manchuria.

In Tokyo at 7:00 A.M. on August 10 Prime Minister Suzuki's translators finished the English-language version of the Japanese government's answer to the Potsdam Declaration. It was sent by international radio to the governments of the U.S., Britain, China, and the U.S.S.R. The message stated that by imperial decree the Japanese government was ready to accept the surrender terms as long as the prerogatives of the Emperor were not endangered. The message was not sent by direct radio, because the government did not want any eavesdroppers. It was sent in code to the Japanese ministers at Bern and Stockholm. The message was picked up by American radio monitors, and decoded and translated.

The Japanese government made no public announcement that day. Prime Minister Suzuki had considered the idea, but rejected it until the time when the imperial rescript on the subject was actually released. He feared an attempt by the Japanese army to overthrow the government and continue the war.

Suzuki's fears were well grounded. Even as the message of surrender went out across half the world, in Japanese army headquarters in Tokyo a revolution was brewing. A band of young army officers faced their superiors and demanded that the war continue. They had everything to lose by surrender; the words of the Potsdam Declaration were clear: after the surrender there would be no more Japanese army and there never would be an army again as far as the Allies were concerned. The officer corps had grown up in complete dedication to a society obedient to the demands of the military. For the officers of the professional class there was no future in the surrender, and to them the concept of death rather than dishonor had a special meaning. General Anami was so worried about rebellion that he summoned all officers in Tokyo above the rank of lieutenant colonel and appealed to them to keep the young officers quiet.

When President Truman in Washington learned the text of the Japanese message, although unofficially, he summoned what might be called the American war council to his office in the White House. The members were Secretary of War Stimson, Secretary of the Navy Forrestal, Secretary of State Byrnes, and Admiral William D. Leahy, the President's personal military advisor. Truman was stumped by one question: could the answer of the Japanese government be construed to be acceptance of the terms of the Potsdam Declaration?

Secretary Stimson said yes. He had been convinced by his recent studies of Japan and the Japanese character that retention of the Emperor was necessary and could be useful in maintaining order.

Secretary Byrnes was doubtful. He recalled that President Roosevelt had specified that the Japanese would have to surrender unconditionally, and that meant without any condition such as the retention of the Emperor.

The discussion lasted an hour, and then Byrnes pointed out that they could do nothing at this time because they had not received the official word, and when they did they must consult the governments of Britain and China, as they were cosigners to the declaration.

Secretary Stimson was not very happy with Byrnes' attitude. He had become convinced in recent days that the more leniently they treated the Japanese—despite all propaganda pronouncements made earlier—the better the world would be for it. Several of his assistants suggested that he ought to draft a reply for the President, and that process began. Advisor John J. McCloy wanted to put into the answer a discussion of the democratic government that would be instituted in Japan, but Stimson vetoed this as premature, possibly subject to a misunderstanding that would upset the whole negotiation and, most important to him, be a cause for delay. General Marshall had discussed the question of Soviet advance. It was too early to tell just how quickly the Soviets would move, but it was a worry. For now that the war was virtually ended and they had seen the color of the Soviet future at Potsdam, Stimson and his associates wanted no part of another joint occupation with the Russians. Already the troubles had begun in Germany and Austria. Anything that delayed the Japanese surrender process would increase the danger of the Russians insisting on having a share of the occupation of Japan. Just now, when they had not reached Japan proper, there was no such danger.

Thus the day was spent in Washington, with the President's principal advisors worrying over the terms of the Japanese surrender. In the end, when the advisors met again in the President's office, all agreed that the version prepared by the State Department was the best.

On Tinian during the day of August 10 Captain Parsons surveyed the atomic parts that had been delivered from the American mainland. He radioed General Groves that starting the next day he would begin the assembly of two more plutonium bombs. The third would be completed by August 12 and ready for drop the next day. The fourth bomb would be ready for drop by August 16.

Back in Washington, General Groves made preparation to send more atomic materials to Tinian. The Japanese were quite wrong, much more so than anyone in Tokyo thought. The Americans had the power to put forth several more atomic bombs and plans for a production system as well. No matter what the Japanese militarists thought, their war machine had run down. The problem, however, even now after the Emperor's decision, was to convince the military men that there was more to life than the war they had been fighting for fourteen years.

16

WAITING

On the morning of August 11, 1945, the Soviet forces in Manchuria penetrated 125 miles past the border and were plunging over the last hills onto the Mutanchiang Plain, despite every kamikaze and every conventional weapon the Japanese could throw against them.

In Moscow, Soviet Foreign Minister Molotov was engaged in a bitter debate with American Ambassador Harriman. On the evening before, the Americans had delivered a copy of the message they proposed to send to the Japanese government, and while the Russians agreed, they tried to get their foot in the door of the coming occupation. Molotov insisted that the Soviets should have an equal voice in the choice of a commander of the occupying force. Perhaps there should be two commanders, he told Harriman: American General MacArthur and Soviet General Alexander M. Vasilevski. Harriman told him coldly that such a demand was out of the question. The Americans had been carrying the war in the Pacific for four years, keeping the Japanese from attacking the Russians while the Russians were fighting for survival against the Nazis. The Russians had been in the war for two days and now asked for equal power in the occupation.

Molotov became angry and insisted that Harriman send Washington the demand. Harriman left the foreign office, but had scarcely arrived at the embassy when a telephone call from Molotov indicated that he had seen Stalin and that Stalin had backed down. He still asked for consultation on the supreme commander of the Allied powers, but withdrew the insistence that the Soviets have a representative.

Back in Washington, President Truman received the Soviet request without warmth. He was determined that there would be no repetition of the mess the Western powers had gotten themselves into in Germany by stopping and waiting for the Russians to come up and capture Berlin, thus paving the way for a four-power occupation that was proving extremely trying to the West.

President Truman had the answer from Britain and from China quickly enough, and on the morning of August 11 he was ready to send a reply to Japan.

Navy Secretary Forrestal and Army Secretary Stimson wanted the President to suspend military activity as an act of good faith to the Japanese while they considered the American message. But Truman refused. The war must continue, he said, lest the Japanese see a sign of American weakness and try to bargain. There would be no cease-fire. If the Japanese surrendered they could keep their emperor, but the Emperor and the Japanese government must be subject to the authority of the American (Allied) occupation force. That was the message that went to Japan on August 11.

At sea, Admiral Halsey was doing just what President Truman wanted, carrying on the war against Japan with the same intensity he had shown in the South Pacific in the days when Japan's position was or seemed to be superior to that of the U.S. The fleet fuelled that morning, but almost at the door of the enemy. Admiral Halsey took the opportunity to call a conference of his senior officers, including the British. For several days, Admiral Nimitz had been sending messages indicating that the war was winding down and that the invasion of Japan might not be necessary. Halsey was warned to be prepared to occupy the Yokosuka naval base with the Third Fleet, and this was the reason for the conference. On the eleventh, when the message went out to Japan, Admiral King suddenly realized that the only American force capable of occupying Japan in case of immediate surrender was Halsey's Third Fleet, and even that would take some doing, since the only "infantry" aboard were a few marines.

But the war was not over yet, so after fuelling and after the conference, the planes of Task Force 38 set out to strike Japan again. Not much was accomplished because Halsey was dodging another typhoon.

In Tokyo on the morning of August 11, *Mainichi Shimbun*, *Asahi Shimbun*, and the other morning Japanese papers carried strange articles that demanded reading between the lines. The Japanese were used to these by now; they had not gotten the word about how badly the war was going from the official pronouncements in the press these last two years, but by comparing the statements of one month against those of the month before. The gaps and retrenchments and retreats then made the situation obvious. On the eleventh the newspapers carried an official statement from the government: "In truth we cannot but recognize that we are now beset with the worst possible situation." These were scarcely the words of *bushido*, the attitude was hardly the "fight to the death" of the militarists. But what was it? The statement was a warning to the public to expect some drastic change. The people were called on "to rise to the occasion and overcome all manner of difficulties in order to protect the polity of their empire."

The usual word "polity"—refering to a system of government—was the tipoff. To the militarists and the careless readers, the message might be interpreted as just another call to national destruction, but to the careful it was a warning that something big was about to break. The concealment was to prevent an immediate uprising by the young officers and handful of senior officers who were determined that if the miltarist system died, Japan would die with it.

As far as the army was concerned, the word was the same as always, even more strident this day. The minister of war, General Anami, issued a public statement to the army noting the declaration of war against Japan by the Soviet Union, and called on the men for renewed efforts to defend "our divine land." It might mean eating grass, eating dirt, sleeping in the fields, but Japan must go on with the promise, so vaguely stated, that somehow the resolution of the people would reveal a way out of their desperate situation.

On the morning of the twelfth of August, the American note was transmitted to Japan by official couriers through diplomatic channels. But it was also broadcast across the Pacific by the Voice of America at San Francisco. The final note said that the Emperor and the Japanese government should be subject to the authority of the Supreme Commander of the Allied Powers from the moment of surrender. This was backward acceptance of the continued existence of the imperial system. It was emphasized by the second point: the Emperor would authorize his government to sign the surrender and must command all his armed forces to lay down their arms.

After the surrender the Japanese must transfer all prisoners of war and interned civilians to safe places where they could be picked up by the Allies.

The final form of the Japanese government would be established by the free will of the Japanese people, said the statement, an indication of the feeling of some Westerners that given a choice between a republic and a monarchy, the republic ought to win out. The last provision called for Allied occupation until the purposes of the Potsdam Declaration had been achieved.

When that message was received in various high quarters in Japan, it created a new frenzy of indecision. Most unfortunately, it said too much. By raising the question of the "ultimate" form of the Japanese government, the Americans had indicated that the future of the imperial system was indeed questionable, although the first provision of the message seemed to gainsay that. It was easy for the opponents of surrender to make the assumption that the Americans were being less than candid. The vague reference to retaining occupation forces until the purposes set forth in the Potsdam Declaration were achieved caused more worry.

The policy of the declaration went back to the Cairo Declaration (by which the Allies vowed to deprive Japan of all territory won by conquest), but was there more to it than that?

That morning of August 12, General Umezu, the chief of staff of the army, and Admiral Toyoda, the chief of the navy, met and travelled together to the Imperial Palace to seek audience with the Emperor. He received them, and they argued pleadingly for him to reject the Allied surrender terms because they would put Japan into slavery. They pointed to the anomalies of the American message as proof of the bad faith of the Allies. As all knew, the Americans despised monarchies and would do anything to overthrow the imperial system, they said. They could also quote such statements as Secretary of the Treasury Henry Morgenthau's plan to turn Germany into a wasteland, and turn that about to apply to Japan. The divine nation would be reduced to slavery under an American occupation, said the chiefs of the military.

That same day, Foreign Minister Togo called at the palace and assured the Emperor that no such calamity was threatened by the American message. He was certain that the Allies intended to respect the Emperor, and their coarse language in reference to the imperial position could only be attributed to their ignorance about Japan and the Japanese people.

Even as he was meeting with officials at the palace, at the war ministry a group of young fanatic officers was calling on General Anami to stage a coup d'etat and overthrow the current government. They did not say it in as many words, but the attitude was clear that if the Emperor resisted them, he too could be held expendable.

Leaving the Imperial Palace, Foreign Minister Togo returned to Tokyo center and called on the prime minister. He found him deep in gloom, tossed from side to side by various interpretations of the American message. Togo told him that the Emperor had agreed that the American message should be accepted, and the prime minister then came around to the Togo position that all would be well with the imperial system.

Having adopted a course of action, Emperor Hirohito then assembled his forces like a general, to do what he could to prevent a coup d'etat. He was as much aware of the dangers as any man in Tokyo. He called together his own family, all the imperial princes and their families, and asked for their support in the troubled days ahead. The plea meant that they should not talk against the surrender, but more than that, that the imperial family should go out into the country and convince key military units that the surrender was at the will of the Emperor and that the will must be obeyed.

That afternoon of August 11, the Japanese cabinet again went into session to make official the decision Togo had wrested from the air that morning. The foreign minister was aghast to see that the prime minister was vacillating again, and at one point, spurred by the militarists, he made the statement that he could see no alternative but to continue the war.

The foreign minister argued, his back against the wall. No one knew how many atomic bombs the Americans had—the army had already been proved wrong in its contention that there was only one. To stall, to refuse to accept the Allied terms, could bring nothing but total disaster, the foreign minister said, and that meant the real destruction of the Japanese nation.

The militarists pressed. At one point they secured the agreement of the majority of the cabinet that the American message meant destruction of the imperial system and the enslavement of the Japanese people for years to come.

For a few minutes the issue hung in doubt; had the cabinet voted on the matter, War Minister Anami's war faction would have won out. Foreign Minister Togo persuaded the cabinet to wait until the offical American message had been received. After all, the government could not take an offical action based on the unofficial reports of action by another government.

After the cabinet adjourned, Foreign Minister Togo went to see Prime Minister Suzuki again and once more made all his arguments for peace and against continuation of the losing struggle. Once again, Prime Minister Suzuki declared himself convinced that the Togo plan was the only sensible way for Japan.

That night the foreign minister buttressed all his arguments, finding more facts that showed how badly Japan was faring.

Back in the United States, the American diplomats were puzzled by the failure of Japan to reply promptly to the U.S. message, which they knew had arrived in Tokyo during the afternoon. The reason was simple: the foreign ministry was holding up the official message (which had actually arrived before the cabinet adjourned) so that the cabinet could not act until Togo had made his last desperate attempt for peace. All night long the lights burned brightly in the foreign ministry as Togo and his assistants tried their best.

17

THE STRUGGLE FOR DECISION

As the Japanese government leaders in Tokyo quarreled and schemed over the American peace initiative and the Potsdam provisions, at sea the war continued unabated.

On the morning of August 12, the Japanese submarine *I-58* dived at dawn; then, after a few minutes below the surface, Commander Hashimoto tentatively poked the periscope up, saw nothing on the sea around him, and brought the boat to the surface again. Commander Hashimoto was in a hurry to find the enemy and press the battle.

The submarine moved along the surface at twelve knots. Suddenly the radar operator announced a contact. Hashimoto changed course to try to get ahead of the enemy and ordered more speed. Fifteen minutes later radar had another contact, and then the lookouts saw a mast on the horizon. Commander Hashimoto gave the order to dive and the *I-58* went down. Hashimoto ordered his last two *kaiten* pilots to stand by. Petty Officer Yoshiaki Hayashi, the pilot of *kaiten* No. 3, had been disappointed several times in the past by the failure of his human torpedo before she was launched, and he had been working on the machine steadily. *Kaiten* No. 6, which had failed in the last attempt to launch it on the tenth when Hashimoto attacked the convoy, was also made ready again. But when Petty Officer Ichiro Shiraki entered the *kaiten*, once more it failed to operate. Commander Hashimoto ordered the pilots to start their engines, and No. 6 would not turn over.

In two minutes *kaiten* No. 3 was launched and moving toward the enemy formation. Through the periscope Hashimoto could see a destroyer and a large merchant vessel. As Hashimoto knew, Petty Officer Hayashi had the same view through his periscope as he sped along at thirty knots.

The captain of *I-58* watched from a distance as the *kaiten* moved. It was soon completely out of sight, and he could not even see a ripple of water to mark the passage of the periscope.

The ship Hashimoto was watching was the dock landing ship *Oak Hill*, a large, slow, and unwieldy vessel that was escorted by a destroyer escort *Nickel*, the U.S. naval authorities in the rear area having learned from the *Indianapolis* incident that the war was still in progress.

Commander Hashimoto's view of the action was very dim. He saw the big ship begin to belch black smoke (which meant the engineers were increasing the fuel consumption rapidly), and then the ship started to zigzag, which indicated to Hashimoto that the *kaiten* had been sighted. At the same time the protecting warship (Hashimoto mistook it for a destroyer instead of a destroyer escort) made what seemed to him to be a depth charge attack, and then he heard explosions which must have been depth charges. Finally he heard one final explosion and saw a column of black smoke rise into the air. He searched the horizon but could see only the destroyer, and came to the conclusion that the *kaiten* had sunk the *Oak Hill*. The big ship must have been concealed from Hashimoto's view by the destroyer escort, because the *Oak Hill* was not sunk. But aboard the *Nickel*, whose crew was indeed searching for an attacker, the lookouts saw an explosion in the water a mile astern of the *Oak Hill*. Something had again gone amiss with Petty Officer Hayashi's *kaiten*, but he did not live to explain.

Much buoyed in spirit by what he thought was yet another sinking, Commander Hashimoto prayed for the soul of the departed warrior, and then surfaced in the darkness that lowered shortly after the attack ended and headed north again, toward Okinawa.

On the morning of August 12, Admiral Halsey was still worrying about the new typhoon that had developed. This time he was well advised by Guam's Weather Central, which tracked the typhoon with a care learned from those two dreadful encounters Halsey's fleet had suffered. At 8:00 in the morning, Halsey's flagship was located about 400 miles east of the town of Sendai on Honshu island, and operations began at that point, although the flagship was prepared to move quickly to escape the typhoon. The course of the typhoon was not determined until later in the day when Guam reported that it was fixed at the moment at a point southeast of the main Japanese islands and heading eastward. It posed no threat to the fleet.

By the time the word was received from Guam it was too late to launch any air strikes, so the fleet moved southwest to hit the Tokyo area the next day. There was no question about letting up on the Japanese.

Back at Guam, Admiral Nimitz was making tentative plans in the event of a Japanese surrender. He announced to Halsey that if it occurred he intended to join the fleet immediately and fly his flag on the battleship *South Dakota*. The ship was made ready, and the commander of the battleship squadron shifted over to another battleship, the *Alabama*.

But Nimitz did not stir from Guam. Nobody knew what was happening in Tokyo.

In Washington the delay in Tokyo created an atmosphere of anxiety unmatched since the early days of the war when the U.S. was suffering one defeat after another. Reporters wandered aimlessly about the White House executive office (the old State Department building, next door to the White House), buttonholing anyone they thought might have information about the delay. No one had any solid report to make, and so the radio reporters and newspapermen speculated as their deadlines approached and passed. It was Sunday in Washington, and most of the offices of government were closed down. But in the Pentagon and at the State Department the lights burned late, as they did in Tokyo but for a different reason. Assuming that a surrender was imminent, the Americans made plans as Foreign Minister Togo prepared his desperate arguments in what seemed to be a losing cause. If, when the cabinet assembled in Tokyo a few hours later, Prime Minister Suzuki could not be expected to hold his position of readherence to the surrender (and Togo had very little confidence), then the cause was indeed lost, and Japan would reject the American message and be subjected thereafter to a renewed onslaught of atomic weapons. But in Washington this crisis in Tokyo was virtually unsuspected. The planning went on.

Truman had designated General MacArthur as supreme commander for the Allied powers, and the word was sent off to China, Britain, and the U.S.S.R. that this had been done. MacArthur would accept the Japanese surrender, and representatives of each of the other three powers would be invited to attend. It had not yet been decided where the surrender would take place. As for local surrenders, the Japanese forces in various areas would surrender to the troops they were fighting.

The skies above Japan were quiet on August 12 for a change. Halsey's planes were waiting out the typhoon, and on the day before President Truman had suspended the operations of the B-29s while awaiting the Japanese reply to the message. The absence of attack in these critical hours certainly did nothing to press the militarists into abandoning their hardline position.

In the north of Manchuria the Japanese Fourth Army was fighting a desperate battle to hold the advancing Russians at Heiho, Hailar, and Aigun. They launched a counterattack at Wuchakou, 175 miles northwest of Taonan, to stop the Russians pushing down from Outer Mongolia. The Second Air Army launched hundreds of kamikazes that day to strike the tanks of the advancing Soviet armored divisions. The desperate attack did not stop the Soviets, and General Yamada could see what was coming. On August 12 he moved the headquarters of the Kwantung Army south from Hsinking, the capital of the Japanese puppet state, to Tunghua, 175 miles south. Hsinking probably would have to be sacrificed for the moment, although General Yamada had no intention of giving up the struggle. He was planning a counterattack that would move from the southeast around to flank the Russians and cut Vladivostok and eastern Siberia off from the invading forces. With Vladivostok in Japanese hands the Soviets could move equipment and troops only overland or via the trans-Siberian rail line, and that narrow corridor was extremely vulnerable. General Yamada was convinced that in the end Japan would score a victory, and the brave and effective attack of the kamikazes in the northwest strengthened his resolve.

Aboard Admiral Halsey's flagship the *Missouri,* orders were being prepared to carry out the sense of the discussions of the possibility of Japanese surrender. Halsey had organized a landing force that consisted of a regiment of marines, three battalions of sailors from Task Force 38, and one battalion from the British Task Force 37. If more men were needed to take over Yokosuka naval base, the symbol of surrender, then Halsey could muster another five battalions. The plans included taking over airfields and manning them with Americans, even manning Japanese naval vessels if necessary. The locations of the prisoner of war camps were spotted, and rescue missions organized to get to work as soon as the word came.

On the night of August 12, Halsey was in his cabin aboard the *Missouri* when Rear Admiral Robert Carney, his chief of staff, came in with an intercepted message. It was a radio broadcast from the Army News Service, announcing that Secretary Byrnes had sent off the acceptance of the Japanese surrender

with the condition that the Emperor be retained. It was unofficial, but the report triggered a staff meeting that night. Most
of Halsey's staff wanted to suspend operations pending the
official announcements. They were sure the Japanese had given
up. Halsey agreed with them, and gave orders to be passed to
Admiral McCain to cancel the air strikes for the morning of
August 13 and hold off until further notice. But Halsey had no
sooner sent off that message than Admiral Carney was back in
the commander's cabin with more arguments. If the Japanese
did not surrender—and Carney reminded Halsey that the Japanese had not proved trustworthy in the past (a position he knew
Halsey had always taken)—then the cost in American lives might
be far greater, for Admiral McCain had steadfastly maintained
that the Japanese had thousands of aircraft still ready to fight
and the gasoline to fight with.

Halsey was susceptible to this argument because he did not
trust the Japanese. And so he countermanded his own order
late that night, and the air strikes for August 13 were back on
the board.

Admiral McCain was worried about kamikaze attacks. He expected that at some point the Japanese would unveil their air
armada, and this time, with all the talk about a surrender that
had not developed, seemed to him a most logical one. He warned
the task force to keep alert for tricks. There had been so much
talk about surrender that some of the pilots were less than wary,
and McCain wanted to reassure them that the war was anything
but over at the moment.

But the problem was complicated that night when Admiral
Nimitz ordered Halsey to cancel his next day's air strike and
then proceed to the Tokyo area "with caution." That represented Washington's hope that the message from the State Department to Japan had already been accepted, and was issued
before the President and others became wary when the Japanese delayed their response.

That message of apparent peace came in to Halsey's flagship
just after midnight on August 13, but was followed almost

within the hour by another, telling Halsey to ignore the first one. Confusing, but Halsey then sent word to the ships that the strike was to be made the next morning as planned.

Five hundred miles away, General Anami, the war minister, was struggling somehow to create conditions of surrender that would leave the army intact. He called on Prince Mikasa, one of the Emperor's closest advisors, and asked him to intercede with the Emperor in behalf of the army. Prince Mikasa was the youngest of the Emperor's three brothers. He had been a soldier in the cavalry but now was serving as a member of the staff of the inspector general of the air army. Mikasa told General Anami to stop trying to subvert the decision of the Emperor and pointed out coldly that the army had been acting contrary to the imperial will since the Manchurian incident fabricated in 1931, which had begun the events that led to the Pacific war.

Earlier in the day, General Anami had called on Marquis Kido, the lord keeper of the privy seal, and another man extremely close to the emperor. Lord Kido had not offered the army any encouragement.

Leaving no stone unturned, the war minister had summoned Marshal Hata, one of the army's most respected figures, to come up from Hiroshima where he was organizing the defense of Kyushu against the planned invasion, to help convince the Emperor that the army must not be dissolved.

At 4:00 on the morning of August 13, the full striking power of the Third Fleet's air task force was launched against Japanese targets, from the Tokyo area north to Sendai. As dawn came the planes were winging their way, and as the sun came up they were crossing the coastline to make the attacks.

The Japanese attitude toward the war seemed to have changed recently on the operational level. As Halsey had noted attacks against the task force the last time it maneuvered near the Japanese coast, so this time too a number of aircraft came out to try to run the gauntlet of the combat air patrol. Most of the

Japanese planes were shot down miles from the carriers, but some did get through to within gunner's distance of the ships, and they were then destroyed either by the guns or by pursuing fighters.

As for the target area, once again there was no opposition from the air to the Halsey planes. The American and British fighters and bombers destroyed 250 Japanese planes that day on the ground and damaged another 150.

Halsey had expected to send planes against some industrial targets on Honshu island, but most of the cities chosen were in areas with thick cloud cover, so the planes concentrated on airfields. After a heavy day, the Japanese tried one old trick. As evening came and darkness began to lower over the task force, the Japanese launched one of those low-level torpedo attacks—but this time using flying bombs—against the force.

The Third Fleet was not caught napping. All the Japanese planes were destroyed before they could damage a single ship.

On August 13 in Manchuria, the Soviets drove toward Hsinking and Mukden with three armies. The Zabaikal Area Army was operating along the Inner Mongolia and western Manchurian fronts. It consisted of four infantry divisions, spearheaded by two tank divisions, three tank brigades, and a cavalry division. In eastern Manchuria and North Korea, the Soviets sent the First Far East Area Army, consisting of ten infantry divisions, one tank corps and one extra tank division, plus two independent tank brigades. General Meretskov was in command. In the north of Manchuria the Soviets operated with the Second Far East Area Army, which consisted of four infantry divisions and one tank brigade under General Purkayev. Although slowed in the west, the Soviets were moving satisfactorily from the north and in the east.

On the morning of August 13, the chiefs of the army and navy were prepared to resist the demands of the civilians in government and insist on the continuation of the war, no matter what the

Voice of the Sacred Crane had said. In a sense they would be destroying the governmental system of Japan, but if they did not do so, the government was going to cause their destruction by surrendering to the enemy—an enemy whose implacability in Germany had already shown that the major military figures could expect to be tried as war criminals; an enemy who had announced flatly that the military system of Japan would be destroyed and would never be allowed to rise again.

General Anami and General Umezu and Admiral Toyoda spoke together and agreed to offer a united front against the surrender. In the meeting of the Supreme War Council that day they did so, and insisted that the surrender offer be withdrawn in view of the new American note. The Emperor could not be subjected to the orders of foreigners, and Japan must not be compelled to submit its form of government to the will of the common people.

Foreign Minister Togo replied that only in terms of the surrender was the Emperor's authority at stake (which was hardly true), and that the Japanese people were so thoroughly loyal to the imperial system that they would never renounce it in favor of some other form of government.

The military men, who distrusted the Japanese people almost as much as they distrusted the enemy, were not convinced.

The argument in the Supreme War Council came to nothing; it went around and around. It was repeated a few hours later at the meeting of the cabinet.

The hours went by, the Americans fretted in Washington, and no answer was prepared in Tokyo. But out of these discussions came enough fragments of information for the Allies to learn that the surrender terms were under serious discussion in Tokyo. That bit of information explained why Japan had not replied to the American note, although it did not give any indication of the ferocity of the discussions or the growing strength of the military party in this matter.

Meeting at the offices of the army military affairs bureau on the evening of August 13, several generals and admirals and lesser officers agreed that something outside the parliamentary system had to be done. They sent Admiral Ohnishi, the man who had devised the idea of the kamikaze corps, to see Prince Takamatsu at the Imperial Palace. Takamatsu, another younger brother of the Emperor, trained for the navy as Mikasa had been trained for the army, was to be asked to urge Navy Minister Yonai and Admiral of the Fleet Nagano to come out for the militarists and force the government to ask the Emperor to change his position. Prince Takamatsu asked Admiral Ohnishi that if the Emperor were to ask that the war be continued, just what would the army or the navy do to change the course of events?

Admiral Ohnishi could offer no realistic plan to strike the enemy the sort of blow that would be needed to stop the invasion of Japan. Prince Takamatsu sent him away with a refusal.

At the same time that Ohnishi went to see Prince Takamatsu, Commander Dohi went to see Admiral Nagano and Admiral Tomioka visited Admiral Koshiro Oikawa. Captain Toshikazu Ohmae called on Admiral Naokuni Nomura and Nobutake Kondo.

After Ohnishi had failed, he returned to his own office in the navy ministry, where he was vice chief of staff. There he found Captain Rikihei Inoguchi waiting in the darkness. He told his weary tale of refusal because neither army nor navy had a plan that might even possibly affect the outcome of the war, except national resistance to the end, which the prince had called suicidal.

Inoguchi suggested that Ohnishi return to see Prince Takamatsu and pretend to accept the Emperor's decision but ask that Hirohito make one last concession to tradition. The tradition to be invoked was a visit to the Grand Shrine at Ise, dedicated to Amaterasu Omikami, the sun Goddess and legendary founder of the nation of Japan. The shrine contains the Mirror, one of the three Great Treasures of Japan, and to this spot all Emperors had come in past to report on grave affairs of state to the imperial ancestors. Inoguchi suggested that Ohnishi persuade the royal family to send the Emperor or a representative on this mission. This delay would give the men opposed to the surrender a few more days in which to prepare. Ohnishi could not make the appointment. He had destroyed his credence in the original interview. But he asked Inoguchi, an intimate of Takamatsu's, to undertake the task. Inoguchi agreed, but the events of the next few days prevented his seeing the prince, and by the time it became possible it was too late.

In Washington as the word filtered through that the Japanese were having internal difficulties with the surrender problem, President Truman began to lose his patience. Among his advisors were some who advocated the drop of another atomic bomb, and the materials were available. He waited, but none too patiently, as the hours ticked by.

18

PLOT

On the night of August 13, as the military faction struggled to regain control of the nation, several members of the Imperial General Staff visited General Anami at his house in Tokyo. Colonel Arao, chief of the military affairs section, was the leader of them, and he came out openly to tell Anami that it was time to strike a coup d'etat, throw out the present cabinet, and set up a military oligarchy that would tell the Emperor what he must do. General Anami listened, and said nothing. But later in the evening he went to the war ministry, where he felt safe from an assassination attempt, and summoned Arao to his office. He told Arao then that he could not agree to a coup d'etat, and the colonel left seething, but still convincing himself that Anami really did not mean what he said and that he supported a coup.

War Minister Anami then summoned Lieutenant General Sanji Okido, the chief of the military police in the Tokyo area. Okido was every inch an army man, once a member of the military affairs bureau of the army. He had been a field commander in China, chief of staff of the North China army in the end, and an official of the war ministry before taking his post as military police chief. He was responsible for the safety of the community. Anami was general in his discussion with Okido, but he warned him to accept no orders that purported to come from the war ministry unless they were issued by himself or his vice minister. The meaning was very clear: look out for something unpleasant.

After dismissing Okido, War Minister Anami called in the commander of the imperial guard division, Lieutenant General Takeshi Mori, and warned him to be more careful than ever before in guarding the Imperial Palace against all comers—no matter how high their rank.

General Anami's apparent contradiction of attitudes was real in a sense. At this late date in history, Anami had adopted the same philosophy about the war that Admiral Yamamoto had at the beginning: Yamamoto had said before Pearl Harbor that if Japan got into war with the U.S., which he bemoaned, then the only solution was to get a quick victory and bring the Americans to the peace table before they could bring their enormous productive potential into full gear. Yamamoto had died lamenting the lost opportunities, and now, more than three years later, General Anami was coming around to the same position. But it was much too late, as he should have known. For Anami was completely familiar with the Japanese army's true situation. He knew of the shortage of metals, the almost total end of the gasoline in the nation except for those reserves for the "last battle." He knew of the massive destruction recently of the military factories, of the inability of the aviation experts to produce enough planes because of power failures and shortages of copper and other materials.

In Washington the leaders of the United States government were growing irritated over the continued Japanese delay. By the morning of August 14 it was apparent that there were serious complications in Tokyo and, knowing this, the American government doubled its efforts to break the deadlock. A few things could be done: one was to continue, even increase, the tempo of air attack against Japan. President Truman ordered the suspended B-29 flights to Japan to resume. Generals Spaatz and LeMay planned to put 1,000 planes over Japan that day. Another move that Truman could make was to authorize the dropping of leaflets announcing the terms of the American offer for the surrender. The Japanese government had not informed the Japanese people of the facts. The Americans had known that all along by monitoring Japanese radio broadcasts, but had refrained from interfering in the belief that it might do more harm than good. But under the circumstances, the wraps were taken off and American planes were dispatched to Tokyo. Seven B-29s appeared that morning to drop five million leaflets announcing the American plan. The ploy succeeded to an extent undreamed by the psychological warriors. Keeper of the Privy Seal Kido picked up one of the leaflets in a Tokyo street and took it to the Imperial Palace and sought immediate audience with the Emperor.

Kido told the Emperor what he knew of the militarists' scheming in recent hours and of War Minister Anami's call on him in the effort to persuade the Emperor to revoke his decision to end the war. Foreign Minister Togo was surrounded by enemies; Prime Minister Suzuki vacillated by the hour but always came back to the militarist point of view, and there was grave danger that the young officers would stage a coup d'etat. Even the Emperor's avowed wish was not enough to stop them at this critical point.

Emperor Hirohito listened to his councillor and agreed that the political situation had reached an ignition point. Kido suggested that the Emperor must take strong and immediate action, to convene an imperial conference. No one, not even General Anami, could refuse to respond to the Emperor's call.

The Emperor agreed, but before he called the conference, he and Kido arranged to notify Fleet Admiral Nagano and Field Marshals Sugiyama and Hata, the senior statesmen of the navy and army who were then in Japan. They came to the palace, and the Emperor explained the gravity of the situation and asked them to see the younger officers and make sure that the army and navy remained obedient to the imperial will.

As all these meetings were taking place, Prime Minister Suzuki arrived at the Imperial Palace in one of his conciliatory moods and agreed that the Emperor must act. So Hirohito summoned the Supreme War Council for an extraordinary session, knowing that no member dare refuse.

In Peking, the North China Expeditionary Army was preparing to transfer six divisions, six brigades, and all available tank units and aircraft to the Manchurian front in support of General Yamada's counteroffensive. The orders were going out on August 14 as the morning wore along.

At 6:00 on the morning of August 14, Admiral Halsey's Third Fleet was moving slowly off the coast of Japan, taking on fuel again. Actually, Halsey should have broken off by now and gone back to Ulithi for major resupply. The fleet had been more than forty days at sea without surcease, and basic stores were running short. But with the thought of impending Japanese surrender, some Allied force had to be on hand, and Halsey's was the only one available. So the men would have to get along on dehydrated foods and whatever was left in cans.

The fuelling was finished in the middle of the afternoon and the task force then headed for a launching point to strike the Japanese early the next morning. The targets would be airfields, rail lines, ports, and industrial plants in the Tokyo area. Several ships were sent back to Iwo Jima to pick up loads of Japanese translators and interpreters, just in case the Japanese surrendered.

On the morning of August 14, as the B-29s set out for Japan, two Dumbo rescue planes were ordered into the air from Ryukyus bases, and five P-38s of the 35th Army Air Force Fighter Squadron were assigned to follow them over the course from Kyushu to the Inland Sea. For once the Japanese air force decided to come out; six fighters attacked the American formation over the Inland Sea. Captain Raymon F. Meyer shot down one in his first pass, and another when he spotted it on the tail of a P-38, gave chase and came up on the enemy's tail, then sent the plane crashing into the sea. Captain Billy G. Moore saw another enemy fighter on the tail of a P-38 and shot it away. Lieutenant Dwight Hollister accounted for one more Japanese fighter, and so did Lieutenant George Stevens.

But the Americans lost one plane and pilot to a very brave Japanese flier. The Japanese fighter was under attack by two P-38s, one flown by Captain Moore and the other by Lieutenant Duane L. Keiffer. They were chasing the single-engine Japanese fighter up the coast, and the P-38s had the advantage of greater speed so they were coming up on the Japanese plane. Captain Moore moved up onto the Japanese plane's tail and began firing. Lieutenant Keiffer came up fast, overshot, and pulled up in a climb directly in front of the Japanese fighter. The Japanese pilot ignored Moore's firing behind him, turned in a climb and fired into Keiffer's right engine, which began to burn. The plane spun into the sea, and the Japanese plane then maneuvered and escaped.

Other pilots of the Air Force Fifth Fighter Command were over Japan. Lieutenant Joe Ozier led a dozen P-51 Mustangs on an antishipping strike off the southwest coast of Kyushu. There was not much out there to attack, but they did destroy some small vessels. They had been warned against attacking shore installations because the war situation was so confused.

The confusion ended at 11:00 on the morning of August 14, as far as Japan was concerned. The Supreme War Council assembled in the palace air raid shelter for the conference called by Hirohito just a few hours earlier. Some of the members had left home in informal summer clothes, open-necked shirts and trousers. They had to scurry around their offices borrowing jackets and neckties from subordinates, since it would never do to appear before the Emperor in informal costume. Under normal conditions they would have been in court uniform, but these were anything but normal hours.

The Emperor again called for the various participants to state their views on the war, and the military party made all the arguments: that Japan would be enslaved by the Americans, that the imperial system would be overthrown, and even that the Emperor might be tried as a war criminal by the enemy. Foreign Minister Togo once more stated his position that the government had no alternative but to surrender.

Then the Emperor began to speak.

He agreed with the foreign minister that the manner in which the surrender was offered did not threaten the continued existence of Japan or the imperial system. But if the government persisted in carrying on this disastrous war, he feared that the nation would indeed be destroyed.

"It is therefore my wish," he said, "that we bear the unbearable and accept the Allied reply, thus to preserve the state as a state and spare my subjects further suffering. I wish you all to act in that intention."

There it was, the direct order of the Emperor. This was not the Voice of the Sacred Crane offering advice to his governors, but the voice of the Son of Heaven directing his subjects on a course.

The Emperor continued to discuss the plight of his poor people, those who suffered from the war and those who had lost so many hundreds of thousands of sons and husbands and brothers. He knew his decision would come as a shock to the military forces, so long trained in the philosophy of total victory and no surrender, but he was prepared to speak directly to the troops. He would indeed break all tradition and speak directly to the nation over the radio. He asked the government to draw up an imperial rescript that would announce the end of the war.

As the Emperor said these words, the men around him began to break down. Several of them wept openly in contemplation of the straits to which Empire and Emperor were reduced. The Emperor arose and left the bomb shelter. The imperial conference ended just after noon in a shattering silence.

On the afternoon of August 14, Foreign Minister Togo's office prepared a translation of the Japanese into several languages, announcing the acceptance of the American terms of surrender. The Emperor promised to issue commands to all military naval and air authorities to cease operations and surrender their arms as required by the Supreme Commander of the Allied Powers. In fact, the Emperor's family was already moving out to various key centers to prepare the way for the shock. Soon the message was radioed to Switzerland, where the Swiss government was asked to relay the word to the Allies.

Late on the afternoon of August 14 in Washington the American minister's office in Bern telephoned the secretary of state to announce the Emperor's surrender. Secretary Byrnes hurried to the President's office as his assistants were preparing a message for the Allied powers. The airwaves began to hum with messages, to the Japanese government, to General MacArthur, to Admiral Nimitz, all aimed at bringing an end to hostilities and preparing for the formal Japanese surrender. The news was released to press and radio, and Americans gathered in the streets to cheer. In New York, London, Chungking, and a hundred other places the joy of victory reigned.

But not in Moscow. The Soviets were scarcely embarked on their conquest of Manchuria. They wanted to reach Mukden and Port Arthur, and Seoul in Korea before stopping their drive. Thus they could assure themselves a special position in the postwar world in Asia.

At midnight on the fourteenth, T. V. Soong, representing Chiang Kai-shek's Nationalist government, and Premier Stalin finally worked out the details of a series of treaties that were supposed to regulate Sino-Soviet relationships in the future. To the Nationalists, the most important part was apparent Soviet acceptance of the position of the Nationalist government as *the* government of China, and the apparent abandonment by Stalin of Mao Tse-tung's Communist Party which actually controlled much of North China and Manchuria. To the Russians, the important matter was a special position that the agreements gave the U.S.S.R. in Manchuria. That latter worried the Americans more than a little, but there was nothing to be done about it.

On the morning of August 14, the American submarine *Spikefish* was travelling on the surface of the South China Sea not far from Shanghai. There had been very little action; the nearest thing to a ship that had been sighted was a Chinese junk. Like all the other U.S. submarines these days, the *Spikefish* was suffering from a shortage of targets. The last important ship to be sunk had been the *Teihoku Maru*, a 6,000-ton passenger freighter torpedoed by the *Jallao* a few days earlier. Since then the American submarines had reported back to Pacific Fleet headquarters that they had found nothing.

But later on August 14, the *Spikefish* had spotted a Japanese submarine travelling on the surface. She approached, fired her torpedoes, and sank her. The war was not over yet.

In the army headquarters center at Ichigaya Heights in the Ushigome district of Tokyo, General Anami and General Umezu dutifully issued the orders demanded by the Emperor: the troops were to lay down their arms and accept the imperial will.

But elsewhere in the offices of the military men at Ichigaya Heights, small groups assembled to discuss the unthinkable decision of the Emperor. Here were located not only the war ministry and the army section of Imperial General Headquarters, but the general staff, the inspector general, the army air force headquarters, and the headquarters of the armored forces. The staff officers were still in shock that afternoon. The disbandment of the army, for this was what must happen, would mean the change in Japanese ways in any fashion that the occupying forces demanded. No one in the world understood the Japanese spirit, said the officers, and thus no one could be expected to appreciate it. The Emperor's decision meant the end of everything.

Did Emperor Hirohito have the right to go against all that the Japanese military had established? The younger officers said no —he had no such right—and because Hirohito had passed the barrier, to disobey his direct order was to act in compliance with the will of his ancestors. Therefore a coup d'etat was the only solution to this intolerable situation.

Foreign Minister Togo was simply parroting the enemy's propaganda. The Japanese people were not going to be wiped out by atomic bombs or even by fighting, not even if it should extend back into the mountains of the homeland. The young officers pointed to the "China Incident": during their invasion of China, in spite of constant Japanese victories and occupation of territory, relatively few Chinese soldiers were killed or captured. Indeed, one of the burdens of the Pacific war had been the implacable struggle of the Chinese. Although Japan had occupied the entire eastern seaboard of China (with a few minor exceptions) and had taken all the major cities, the Nationalists had simply moved and moved, finally to Chungking in the far west. In the north, Mao Tse-tung's communist forces had holed up in the caves of Yenan, and their Eighth Route and Fourth Route Armies had made life miserable for the Japanese occupation forces for four years.

The Emperor was behaving in a wrong-headed fashion, said the officers talking in the rooms of Ichigaya Heights that evening. The Emperor was under the influence of evil advisors. They must be destroyed, the Emperor must be rescued from his error, and the war must go on to preserve the Japanese spirit. For even if the whole nation were virtually destroyed, that spirit would be forever recorded in history, and the souls of Japanese departed could rest. The national will must not be sacrificed on the altar of materialism.

This religious haranguing by the few appealed to the deep-seated longings of the young officers at headquarters, and soon the officers were talking about killing the members of the peace faction immediately and establishing a military dictatorship under General Anami to carry on the war. The fervor grew. The nucleus of officers announced readiness to act.

In various headquarters offices on Ichigaya Heights the lights burned late, for opposing reasons. In some offices, men in khaki uniforms were burning secret papers. The rumor spread through the headquarters that a powerful American landing force was standing just off Tokyo Bay and that the Americans were prepared to pounce at any moment. Someone said that the Americans would send in paratroops to Ichigaya Heights at dawn, to captured imperial headquarters.

The military affairs bureau was the center of the revolutionary spirit that night. The plan was made: first the imperial guard division would be taken over and the Imperial Palace surrounded, the Emperor made prisoner within his compound. Whether or not the Emperor's person would be touched was a matter not developed. Once the palace was in the conspirators' hands, they would seek the Eastern Army's adherence.

Late that night the young officers set out on their "holy" mission. They went directly to the headquarters of General Mori, the commander of the division. Their visit was not unexpected: they had come to call on General Mori two days earlier to sound out his views on the projected revolution. He had told them then that no matter how little he liked the prospect of surrender, as commander of the imperial guard he had a special obligation to the Emperor. Even if General Anami gave him a direct order, if it contravened the decision of the Emperor, General Mori was unable to act.

Late on the night of August 14, the young rebels came again. The die was cast. They were committed to their plot.

19

THE SMELL OF DEFEAT

At around midnight on August 14, Major Hataka of the war ministry staff and a group of other young officers returned to General Mori's headquarters and demanded entry. Other young officers and some guards went to the homes of Prime Minister Suzuki and Marquis Kido, both known to be ardent advocates of surrender. Their intention was to find the two men and murder them, but they did not find them. Others went to talk to officers of the imperial guards, persuaded them that General Mori was being enlisted in the plot, and set off for Radio Tokyo to try to seize and suppress any information about surrender, including the recording the Emperor had finished that evening at the palace in which he read his own imperial rescript.

At Atsugi airfield, about thirty miles south of Tokyo, young kamikaze pilots, learning of the surrender plan, made up thousands of leaflets demanding the continuation of the war, and then flew them over Tokyo and dropped them.

At 2:00 in the morning, the young officers led by Major Hataka burst into General Mori's presence and demanded that he join their rebellion. The general said he was just on his way to the Meiji Shrine where he intended to pray and seek divine guidance as to the role he should adopt.

Was that the final answer, Major Hataka used. The general indicated that he was going to the Meiji Shrine before he did anything else, whereupon Hataka pulled out a revolver and shot him to death. He then walked outside and told the others, "I have disposed of him for fear that we may only waste more time."

The young rebels, joined by some of the imperial guard, then went to the imperial palace to force entry. What they would do with the Emperor if they were successful was never stated, but the implication was clear in the plot that Hirohito's life might be sacrificed in the interests of the militarists. False orders to the imperial guards persuaded some of the guards around the palace that the rebels were acting on orders—but not all, and a confrontation followed between the rebels and the royal guardsmen. The rebels tried to bluff their way through, but General Shizuichi Tanaka, commander of the Eastern Army, got word of the false orders that had been issued. Fearing for the life of the Emperor, he rushed with troops to the palace in time to confront the plotters. There, inside the palace grounds, loyal guardsmen and the disloyal scuffled. General Tanaka made it quite clear to the plotters that the palace was surrounded and their coup was at an end. Major Hataka, seeing that the move had failed, took his own life with his pistol on the imperial plaza.

Even as the scuffling occurred, War Minister Anami was at his home in Tokyo, committing hara-kiri. He left a private will for his family and a public will for the nation; in the latter he apologized for all that had happened. If there had been any further thought by others of rebellion, it ended then.

As the sun broke out over Tokyo the next morning of August 15, the Emperor's aides prepared for the announcement. The transcription of the Emperor's rescript was taken to Radio Tokyo and at noon it was broadcast to Japan and the world.

The vast majority of the Japanese people had never before heard the voice of their Emperor, but there was no mistaking the message. Surrender. Japan must face the agony of total defeat, and the Emperor called on his people to do so with fortitude.

In Washington the plans had already been made and there were no surprises. Relieved by the knowledge that there were no serious complications in Tokyo, President Truman turned his attention to other matters. His experience at Potsdam had given him a clear distrust of the Soviets, and now on August 15 he directed the cabinet and the Joint Chiefs of Staff to take steps to be sure that no information about the atomic bomb be released except by Presidential order.

In Manila, General MacArthur issued his first directives as Supreme Commander for the Allied Powers. He sent a message to the Emperor, the prime minister, and Imperial General Headquarters, directing them to order Japanese troops everywhere to lay down their arms at once. As soon as he had a time given by the Japanese for cessation of warfare, he would issue orders to the Allied troops.

MacArthur then sent preparatory messages to all commanders of units fighting the Japanese. To Moscow he sent a message through the U.S. embassy and the Russians ignored it. General A.I. Antonov, the Soviet chief of staff, said only the supreme commander of the armed forces of the U.S.S.R. could issue such an order. The reason, of course, was that the Russians were still moving south in Manchuria and intended to continue doing so until they had captured the rich industrial area of the southeast, which they would milk to replace industry lost in the war against Germany.

At least that is one interpretation. Another is that the Russians were extremely touchy and simply resented MacArthur's general order.

At dawn on August 15, a rash of suicides decimated the ranks of the militarists. Vice Admiral Matome Ugaki, commander of Japan's Fifth Air Fleet at Kanoya, had been one of the leading organizers of the kamikaze flying corps. He had moved his headquarters many times, and most recently in the face of the determined attacks on the airfields by Admiral McCain's Task Force 38, Ugaki had taken Fifth Air Fleet headquarters from Kanoya in southern Kyushu to Oita in the northeastern section of the island. The base was nothing like the air bases of the past. The command post was established in a bunker in a hillside southeast of the airstrip. The aircraft were stored underground, in the hillside, and in concealed revetments miles from the field.

Although little attention was paid to the operations of the kamikaze corps in the last weeks of the war, the attacks had continued. Japanese records showed that after the attack on the *Borie* on August 9, Admiral Ugaki had ordered a flight off on the eleventh to attack Okinawa, and another on August 13. American records did not indicate that any of these missions were successful, but they were a part of the continued Japanese war effort of the early days of August.

After the abortive coup of the night of August 14, Admiral Ugaki and his staff knew that next day would come the Emperor's call for surrender. In Ugaki's view, that decision made a mockery of his life, and subjected him to the most severe sort of criticism for trying to preserve Japan's sense of honor above that of life. Under those conditions he felt he could not live out the day.

As dawn came, Admiral Ugaki announced plans for a kamikaze attack that very morning on Okinawa. He told his staff that he intended to lead this attack himself.

The staff and other officers argued with the admiral, but without success. They came to his quarters, which consisted of a couch and a desk in a cave in the hillside. They protested that the war was now over and that the admiral had a responsibility to live and help rebuild Japan.

Ugaki was implacable. All that he had stood for during his professional life had now been denied by the Emperor's decision to surrender. That decision had made a mockery of the militarist position from the day of the Manchuria Incident trumped up by the Kwantung Army to begin Japan's conquest of China.

The younger officers hoped that Admiral Yokoi, chief of staff and second in command of the Fifth Air Fleet, could have some influence on Ugaki, and they got him out of a sick bed to plead with their commander. But neither could Yokoi sway the admiral.

"Please allow me the right to choose my own death," he said. In the Japanese tradition there was no answer to that argument. But Yokoi then sought out Admiral Ugaki's close friend Admiral Takatsugu Jojima. The latter approached Ugaki one more time, but again Ugaki refused him. "This is my chance to die like a warrior," he said. And in these hours of failure that was the only matter of importance to him; honor gone, success denied him, hundreds of young lives sacrificed in what now turned out to be useless suicides, Admiral Ugaki had no will to live, and a great will to die.

But the admiral did agree to wait until the Emperor had actually made his broadcast before taking off on the last suicide mission. His subordinates, playing every chord, convinced him that there was at least a chance that the Emperor would change his mind at the last minute and decide to continue Japan's path to glory.

During the morning, Radio Tokyo announced repeatedly that at noon the Emperor would address the nation. At Oita as everywhere else across the Japanese islands, the radios were tuned. As noon approached the senior officers of the command assembled at headquarters to hear the Emperor's words. The speech began with heavy static, and the playing of the Japanese national anthem. Then came a hoarse voice through the static, identified as that of Prime Minister Suzuki. Finally, someone else began to speak, in a high-pitched but melodic tone. The airmen, who had never heard the imperial voice before, realized it was their Emperor. Much of what the Emperor said was lost in static and much of the rest of it was cloaked in the special language of the imperial court, but the idea came through plainly: Japan had lost the war and must surrender to force majeure.

Until that moment, Admiral Ugaki seemed to have a ray of hope that the Emperor would reconsider, but with those words from the radio, hope was extinguished.

It did no good for others to argue duty to the Emperor as one of his senior officers, to assist in the dissolution of the navy in the most honorable way and then try to rebuild. Some around him wondered how he could conceivably make an attack on the enemy after the Emperor's direct order for every military man to lay down his arms. But Ugaki did not answer these questions, and in the final analysis only he knew what he was about to do.

His staff, assembling the last of the delicacies left to any of them, gave a small party for the admiral. His main thought was the failure of the kamikaze effort, and he apologized to them and called on them to cooperate with each other during the difficult days to come. The admiral then stripped off all his insignia of rank, and, armed with a short samurai sword and a pair of binoculars, he prepared for his last flight.

At the airstrip, although he had ordered up a unit of only three planes, he found eleven planes on the line and twenty-two fliers who insisted on accompanying him to his death. He climbed into one of the planes, taking the place of one of the observers. The young man refused to be left behind, and squeezed into the narrow seat beside the admiral. Thus the eleven planes took off, heading for Okinawa.

On the way, the Admiral sent his farewell message, revealing clearly what had been on his mind all these last hours. He alone was to blame for the failure to defend Japan against the Americans, he said. He would now attack the enemy in the true spirit of *bushido*, in the faith of the eternity of Japan, but his men must stay and rebuild so that Japan would survive.

The sun was going down when that last message came through, and then a brief report by one pilot that the force was "attacking the enemy."

What Admiral Ugaki or the others saw that evening in the growing darkness is unknown, but there was no American record of any kamikaze attack on the night of August 15. No one can ever know precisely what happened, because none of the eleven aircraft of Admiral Ugaki's little squadron ever came home.

On the morning of August 15, as Admiral Ugaki prepared for death, Admiral Halsey's Third Fleet was preparing to hammer Japan again. At 4:15 in the morning the combat air patrol was put up over the task force, and 103 planes of the first sweep set out for the Tokyo area. They attacked airfields in the area.

Much to the surprise of the Americans, the Japanese air force men decided to oppose the attacks. The first wave was met by determined opposition, and air fights began, near Kashima and Hyakurigahara.

Aboard the *Yorktown* (and other carriers) the first strike was off by 5:00 and soon began hitting the target. The second strike was scheduled to fly off at about 7:00, but at 6:30 orders were received from Admiral Nimitz to cease operations. The Japanese had surrendered, said the message. The war was over.

The war was not over yet, however, for the airmen of the first strike. As the message came through, many of them were locked in combat with Japanese fliers, and men were still dying on each side.

When the call came from the carrier to return to base, the pilots of the *Yorktown* turned back, but were intercepted by about twenty Japanese fighters. Lieutenant (j.g.) Joseph G. Sahloff was shot down by flak over Atsugi airfield. Three other *Yorktown* pilots were shot down by Japanese fighters—Lieutenant H. M. Harrison, Ensign W. C. Hobbs, and Ensign E. E. Mandeburg —and a number of pilots from other carriers were also lost.

Eight P-51s from the 35th Army Air Force Fighter squadron were also in the air over Japan that morning of August 15, escorting Dumbos which were sent out to guard the escape routes of the carrier pilots. They returned without incident.

By late afternoon, the planes of Task Force 38 had fought their way back to the carriers, shooting down about fifty Japanese planes. Officially the air war had ended.

DEATH AND HONOR

After the Emperor's radio broadcast was over, Admiral Ohnishi prepared for a party. That evening a number of officers of the Imperial General Naval Staff came to Ohnishi's Tokyo house to talk over the past. Ohnishi told the others he blamed himself for the failures of the special attack corps that had cost the lives of so many of Japan's young men. To be reckless, he said was only to aid the enemy. Had he been reckless? In a way it so seemed, but in the final analysis Ohnishi was not really sorry for his part in the war. He was sorry only that Japan had lost.

His more intimate friends remained late at the house talking about the good times until about midnight. Then the guests went home and Ohnishi went to his second floor study.

An hour before dawn, someone in the Ohnishi household saw the light burning and entered the room. In a moment the household was alerted: the admiral had tried to kill himself. A servant hurried to the house of his aide and roused that officer. The aide came immediately to the Ohnishi house, where he found the admiral lying on the tatami mat, blood exuding from a comma-shaped cut in his abdomen. He had used the short samurai sword in the traditional manner, plunging it into his belly and then turning it upward to destroy the vital organs. Then he had attempted to cut his own throat, but in this he had missed the carotid artery, and was bleeding only moderately from the veins. He was conscious and grimacing with the pain of the belly wound.

"Don't try to help me," he ordered the aide, and refused to let him send for a doctor. He remained as he was, then, by his own order, until he fell unconscious. But then the household respected his last wish, to be let alone to die. He lingered until nearly dark that day, and then he died.

His last written words were addressed to the young men he had exhorted so ardently in times past to commit suicide for the welfare of the nation. Now he told them they must abide by the spirit of the Emperor's decision and strive for the welfare of Japan and for peace throughout the world. Thus passed one of the most warlike of the new breed of officer class spawned in the twentieth century, and one of the architects of the Japanese sneak attack on Pearl Harbor. In the end, he had lived up to the philosophy he had urged upon the young men of his *shimpu* (suicide or divine wind) special attack corps:

> In blossom today, then scattered;
> Life is so like a delicate flower.
> How can one expect the fragrance to last forever?

On August 15, the officers and men of *I-58* were too busy to pay attention to the radio. They were running on the surface all day, searching for targets, and since they were approaching Okinawa they expected to find American ships at any moment. But finally in late afternoon, the senior radio operator caught a broadcast from Radio Tokyo's overseas station. It was a communiqué from the general staff announcing the end of hostilities and calling on all vessels at sea to return to Japan.

At first Commander Hashimoto refused to believe that the broadcast had come from Imperial Headquarters. It was an enemy trick, he announced, to force them to give away their position so they could be destroyed. Several of his officers said they believed it was real. In the past few days the news coming from Japan had been completely strange, and it seemed logical to them that somehow hostilities had ended.

Commander Hashimoto still refused to return to Japan. There was more time left on their patrol, and they must make use of every moment to strike decisive blows against the Americans. He could not make a decision on the basis of a public radio broadcast. He had no orders, and in their absence, he would follow the orders written and given him before he left Japan.

He did, however, ask the senior radioman privately to bring all wireless messages to him personally just as they came in, but to inform no one else of the order.

By this time, Commander Hashimoto was beginning to believe that the war had indeed ended, but his concern was for the safety of his boat. If the men learned of the fact and relaxed their vigilance, they might all be lost before they returned to Japan. So the *I-58* continued on patrol and continued looking for American ships, but did not find any. Had they done so, it seems likely that Commander Hashimoto, with no direct orders to the contrary, would have attacked.

Despite the commander's vigilance, the secret of the surrender was out within twenty-four hours, and one of the officers remarked slyly to Hashimoto that they seemed likely to find something surprising when they reached home. He did not reply.

At various army and navy bases around Japan officers assembled at noon on August 15 to hear the Emperor, but their reactions to the imperial rescript were mixed. At the Otake submarine school on the Inland Sea, Commander Zenji Orita had been telling students that they must fight on for Japan as long as they were alive.

Orita and other officers and men of the school were notified early in the morning that the Emperor would address the nation at noon, and were ordered to appear before the school administration building a few minutes earlier. Loudspeakers would be set up outside the building. They would appear in full uniform in parade formation, and their commander, Vice Admiral Noboru Ichikawa, would attend and preside over the occasion.

A rumor had been out for hours. Orita had heard it in mid-morning when one officer had burst into headquarters after a trip to Tokyo to announce that the Emperor had fallen prey to a handful of false advisors who had been telling him lies: that the Japanese people would not fight, and that the nation was already defeated. The officers of the submarine school were aghast: how could anyone say such a thing? Orita went to the parade believing firmly that the Emperor was going to make an appeal to the Japanese people to fight on through the one great last battle that would throw the invaders off the shores of Japan as the great wind had done in the thirteenth century when Kublai Khan tried to invade Japan.

Just before noon the officers and men assembled, and the squawking of the radio began. They heard the announcer from Radio Tokyo, then the prime minister and finally the strange voice that was their Emperor's. The electric power supply was so diminished that the static made the broadcast very hard to understand, but the terms *kofuku suru,* surrender, were unmistakable.

When the radio went dead, Admiral Ichikawa dismissed his men. They gathered in small knots outside the headquarters and in the offices, discussing the Emperor's speech. Most of them insisted that they must fight on; the Emperor had been misled, they said, and all would soon change. But others counselled that they must wait for some official word from the naval general staff before they took any action.

In an atmosphere of gloom and shock, the officers returned to their classrooms, talking again of the tactics and strategy of submarine operation as if nothing had occurred.

That afternoon and evening, rumors flew through Otake. Most of them concerned units of the armed forces which had vowed to resist surrender to the last man.

When the news of the surrender and the order to cease bombing and strafing Japanese targets was disseminated through the Third Fleet, it was greeted with sounds of joy. Admiral Halsey shouted "Yippee" and began clapping the members of his staff on the back in a most unmilitary fashion. By 10:30 all the air strikes had returned, some of them tailed by Japanese fighters, which were shot down by the combat air patrol circling above the fleet. It was apparent that if the war was over the Japanese air force still did not know it. Halsey obeyed the order to fire only in self-defense, but he told McCain to spot the decks of the carriers with fighter planes that would resist any attack "in a friendly sort of way."

It was not long before another message came from Admiral Nimitz, verifying the end of operations, but warning very clearly:

"Beware of treachery."

Halsey was already aware. Half an hour after the Nimitz message was received, a Japanese dive-bomber appeared near the fleet, coming down to attack. One of the combat air patrol planes shot the dive-bomber out of the air. During the afternoon, the combat air patrol shot down another eight planes whose pilots were carrying their personal war to the very end.

On the morning of August 16, Captain Yasuna Ozono, the commander of the Atsugi naval air base, sent half a dozen fighters over Otake base, where they dropped leaflets announcing that the Japanese naval air force was going to continue the fight against the American enemies. Captain Ozono sent other planes over other naval bases urging the officers and men to continue to fight with him in the spirit of *bushido* to the final victory of Japan over its enemies.

The leaflets raised a new storm of discussion among the submariners at Otake base. Commander Orita, who had first been inclined to join the hotheads and fight on, had reconsidered during the night. It came to him that the Emperor had made a most unpleasant decision to "bear the unbearable" and that as a Japanese officer he had an obligation to the Emperor and the nation that transcended his personal wishes. He came to Otake that morning prepared to follow the Emperor's orders, but just then the situation in Tokyo was so confused, and the Imperial General Staff so delayed in action by discussions of the high-ranking officers, that no orders were waiting.

Some of the Otake officers were determined to fight on. At the submarine station at Hirao, near the school, Lieutenant Takesuka Tateyama assembled a crew and took the *I-159* out into the Inland Sea. He had torpedoes and two *kaiten* aboard, and he vowed to find American ships and sink them.

The suicides continued on August 16. Field Marshal General Sugiyama and his wife sat down in their Tokyo house that morning and discussed the problem. Marshal Sugiyama had served as war minister, chief of the North China armies, and at the end was commander of the First General Army entrusted with the defense of Japan. Now there would be no defense. He committed suicide that day, and his wife followed him.

On August 16, the Soviet armies were moving with ease deep into Chahar province, deep into southern Manchuria and down into Korea. The western army had penetrated to within 150 miles of Peking, when at four o'clock in the afternoon radio monitors at Marshal Vasilevski's headquarters picked up a broadcast from Radio Tokyo announcing that the Emperor had ordered all forces to stop fighting, Marshal Vasilevski slowed his advance and radioed Moscow for instructions. While he was waiting he heard from General MacArthur, who had ignored the refusal of Marshal Antonov to accept the MacArthur orders. The Japanese Kwantung Army headquarters, which had just received the word from Japan that the fighting was to end, was putting the information out to the troops in the field. There was the usual tension between those officers who wished to continue the war at any cost and those accepting the Emperor's will, but General Yamada maintained control.

Thus two days after the decision to accept the American surrender terms had been made, the Emperor's decision was beginning to take effect in most places. Members of his family were on their way to Manchuria to deliver the message personally to the high officers of the almost independent Kwantung Army. The Emperor was doing his best.

MARGIN OF SAFETY

The plans that Admiral Halsey and his staff had made for occupation of Japan became reality on August 15, but soon evaporated in interservice rivalry. General MacArthur was not willing to give the navy credit for "occupying Japan," even though Halsey had the only force available and ready. The 2,000 marines aboard Third Fleet ships had been organized into a provisional regiment. The ships had provided 1,200 men for three naval battalions (one of them British). Five reserve battalions were to remain on the ships unless needed. Rear Admiral Oscar Badger had been appointed to command the expeditionary force which would move into Yokosuka naval base.

But MacArthur stopped the move. It would be ten days before he could prepare to get his troops moving from the Philippines. Halsey would simply have to wait.

While Halsey waited, troopships were brought up from Okinawa to move the navy force and the marines, and navy battalions boarded them. Bombers and fighters from the task force flew daily missions over Japan to spot prisoner of war camps, and when they had found them, they returned with the word, whereupon supplies and medicine were flown in by the bombers and dropped for the prisoners.

On the morning of August 17, Commander Orita appeared at the Otake submarine school headquarters to find that Admiral Mitsuru Nagai had come from Tokyo with orders to close down the school. He assigned Orita the task of calming down the young submariners, many of whom were talking wildly of staging personal attacks on the enemy with whatever weapons they could find. He was also assigned to burn all official records and secret documents. The same sort of orders went out to every army and navy command. (The reason for the destruction of records was multifaceted. Some officers were determined that the Americans should have no pleasure in their victory. Some were seriously concerned about war criminal charges, quite rightly as it turned out, for the Allies had already shown their attitude in the prosecution of the German leaders. Whatever the reasons, the result was destruction so complete that when in later years the Japanese self-defense agency history room undertook to write an official history of the Pacific war, in many instances the historians had to rely on Allied accounts—there were no Japanese versions extant.)

On August 16, Prince Takamatsu appeared at Atsugi airfield, where many of the young fliers were threatening to organize a mass flight to attack the Third Fleet. He roused the loyal troops, and they punched holes in the fuel tanks of aircraft and removed the propellers of others so the young hotheads could not upset the agreement to which the Emperor had become a party. Captain Ozono, who had insisted publicly on carrying on the war, simply disappeared in the prince's wake and did not surface for many months, when he was tried by a Japanese court for disobedience to the imperial order.

At Kure naval base Lieutenant Akira Kikuchi led a delegation of officers to demand that the submarine fleet keep fighting. The senior officers of the Sixth Fleet (which was the submarine organization for all Japan) told Kikuchi to quiet down and obey orders. Thereupon, the young officers commandeered six small coastal submarines and set out for the sea to attack the Third Fleet.

On August 17 the Allies were quarreling among themselves. The Americans laid out the system of surrender and the Russians did not like it. They wanted to occupy the Kuriles Islands and northern Hokkaido, one of the Japanese home islands. The Americans allowed them the Kuriles, but would not let the Soviet foot enter the door of Japan. The distrust was growing almost hourly.

Korea was a principal victim of the manner of surrender. The Soviets had been marching south, and the Americans had not landed. But the surrender called for American occupation to the 38th parallel (chosen because it was regarded as the furthest point the Americans could reach and included the Korean capital, Seoul). By the seventeenth of August the Soviets had spread through Manchuria, and instead of concentrating his efforts in the northeast, Chiang Kai-shek was more concerned about the wealth of south China. Consequently as the Soviets came in, the Chinese communists were right behind them, taking over, organizing the villages and towns, and making ready for another war.

The arguments also involved the Americans and the British to a certain extent, because the British were feeling very unhappy that the Americans, and not they, were taking credit for winning the Pacific war. But that was minor compared to the division between the U.S. and the U.S.S.R. After some vacillation the Americans helped the British regain control of Hong Kong (the Chinese had expected to take it over). A degree of harmony was restored to American-British relations, but American-Chinese relations were not helped. The French were also unhappy because they wanted to step right back into Indochina although they had played no part in the Pacific war nor had they any forces in the area that could occupy Hanoi or Saigon. The best they could do was secure representation at the coming surrender.

So on August 17, the victors were already quarreling about the spoils—the Japanese empire. Everywhere, in Indochina,

Formosa, Manchuria, the Japanese were preparing to lay down their arms, except for those few diehards who still believed they could carry on the war by themselves.

That day Commander Hashimoto brought the *I-58* back into home waters. They returned first to the base on the Inland Sea, on the Bungo channel, where the *kaiten* crews were trained. Stopping there to unload his single remaining *kaiten*, Commander Hashimoto was shown a copy of the imperial rescript that announced the end of the war. He went ashore briefly to report on his voyage and on the sinking of the American "battleship." It all seemed hollow in view of the dreadful news he had just read.

On August 18, Admiral Nimitz and General Albert C. Wedemeyer, the commander of American forces in China, met at General MacArthur's headquarters in Manila. Wedemeyer needed American troops in large number if an orderly surrender was to take place. The Chinese Nationalists did not have the resources to take over all the country and Manchuria in a hurry. But MacArthur was bemused by Japan, not knowing what to expect there or sure of his own resources. He believed he would need twenty-five divisions to occupy Japan and South Korea. Wedemeyer would have to wait until the end of September for American troops. That decision was one of the most costly of the postwar period in terms of the American aspirations in the Far East. The Russians had already violated the Sino-Soviet treaty, signed a few days before, by demanding the surrender of all Japanese troops to the Soviet forces. The moment they reached Mukden, the industrial center of Manchuria, the technicians came in and began tearing up the factories and shipping them, piece by piece, back to the Soviet Union. They took everything down to the concrete floors of the buildings.

The Japanese cabinet resigned. Prince Naruhiko Higashikuni, the Emperor's wife's uncle, became the new prime minister. He tried to get Prince Konoye to come into the cabinet, but the prince felt he was too closely associated with the past, and particularly with General Tojo, the prime minister who had led the war effort in the victorious years. Mamoru Shigemitsu, a known enemy of the militarists, became the new foreign minister.

The Japanese were ordered by General MacArthur to send a mission to Manila to discuss the mechanics of the coming surrender. Prime Minister Higashikuni appointed General Kawabe, deputy chief of the army's general staff, to lead the mission, but it was delayed for two days. Prince Takamatsu reported that he had not yet secured all the air units and aircraft in the Tokyo area, and that a number of brash young fliers threatened to shoot down any plane that tried to take off to fly to Manila. Until the authorities could bring the young militarists under control, the danger was real, but this could not be explained to the Americans. Consequently, as the hours passed and the mission did not appear, at MacArthur's headquarters officers began to talk of the Japanese "stalling."

Finally, after two days of fruitless waiting, General Kawabe and his staff took off under cover of darkness from a heavily guarded field. Their two twin-engined bombers had been painted white, with green crosses. They flew in the early hours of August 19 to Ie Shima, near Okinawa, and there transferred to an American plane that took them to Manila.

At Clark Field the Japanese delegation was met by MacArthur's representatives. They were given copies of the instrument of surrender, and told that the first American troops would land on August 23. The Japanese nearly panicked. That could not be— the Japanese were forced to admit that government authority over the armed forces was still hanging in the balance. They needed more time to bring the hotheads under control. MacArthur gave them until August 26.

On August 18, as the mission to Manila assembled, Commander Hashimoto was moving his submarine back to Kure. Just outside the *kaiten* base, he encountered the six submarines led by Lieutenant Kikuchi, who tried to persuade him to join them and continue the fight. Commander Hashimoto refused. He turned his submarine toward Kure, and when he looked behind he noticed that the six small submarines were also turning. Lieutenant Kikuchi had suddenly seen the error of his ways.

General MacArthur had planned that the 11th Airborne Division land at Atsugi airfield to begin the occupation officially. But another typhoon came up and the division was stalled for two days.

For a week Halsey's Third Fleet had been preparing to go into Japanese bases. On August 22 all available aircraft were flown off for a "flyby," or aerial parade, for photographic purposes. It was time to think of the folks back home. On August 23 and 24 the carriers stood off Honshu, close enough to furnish air cover for the occupying troops—but the troops did not come. On August 26 the weather was so foul that the planes were shipbound. On August 27 the carriers again furnished air cover, and on this day one pilot, ignoring his orders, landed at Atsugi airfield and instructed the welcoming Japanese ground crew that they were to paint a large sign to guide the troops of the 11th Airborne Division.

On August 28 the advance units of the 11th Airborne Division arrived at Atsugi airfield, to be greeted by the sign: Welcome to the U.S. Army from the Third Fleet.

That day Captain Otani and Captain Takasaki of the Japanese navy boarded the Japanese destroyer *Hatuzakura* and were taken to the *Missouri*, where Admiral Halsey's staff instructed them in the procedures that would be followed, and secured information about tides and mine fields. That day the *Missouri*, the HMS *Duke of York*, and several other ships moved into Sagami Wan (bay), and the minesweepers began work in the Uraga Suido channel. No one still knew quite what was going to happen, and the atmosphere aboard ship varied between tension and exultation.

On August 28 Halsey sent his minesweepers into Tokyo Bay and the next day Admiral Nimitz arrived in the *South Dakota*, and he and Halsey anchored that night off Yokosuka naval base. The two battleship crews were instructed that they were to provide bombardment support if necessary for the landings of the main group of the 11th Airborne Division on August 30.

The next day there were no incidents. Admiral Halsey took command of Yokosuka naval base when his chief of staff, Admiral Carney, accepted the Japanese surrender on the waterfront. That day Third Fleet units began rescuing prisoners of war from camps in the Tokyo area.

In Tokyo, the loyal officers of the Emperor were still having their difficulties as of the end of August. A number of ardent young fliers made a suicide pact. They were to rush one of the outlying airfields, steal fighter planes, and make a mass suicide attack on the *Missouri,* which was to be the place of signing of the surrender.

Fortunately the plot was uncovered and the military authorities were able to stop it.

The official surrender of Japan was signed aboard the USS *Missouri* on Sunday, September 2, 1945. Foreign Minister Shigemitsu, who had lost a leg to a bomb earlier, stumped his way up the ladder. General Umezu, who had to be restrained personally by the Emperor from committing suicide rather than accept the task, followed him up. General MacArthur made a little speech about war and peace, and the Japanese then signed the surrender and the Allied representatives followed them.

At last, after nearly four years for the Americans and the British, fourteen years for the Chinese, and twenty-four days for the Russians, the war was over. If there was a symbol of it that was meaningful to the common man, it was in a joke played on Admiral Halsey the night before he left Japan for home. Months earlier, in his gruff way, Halsey had replied to a reporter's question about the war with the suggestion that he wanted to ride the Emperor Hirohito's white horse. Traditionally, the Emperor appeared on national holidays in the uniform of a Japanese field marshal, riding Shirayuki (White Snow), his favorite horse, a big handsome white Arabian. On that last day in Tokyo the commander of the First Cavalry Division brought forth a white horse, and Bill Halsey, son of an American naval officer and father of a naval officer, rode "the Emperor's horse" through the streets of Tokyo.

NOTES

This book is a part of my continuing study of the Pacific War (1941–45 as far as America is concerned). The basic source for the naval material, and the impetus for the book, came from the files of the Operational Archives of the United States Navy in the Washington Navy Yard, and as with so many of my books I am deeply indebted to Dr. Dean Allard, chief of the archives, and his staff.

Specifically I made use of the following military documents: the war diary of the Third Fleet, *The History of the Joint Chiefs of Staff in World War II* by Lieutenant Grace P. Hayes, the action reports of the Third Fleet and the various ships of the fleet, especially the *Independence* and the *Enterprise, Yorktown,* and *Wasp,* the action reports of the Task Unit 34.8.2 and of the Second Carrier Division of Task Force 38, and the action reports of Task Force 38, all for the period of June-September 1945.

I also used the two volumes of the official Japanese Pacific War history concerned with the last days of the war and the home defenses of Japan, *Hondo Kessen Jumbi,* or the "Preparations for the Deciding Battle of the Homeland," Volumes One and Two. This is part of the 101-volume history prepared in the 1950s and 1960s by the War Room of the Imperial Defense Agency in Tokyo.

1: Re-enter Halsey

Halsey's planning in the spring of 1945 is described in his *Admiral Halsey's Story.* The command relationships are described in my *How They Won the War in the Pacific.* So is the note about the army-navy quarrel over Major General Ralph Smith's relief at Saipan. The assessment of Halsey as a commander is my own, based on a study made for a possible as yet unwritten biography of the admiral. The details of his early years come from Halsey's own story. His adventures in flight training come from his own book and from *How They Won the War . . . .* Halsey's attitude toward the regulations comes from the same sources. So does the note about the aftermath of the Doolittle raid. The sign "Kill Japs, Kill Japs and Kill More Japs" became a sort of general slogan in the South Pacific. The notes about American and Japanese fighting men are my own observation based on studies for several books. The furor created by Halsey's interview with the New Zealand press made a lasting impression in America. The notes about Admiral Kinkaid's reaction and Halsey's situation at Leyte come from a long interview I had with Admiral Kinkaid in 1968, and correspondence with Admiral Robert W. Carney, Halsey's last chief of staff, in 1968 and 1969. The analysis of Halsey and Spruance as commanders comes from *How They Won the War* . . . . Halsey's actions in the spring of 1945 are detailed in his own book. The story about Admiral Clark's activities comes from *Carrier Admiral*, by J. J. Clark and Clark Reynolds. The notes about Japanese defense plans in the spring of 1945 come from *Hondo Kessen Jumbi* (Homeland Decisive Battle Preparations), the two volumes of the Japanese Self-Defense Agency's history of the Pacific War that deal with plans for the battle of Japan.

Halsey's movements in May are detailed in the U.S. Third Fleet War Diary for that period. Halsey's intentions to carry a strong effort against the kamikazes are indicated in his own book. The operations of the kamikazes are described in Inoguchi's *The Divine Wind*. Halsey's actions of May 26 and May 27 come from the Third Fleet War Diary.

2: Hit the Enemy; Get Those Planes!

The first paragraph is from Halsey's own memoirs. The second comes from Morison's *History of U.S. Naval Operations*, Vol. 13. The notes about Admiral McCain's career come from my own *Guadalcanal*, and *How They Won the War in the Pacific*. The story of the Third Fleet Operations on June 1 is from the Third Fleet War Diary. For other materials on the operations I used the action reports for the period of the USS *Independence*, the USS *Yorktown*, Task Force 38, the Third Fleet War Diary. The story of Jimmy Doolittle's impact on the war comes from a long interview with Jimmy Doolittle in 1971. The reaction of the Japanese to the carrier raids is told in *Hondo Kessen Jumbi*, Vol. 2. The Koeller story comes from the action reports of the *Yorktown*. British and U.S. Fleet operations are described in the Third Fleet War diary. The story of Halsey and the typhoon is from my own *How They Won the War* . . . . A whole book has been devoted to the subject of Halsey's typhoons for anyone interested in pursuing this aspect of the war, which was more costly than any Japanese action in the last stages. Halsey got the blame for the damage, but it seems clear years later that the American system of weather reporting was the major culprit. In the final analysis the proof is that in the last days of the war, Nimitz revamped it completely.

3: The Waters of Japan

A basic course for this chapter was the Third Fleet War Diary for the period of June, July, and August, 1945. For the Japanese story of troop movement, *Hondo Kessen Jumbi* was the source. Herbert Feis' book and that of Lester Brooks on Japan's surrender were also important. For matters pertaining to the Japanese army, *Kogun* was basic. Much of the background material about Korea and Manchuria comes from the author's period as a war and foreign correspondent in the Far East (1945–47). The material about Japanese home production and distribution is from *Hondo Kessen Jumbi*, Feis, and Brooks. The material about Admiral Yamamoto is from *The Reluctant Admiral*. The stories of the Japanese submarine service come from *I-Boat Captain*. The material about Koinawa is from Morison and from Halsey's book.

4: Destination: Tokyo

The sources for the early part of the chapter are the Third Fleet War Diary for the summer of 1945, and my own *Blue Skies and Blood*, the story of the battle of the Coral Sea. I used the *Yorktown* action reports for July. *I-Boat Captain* and Morison, Vol. 13, are the sources for the *I-53's* activities just then. *Hondo Kessen Jumbi* and *Kogun* were used to get the flavor of the Japanese activity. Richard Crommelin's story is from the *Yorktown's* reports and from Morison. The detail about the strikes against the Japanese homeland is from the Third Fleet War Diary. Admiral Halsey's special report of October 6, 1945, on the Third Fleet's Operations in the summer was the source for some of the reconstruction of Halsey's thoughts during this time. *Kogun* is the source of the story about Japanese negotiations with various Chinese peace factions. *Kogun* and *Hondo Kessen Jumbi* are the sources for the notes about the Japanese forces. The Third Fleet's action reports and *I-Boat Captain* were basic sources for Japanese naval activity in the middle of July, and Captain Ariizumi's abortive plans. *I-Boat Captain* gave the details of the attack on the American convoy, and Morison gave the American side of it. *Hondo Kessen Jumbi* and *Kogun* were basic to the notes about the kamikaze units, as was *The Divine Wind*.

5: Battleship Shock

Enola Gay and the Marx book were used for this material about the atomic bomb. Feis also has some discussion in *Japan Subdued*. The knowledge of the military comes from *How They Won the War in the Pacific*. The story of Allen Dulles and negotiations about Japan comes from Feis, *Kogun*, and *Enola Gay*. The voyage of the *Indianapolis* is from *Enola Gay* and *How They Won the War in the Pacific*. The operations of the Third Fleet come from the action reports. The story of Lieutenant Takahashi's adventures is from *I-Boat Captain*. The account of the B-29 raids is from Morison's book on the 20th Air Force. Feis is the source for the material on the situation at Potsdam in mid-July. The Third Fleet's War Diary is the source for the Fleet's various activities in mid-July.

6: The Ultimatum

The Byrnes, Truman, and Feis books were the sources for the observation on American attitudes. *Enola Gay* was used for the story of the 509th Air Group here, and the Morison book on the 20th Air Force. *The Divine Wind* and *Born to Die* are sources for the stories about the kamikaze pilots. *Kogun*, *Brooks*, and *Enola Gay* were sources for the activities on July 20 in Japan, Moscow, and Potsdam. The Third Fleet's activity comes from various action reports of the units, and the Third Fleet War Diary. McCain's observations about carrier warfare and Okinawa come from his final report of Task Force 38 activity at the end of the war. Again, the account of the *I-58's* activity is from *I-Boat Captain*. Leahy's observations are from his own book, *I Was There*. Truman's activities and those of the others at Potsdam are from Truman's book and Feis. The activities of Japanese submarines are from *I-Boat Captain* and Morison. Political notes about the Allies and the commanders come from all these sources, and from the author's own observations over the years. The reports on King's activity come from *The History of the Joint Chiefs of Staff in World War II*. The activities of various submarines come from Holmes *Undersea Victory*, and Blair's *Silent Victory*, and from the war patrol reports of USS *Bowfin*, which I studied for another book. The material about General Groves and the atomic bomb came from Feis and Morrison and from *Enola Gay*. The terms of the Potsdam Declaration are from Feis. Notes on the activities of the *Underhill* come from Morison, Vol. 13. Halsey's attitude and actions is from his own book, from the Third Fleet War Diary, and from *How They Won the War in the Pacific*. King's and Nimitz' attitudes come from the latter; the original source is the record of the King-Nimitz meetings during the war. The story of Lieutenant Harrison comes from the action reports of the *Yorktown* for July 1945. The politicking in Tokyo is from Brooks and *Kogun*. The notes about Halsey and the A-bomb late in July are from Third Fleet War Diary, Halsey, and *How They Won the War* .... Notes about the B-29s come from Morrison on the 20th Air Force. Observations about the politics on July 26 come from Feis. The *Indianapolis* story is from *Enola Gay* and *How They Won the War* .... The activity in Tokyo is from Brooks and *Kogun*.

7: The Hunter and the Hunted

I used *I-Boat Captain* as the basic source for the *I-58*'s voyage. For the story of the *Indianapolis* I used Morison, Vol. 13, and *How They Won the War in the Pacific*. *The Divine Wind* is the source for the tales of the kamikaze pilots. The Third Fleet action reports and Morison are the sources for the destroyers off Okinawa, and for Halsey's activity in late July. The story of the *Barb* is from *Silent Victory*. Events in Japan come from Brooks, *Kogun*, and Feis. Events in Potsdam come from Byrnes and Feis and Truman.

8: The Hunter Strikes

Events in the Third Fleet are from the War Diary. The Potsdam situation comes from Byrnes and Feis. The story of the *I-58* and the *Indianapolis* is derived from *I-Boat Captain* and Morison.

9: The Halsey Fury

The source for the *Indianapolis* story is Morison and *How They Won the War in the Pacific*. The story of the Third Fleet is from the War Diary and carriers' action reports. Colonel Tibbets' activities comes from *Enola Gay*. The source for the report of events in Washington are Feis, Truman, and Byrnes. The notes on the events in Japan come from Brooks, the details of *I-58* from Commander Hashimoto's book, and Third Fleet activities from the War Diary. The B-29s activity is from Morrison's book on the 20th Air Force. The notes on the *kaiten* are from *Kamikaze Submarine*, and from *Sunk*. The *Indianapolis* survivors' story is from Morison.

10: The Tragedy of Delay

The continued story of the *Indianapolis* is from *How They Won the War in the Pacific* and, originally, from the naval record of the inquiry into the sinking of the *Indianapolis*. The material about Colonel Tibbets and the 20th Air Force is from *Enola Gay* and Morison. The material about the Japanese economy is from *Hondo Kessen Jumbi* and Brooks. Commander Hashimoto's book, *Sunk: The Story of the Japanese Submarine Fleet, 1941–45*, is the source for his continuing story.

The Third Fleet War Diary detailed the activities of Halsey's fleet for early August. Colonel Tibbets' running story continues, from *Enola Gay.* The material on the Japanese planes and pilots is from *Samurai* by Saburo Sakai, Japan's leading living aerial ace. The material about Nagasaki is from *Hondo Kessen Jumbi*, Vol. 2, and from *Seven Hours to Zero.* The details of the end of Potsdam and of Truman's travels are from Truman and Feis. The story of the *Indianapolis* survivors comes from the record of the investigation, and from Morison, Vol. 13.

11: Alarums and Excursions

The material of the results of the *Indianapolis* sinking comes from *How They Won the War in the Pacific* and from Holmes' *Undersea Victory.* The observation that the navy was half asleep is my own, as is that about the politicization of the war. The details of the Japanese-Soviet negotiations are from Feis, and the Manchuria Army situation is from *Kogun.* The story of the planned Japanese suicide attack comes from brief notes in Morison, the Third Fleet War Diary, and Halsey's story. The notes about the invocation of God by the American chaplain represent a personal crotchet of the author's: in all the wars about which I have ever written the chaplains of each military force claim that God is on their side. I suggest that God is neutral.

12: The Day of the Big Bang

The sources for the story of the B-29s are *Enola Gay,* Morrison's book on the 20th Air Force, and *Seven Hours to Zero.* The translation of the paragraphs from *Hondo Kessen Jumbi,* Vol. 2, is my own, and the material about the Japanese reaction comes largely from that book. The Truman material is from his book and from Feis.

13: Days of August

Feis, *Enola Gay, Hondo Kessen Jumbi,* and Brooks were all sources for the material about Hiroshima, as well as John Hersey's long magazine article in the *New Yorker* in 1946, which was later published as a book. Hashimoto is the source for the submarine material. Third Fleet War Diary and *Kogun* were also vital to this chapter.

14: The Second Bomb

Seven Hours to Zero, Kogun, Third Fleet War Diary, *Hondo Kessen Jumbi* were all important to the material on the progress of the war and the dropping of the Nagasaki bomb. The political material is derived from Stimson's book, Butow, Truman, Brooks, and *Kogun.* The naval sources, war diaries, and the action reports of the ships are obvious. The material about Japanese submarine operations is from *Kamikaze Submarines.*

15: Agony

Feis and Brooks were vital to this chapter. The action reports and War Diary of Task Force 38 and of the individual carriers was also important. For the student of naval

NOTES

229

history, Admiral McCain's reports and analyses of the air side of the war and weapons make interesting reading. One of the discoveries I made in comparing American
and Japanese reports (where comparable) on air raids and fighter sweeps, is the number of actual planes destroyed on the ground and clever fakes. The Japanese built
some excellent Zeros and Bettys and Jills—out of bamboo and paper. They burned
nicely and gave the American pilots a good feeling. As Admiral McCain had suspected,
when the war ended the Japanese had thousands of aircraft left with which to fight.
It also seems apparent, from the reports of the big I-boats, that the Japanese had
developed a superior technology in submarines, incorporating the German schnorkels.
But American submarines and bombers had so devastated their resources by the summer
of 1945 that the Japanese navy could not take advantage of these developments.

16: Waiting

Kogun was vital to the chapter. The various political studies—Truman, Byrnes,
Stimson, Feis—were used to trace the course of American actions and reactions at
home. Admiral Halsey's war diary told what was happening at sea. Brooks was in-
valuable for detail inside Japan. *Kogun*, Brooks, and Feis were all used in tracing
the final developments in the cabinet.

17: The Struggle for Decision

Hashimoto's story of the *kaitens* is poignant and also indicative of the blind
patriotism that led these suicide-prone young men in the last days of the war. Pacific
Fleet War Diary, Third Fleet War Diary, and Halsey's book were the basis for the
American preparations for the surrender of Japan.
Kogun tells of the progress of the war in Manchuria. Halsey's story tells of his
discussion with Admiral Carney. Admiral Ohnishi's story comes from *The Divine
Wind* and from Brooks.

18: Plot

The militarists' plot against the peace faction, their intention to take control of the
Imperial Palace and dictate to the Emperor the course of the war, is detailed in Brooks.
I also used Yamamoto, Morrison, Feis, and *Kogun* in this. The Third Fleet War Diary
tells of the American activities off the coast of Japan. *Fighter Sweep* gives the U.S.
air force movement. I cited Chungking among the cities where joy reigned at the premature belief that the Japanese had surrendered because I was there at the time.
The notes about the *Spikefish* war patrol are from Holmes.

19: The Smell of Defeat

Kogun, Hashimoto, and *Kamikaze Submarines* were all used to trace the sort of
activity that went on in the armed forces when the war ended. Brooks continues the
story of the plot. Feis has several comments about the American-Soviet misunder-
standings of the period, which were to color the whole U.S.-Soviet relationship in
the Far East in the coming year. Ugaki's last flight is detailed in *The Divine Wind*.

20: Death and Honor

The death of Admiral Ohnishi is told in Brooks and in *The Divine Wind*. Commander Hashimoto's reluctant final voyage is described in his own book. Commander Orita's story comes from *Kamikaze Submarines* and *I-Boat Captain*. Halsey's enthusiasm for the surrender is noted in his book.

21: Margin of Safety

The difficulties about Halsey's "occupation of Japan" are shown clearly in the Third Fleet and Pacific Fleet war diaries, and Halsey makes some mention of it in his own book. Brooks tells of the difficulties within Japan, as does Hashimoto.

BIBLIOGRAPHY

Beasley, William G., *The Modern History of Japan*, New York, Praeger Publishers, 1963.

Belote, James H., *Typhoon of Steel: the Battle of Okinawa*, New York, Harper & Row, 1970.

Blair, Clay, Jr., *Silent Victory*, Philadelphia and New York, J. B. Lippincott Company, 1975.

Brooks, Lester, *Behind Japan's Surrender*, New York, McGraw-Hill, Inc., 1967.

Butow, Robert J. C., *Japan's Decision to Surrender*, Stanford, Stanford University Press, 1954.

Byrnes, James F., *All in One Lifetime*, New York, Harper & Brothers, 1947.

————, *Speaking Frankly*, New York, Greenwood Press, Inc., 1974.

Chinnock, F. W., *Nagasaki, the Forgotten Bomb*, New York, World Publishing Co., 1969.

Clark, J. J., with Reynolds, C. G., *Carrier Admiral*, New York, David McKay Co., Inc., 1967.

Dyer, George C., *The Amphibians Came to Conquer: The Story of Admiral Richmond Kelly Turner*, Vol. II, Washington, D. C., U. S. Government Printing Office, undated.

Feis, Herbert, *Japan Subdued: The Atomic Bomb and the End of the War in the Pacific*, Princeton, Princeton University Press, 1961.

————, *Between War and Peace*, Princeton, Princeton University Press, 1960.

Hagoromo Society, The, *Born to Die, The Cherry Blossom Squadrons*, Ed. by Adams, Andres, and Alston, Pat. Translated by Nobua Asahi, Tokyo, Ohara Publishers, 1973.

Halsey, William F., and Bryan, J., III, *Admiral Halsey's Story*, New York, McGraw-Hill Book Co., 1947.

Hashimoto, Mochitsura, *Sunk: The Story of the Japanese Submarine Fleet, 1941-45*, Translated by E. H. M. Colgrave, New York, Henry Holt and Co., 1954.

Hayashi, Sabura, *Kogun, the Japanese Army in the Pacific War*, Virginia, Marine Corps Association, 1959.

Hess, William N., *Pacific Sweep, the 5th and 13th Fighter Commands*, New York, Zebra Books, Kensington Publishing Corp., 1974.

Holmes, W. J., *Double-Edged Secrets*, Annapolis, Naval Institute Press, 1979.

————, *Underseas Victory*, New York, Doubleday & Co., Inc., 1966.

Hoyt, Edwin, P., *How They Won the War in the Pacific*, New York, Weybright and Talley, 1970.

————, *Blue Skies and Blood, The Battle of the Coral Sea*, New York, Paul S. Eriksson, Inc., 1975.

Hull, Cordell, *Memoirs* (2 vols.), New York, The Macmillan Co., 1948.

Inoguchi, Rikihei, and Nakajima, T., *The Divine Wind, Japan's Kamikaze Force in World War II*, Annapolis, Naval Institute Press, 1958.

Ienaga, Saburo, *The Pacific War, 1931–45*, New York, Pantheon Books, 1968.

Kase, Toshikazu, *Journey to the Missouri*, New Haven, Yale University Press, 1950.

Kodama, Yoshio, *I Was Defeated*, Tokyo, Booth and Fukuda, 1951.

Leahy, William D., *I Was There*, New York, Whittlesey House, 1950.

MacArthur, Douglas, *Reminiscences*, New York, McGraw-Hill Book Co., 1964.

Marx, Joseph L., *Seven Hours to Zero*, New York, G. P. Putnam's Sons, 1967.

Morison, Samuel E., *History of United States Naval Operations in World War II, Vol. XIV, Victory in the Pacific*, Boston, Atlantic, Little Brown and Company, 1945.

Morrison, Wilbur H., *Point of No Return, The Story of the 20th Air Force*, New York, Times Books, 1979.

Orita, Zenji, with Harrington, Joseph D., *I-Boat Captain*, California, Major Books, 1976.

Sakai, Saburo, with Caidin, Martin, and Saito, Fred, *Samurai!*, New York, Bantam Books, 1975.

Sanson, Sir George, *Japan: A Short Cultural History*, New York, Appleton Century-Crofts, Inc., 1962.

Thomas, Gordon, and Witts, Max Morgan, *Enola Gay*, New York, Stein and Day, 1977.

Truman, Harry S, *Year of Decisions*, New York, Doubleday & Co., Inc., 1955.

Yokota, Y., with Harrington, Joseph D., *Kamikaze Submarines*, New York, Leisure Books, 1962.

INDEX

238

INDEX